UNDER THE BODHI TREE

UNDER *the* BODHI TREE

Buddha's Original Vision of Dependent Co-arising

BUDDHADĀSA BHIKKHU

Translated. edited, and introduced by Santikaro

Wisdom

Wisdom Publications
199 Elm Street
Somerville, MA 02144 USA
wisdomexperience.org

Library of Congress Cataloging-in-Publication Data

Names: Phra Thēpwisutthimēthī (Ngūam), 1906–1993, author. | Santikaro, Bhikkhu, 1957– editor.
Title: Under the Bodhi Tree: Buddha's original vision of dependent co-arising / Buddhadāsa Bhikkhu; edited and introduced by Santikaro.
Description: Somerville, MA: Wisdom Publications, 2017. | Includes bibliographical references and index. | Includes translations from Thai.
Identifiers: LCCN 2016031571 (print) | LCCN 2016049186 (ebook) | ISBN 9781614292197 (pbk.: alk. paper) | ISBN 1614292191 (pbk.: alk. paper) | ISBN 9781614292371 (eISBN) | ISBN 9781614292371 () | ISBN 161429237X ()
Subjects: LCSH: Pratītyasamutpāda.
Classification: LCC BQ4240 .P58 2017 (print) | LCC BQ4240 (ebook) | DDC 294.3/42041—dc23
LC record available at https://lccn.loc.gov/2016031571

ISBN 978-1-61429-219-7 ebook ISBN 978-1-61429-237-1

21
5 4 3 2

Cover design by Phil Pascuzzo. Interior design by Barbara Haines. Set in 10.75/14.25 Garamond Premier Pro.

Wisdom Publications' books are printed on acid-free paper and meet the guidelines for permanence and durability of the Production Guidelines for Book Longevity of the Council on Library Resources.

Printed in the United States of America.

The Buddha, recently awakened, remained seated at the base of the Bodhi tree, near the bank of the Nerañjarā River, in the vicinity of Uruvelā. The Splendid One occupied a single seat beneath the Bodhi tree for all of seven days savoring the joy of liberation.

At that time, the Splendid One reflected upon *paṭicca-samuppāda* forward and backward throughout the first . . . middle . . . and final watches of the night . . . and uttered this verse:

> Whenever dhammas manifest clearly
> to a supreme one ardent in focused contemplation,
> this excellency incinerates Māra and his armies
> just as the rising sun vanquishes darkness.

—Vin.i.1 (Mahāvagga) and Udāna 1:1–3
(Bodhi Suttas 1–3)

Contents

Translator's Preface and Acknowledgments

Setting and Provenance

The morning bell sounds through the coconut palm grove containing Suan Mokkh's International Dhamma Hermitage at 4 a.m. Just inland from the Gulf of Siam, the climate is warm and tropical, though relatively cool so early in the day. The monthly meditation course's participants awake, dress, and assemble for a mile-long walk in the dark. As in many of the months between February 1986 and October 1991, Ajahn Buddhadāsa will be speaking during this retreat. Many of those filing down the laterite road between marshes and mangroves, know little if anything about the octogenarian monk they are about to meet, though he is the founder of the "Garden of Liberation," *Suan Mokkh* in Thai, where they've come to learn about Buddhism and meditation. Perhaps a third of them are brand new to Buddhism, having stumbled into this retreat from beaches in southern Thailand. Responding to the hospitality of their Thai hosts and the kindness of the retreat guides, mostly Westerners like themselves, they good humoredly follow the program.

The line of meditators enters under the large trees of Suan Mokkh proper. By 5 a.m. they are seated on concrete benches outside a simple two-story building. An elderly, rotund monk slowly walks to his own seat with the aid of a cane, followed by a dog who seems to own the place. As he arranges his robes and legs, a skinny American monk takes a seat beside him. After clearing his throat, Ajahn Buddhadāsa begins with a brief welcome and then launches into his topic. The American—myself—translates first sentence by sentence, then a few sentences at a time, and eventually minutes at a time. If the translator leaves anything out, Ajahn Buddhadāsa repeats it. Occasionally, he interrupts the translation with a cough and correction. As the American monk has been translating like this for over two years he is only slightly discomfited by the corrections, grateful for the warning coughs.

Ajahn Buddhadāsa is in no hurry, having over a week to work with. Assuming that his audience knows little about Buddhism and is therefore free of the preconceptions that many born-Buddhists carry, he lays a foundation of what Buddhism is and is not. Far more familiar with Western philosophy and literature than other Thai forest masters, he works around our assumptions about "isms" (ideologies), philosophies, and religion. Understanding "religion" in a way that fits with the Buddha's teaching rather than cramming Buddhism into Western categories, he explains what sort of religion Buddhism is. He even broaches the topic of "God," although the American translator has informed him that few of this audience believe in the God Ajahn Buddhadāsa has read about in The Bible and known from Muslim friends in southern Thailand. His two introductory talks conclude with the coolness and freedom that is the purpose of Buddhism.

In the third talk, he takes up his primary theme, dependent co-arising (*paṭiccasamuppāda*). He explains how this unifying thread runs through all of the Buddha's teaching and points to its deepest insights through the remainder of the seven talks. Each talk lasts two hours, including translation. A few dogs wander in and out. Dawn rises about halfway through with roosters serenading. In the background, monks leave on almsround. At 7 a.m. the retreatants return to the International Dhamma Hermitage for breakfast, followed by a full day of meditation practice along with instruction in mindfulness with breathing (*ānāpānasati*). Ajahn Buddhadāsa liked to send them on their "morning walk" with advice such as "Walk without a walker."

Dependent Co-arising in Buddhism

The Buddha's vast corpus of teaching is anchored by a handful of core insights and principles. He stated that his teaching is only concerned with distress, dissatisfaction, or suffering (*dukkha*) and its quenching (*nirodha*).

> Friends, there are groups of wanderers and priests that misrepresent me with deceitful, empty, baseless, insincere words: "The wanderer Gotama, who leads people astray to their ruin, lays out a creed of the vacancy, destruction, and nonexistence of beings."
> These wanderers and priests misrepresent me with deceitful, empty, baseless, insincere words because I have never said such things. You'll never hear me saying such things.

> In the past as well as now, friends, I teach only dukkha and the remainderless quenching of dukkha.[1]

This core concern is investigated through the prism of a subtle understanding of conditionality (*idappaccayatā*)—that everything happens, changes, and ceases dependent on other things that share the same essenceless nature.

> When this exists, this naturally exists;
> due to the arising of this, this consequently arises.
> When this does not exist, this naturally does not exist;
> due to the quenching of this, this consequently is quenched.[2]

When we view ourselves and our world this way—more as processes than entities, as natural law—we see the Dhamma, we see the Buddha.

> One who sees dependent co-arising sees the Dhamma.[3]
> One who sees the Dhamma sees the Buddha.[4]

Citing these statements of the Buddha, Ajahn Buddhadāsa continually reminded and emphasized how dependent co-arising (*paṭiccasamuppāda*) is the very core of Buddha's teaching. It provides the definitive perspective of the Buddha's insights and awakening. Realize dependent co-arising and one realizes the natural truth that sets life free. Consequently, whether informing foreigner visitors new to Buddhism or reminding Thais born into Buddhism, Ajahn Buddhadāsa insisted that dependent co-arising is central to the Buddha's experience and teaching, and therefore to our own study and practice. Having taken these words to heart, Ajahn Buddhadāsa endeavored to return dependent co-arising to a central place in Dhamma teaching and practice.

Having committed his life to service of the Buddha, he felt a responsibility to do everything in his power to proclaim the teaching of dependent co-arising, even when warned by elders in the monastic hierarchy that ordinary people will not be able to understand. Further, he thought getting to the core of the Buddha's original awakened understanding of dependent co-arising was more important than adhering to later orthodoxies, let alone pieties and dogmas. Lastly, he believed in making a teaching as accessible as possible without watering it down. These are tasks Ajahn Buddhadāsa accepted as a "Servant of the Buddha."

Thus it made perfect sense for Ajahn Buddhadāsa to introduce foreign meditators attending monthly retreats at Suan Mokkh, many of them brand new to Buddhism, to core Dhamma teachings that were more often than not centered on dependent co-arising. He felt that such newcomers, unencumbered by traditional Buddhist beliefs, yet familiar with scientific thought, should understand what is central and unique to Buddhism. He skipped the articles of faith that appeal to traditional Buddhists and went for the heart. This book captures that approach.

Among traditional assumptions about dependent co-arising is the belief that this teaching is too difficult for lay people, that they will get confused and be lead astray by it. After all, the Buddha told Ānanda, "Dependent co-arising both has the outward appearance of being profound and is truly profound. Through not understanding deeply and not penetratively realizing this Dhamma of dependent co-arising, minds of the many kinds of sentient beings are like a tangled skein of thread, are entangled like thread all tied up in knots, are like muñja grass and pabbaja grass all matted together."[5] As beings, we remain trapped in suffering and distress because we do not understand dependent co-arising. Investigating dependent co-arising is crucial to liberation from dukkha, which is the sole purpose of Buddha's teaching. This makes it incumbent upon teachers to make this vital teaching available to all sincere practitioners, including those without monastic status. Rather than taking its profundity as a reason to be silent about dependent co-arising, Ajahn Buddhadāsa took it as a challenge to do everything in his power to make it better known and understood.

Dependent co-arising is also about not-self or selflessness (*anattā*) and voidness or emptiness (*suññatā*). Ajahn Buddhadāsa's *Heartwood of the Bodhi Tree* surveys the role of emptiness in the Pāli suttas of early Buddhism. *Under the Bodhi Tree* provides the complementary perspectives of conditionality (*idappaccayatā*) and dependent co-arising found in those suttas. All of these help us recognize that nothing can be found to be truly self (a substantial, independent lasting something that is me) and therefore nothing is worth clinging to as "me" or "mine." This is what Buddha's Dhamma is truly about, rather than religiosity, moralism, tradition, clericalism, philosophy, or belonging. For many decades Ajahn Buddhadāsa did what he could to cut through such secondary concerns and focus on the core meaning and purpose of dependent co-arising. The current work expands that effort for English readers.

Ajahn Buddhadāsa's Dependent Co-arising

Ajahn Buddhadāsa's work in Theravāda Buddhism has been to recover the core perspectives that have been ignored, lost, or obscured as Buddha-Dhamma was encumbered with the trappings of religious rituals, moralistic beliefs, afterlife speculations, donation-seeking rationalizations, and quick-fix meditation techniques. As a clerical caste emerged over the centuries following the Buddha's passing, Dhamma was segregated into Dhamma for those identified as renunciate wanderers (bhikkhus and bhikkunīs) and Dhamma for householders (upāsakas and upāsikās). Further, a moralizing tone crept in and emphasis began to shift from liberation in this life to earning a better life after death. While such developments may have their place, something crucial was muddled in the process. Ajahn Buddhadāsa did not accept the segregation of practice and the bias underlying it, nor the superficial moralizing that overlooked the subtler perspectives found throughout the Pāli suttas.

After intentionally flunking out of the Thai monastic education system—he never wanted a position in a big Bangkok monastery anyway—Ajahn Buddhadāsa moved to an abandoned temple near his natal village, dug deep into the suttas, and refined his studies in the crucible of his own practice. Along the way, he discovered dependent co-arising as he thought the Buddha intended, rather than how traditional, pedantic orthodoxy has interpreted it. This required exploring dependent co-arising in light of other core teachings: "only suffering (*dukkha*) and the quenching of suffering," "nothing is worth clinging to (as me or mine),"[6] voidness, thusness, and the middle way. Most of all, one's understanding must be practical rather than metaphysical, ontological, or cosmological; a matter of experience rather than merely accepting the assertions of authorities; and must lead to liberation in this life.

To aid his investigation, he compiled over eight hundred pages of passages translated from the Pāli suttas that concern dependent co-arising in one way or another.[7] These were published as *Paṭiccasamuppāda from His Own Lips*, a volume that allows one to read the wonderful variety of perspectives and details on dependent co-arising in its own terms, largely free of later interpretive assumptions and biases. In translating the Pāli into Thai, Ajahn Buddhadāsa left key terms in Pāli rather than rendering them with an interpretative twist. For example, consciousness (*viññāṇa*) remains just consciousness, and is not twisted into "relinking consciousness," a term the Buddha himself never used. Also, birth is just birth (*jāti*), and need not be assumed to mean "rebirth"; after all, there is no "re-" in *jāti*. If a sutta passage was somewhat ambiguous, he left it to the reader to explore the ambiguity. His own views were appended as comments. This book includes a number of such passages translated from his Thai translations.

Choosing to put the orthodox Theravāda commentaries back in their rightful place—secondary to the Pāli suttas, yet potentially helpful in understanding the originals—left him open to constant sniping from those who had been raised on and never questioned the commentarial system. The commentaries had come to be accepted as the Buddha's word, rather than remembered as derived from the original teachings. In response to those who felt threatened by his approach, Ajahn Buddhadāsa insisted he was hewing to the Buddha's intent—liberation from dukkha. His critique of the commentarial system does not take up much space in this book, as the original talks were given to a largely Western audience unfamiliar with the Pāli suttas and their commentaries. It was not as necessary to clear up traditional obfuscations for his Western audience, as was usually the case with Thai audiences. Nevertheless, he does refer to that system and readers will have some sense of the controversy that existed in relation to it.

Certain writers who adhere to the commentarial understanding of dependent co-arising, which spans at least three physical lives, often warn and scold those who do not follow their beliefs. While the better scholars among them have valid points that serious students of Buddhism should not ignore, there is a tendency among such scholars to over-simplify, if not flatly misunderstand, critiques of their beliefs. To imply, as has happened, that thoughtful teachers such as Ajahn Buddhadāsa are amoral, irresponsible, or heretical smacks of the authoritarianism that often goes with scholarly hubris and patriarchal positions. Rather than dogmas and defenses of the faith, Ajahn Buddhadāsa advocated reasoned debate and honest disagreement with a spirit that never forgets that we are aiming for the end of suffering as soon as possible. Perhaps none of us truly and fully understand dependent co-arising and can enjoy exploring it for the rest of our lives, as the Buddha appeared to have done. Careful, unbiased translations of the relevant suttas are crucial here.

Exponents of the "the three lifetimes interpretation" assert that it is consistent with *anattā* or not-self. Ajahn Buddhadāsa found their explanations unconvincing, as they have not escaped the implications of something that remains the same as it carries over from one life to the next. This vehicle for karmic results smells rather like a self (*attā*)—that is, an individual, separate and lasting entity. Such presentations fail to explain, although they claim to, how karma works over lifetimes without implying such an entity. In Ajahn Buddhadāsa's view, the karma and rebirth emphasizing approach sacrifices the liberating value of a not-self understanding of dependent co-arising for a moral version of dependent co-arising. It may conventionally be correct from an ethical perspective, and therefore may be of value, but it misses out from an ultimate perspective. Ajahn Buddhadāsa found this unfortunate.

There is no doubt that passages that describe "rebirth" appear in the suttas.[8] What are we to make of them? Do we take them to be literally, materially true? If so, how do we deal with the fact that they seem to contradict the notion of not-self? Do we fudge one to protect the other? Are the suttas any less contradictory when we read them less literally? Do suttas present ultimate truth or conventional truth? Might there be value in understanding dependent co-arising in a variety of ways, wherein no single way of understanding it, even Ajahn Buddhadāsa's, is the sole and whole truth?

Ajahn Buddhadāsa is not the only intelligent, thoughtful student of Buddha-Dhamma to have questioned an apparent logical contradiction in the standard view, though he was the earliest and most prominent of Theravāda teachers to do so. He had discussed such contradictions privately with a personal confidant of his who enjoyed a very high rank in the monastic hierarchy, but his confidant would not discuss it publicly. In recent decades, a growing number of scholars and Dhamma students, lay and monastic, Asian and Western, have raised the same questions in various ways as well. Fortunately, when those who raise such questions have studied the matter at least as much as traditional apologists have, dismissing such questions on the grounds that the questioners simply do not understand the matter is no longer accepted as an honest response.

The Buddha was not one to fall back on mysticism. Ajahn Buddhadāsa recognized that religious teachings, including the Buddha's teaching, use ordinary language in ways that express perspectives and realities less obvious than the perspectives and realities that ordinary language is typically used to express. Fundamentalist minds seem unable or unwilling to consider this natural fact of language and instead seek to interpret all teachings literally. Ajahn Buddhadāsa, being more creative and skillful, recognized two levels in the Buddha's language: an ordinary level of language that speaks of people and beings, and a Dhamma level of language that expresses not-self and dependent co-arising. Sensitivity to language and the meanings of key terms, which have changed over time, is central to understanding the vital teaching on dependent co-arising, in particular.

In short, Ajahn Buddhadāsa consistently read the suttas from a not-self perspective and was consequently the first major figure in Thai Buddhism to publicly question the many lifetimes view of dependent co-arising that has long dominated Theravāda teaching. One need not agree with him in order to appreciate the serious reflection he has given the matter. If seeing dependent co-arising is to see the Dhamma, Ajahn Buddhadāsa's perspectives challenge us to examine whether we actually see dependent co-arising or not. May this translation of his work serve the ending of egoism and suffering.

The Process of Creating the Text

As with Ajahn Buddhadāsa's earlier book *Mindfulness with Breathing*, this book was edited from transcripts of live oral translations.[9] The transcripts were compared with the audio recordings of Ajahn Buddhadāsa's original Thai discourses to make sure that nothing significant was omitted and that elaborations introduced into the translation were not inappropriate. The book that you hold in your hands includes everything he said. The natural redundancies that come with extemporaneous, oral teaching have been somewhat consolidated, but some redundancy is retained as a natural reflection of Ajahn Buddhadāsa's style.

As editor, I worked to shape these talks into a book with the help of friends acknowledged below. I have added chapter titles and section headings to make the book easier to navigate for readers. Endnotes have been added to the text to mark the terms and principles discussed within the chapters, and are, as much as possible, comprised of translations or paraphrases from other talks and writings of Ajahn Buddhadāsa. At times, I have relied on my own memory and understanding of his teaching, and to the best of my knowledge the explanations are in line with his understanding of Buddha-Dhamma and life.

I have resisted suggestions to soften occasional provocative language that might be jarring for some Western readers, for example, "stupid" and "foolish." I would rather preserve his own words, as Ajahn Buddhadāsa is saying important things in his own way. Over polishing and prettying would result in someone else's book, and a more common Dharma book at that.

The original talk and translation was a collaborative process. It usually began with Tan Ajahn, as we usually referred to him there, thinking about his theme for an upcoming retreat series and discussing it with me. He would often try out certain themes and terms on me in the week preceding a retreat, without actually telling me what his talks would be about. He would have me look up key terms in the dictionary and discuss them with me so that I would have the appropriate translation available. During the talks, he would listen as I orally translated to make sure I didn't leave out anything important. If I did, he would remind me. Occasionally, when I would get carried away with one of my additions ("improvements" he called them), he would politely clear his throat. In this way, Ajahn Buddhadāsa's talks and my translation of them happened in collaboration with one another. However, in the end, as the translator and editor of this book, the responsibility for any additions to his talks that were not there in the Thai falls on me. I can only offer my sincere apologies for any errors or inclusion of any extraneous material that I have failed to excise.

Pāli Terminology

To encourage a common basis of understanding central terms, Ajahn Buddhadāsa emphasized the importance of the Pāli terms that appear in the traditional discourses of the Buddha and used them as much as possible. Becoming familiar with them is a great aid to careful reading of the teachings. Nevertheless, this can be daunting for new students, especially Americans who only know their native tongue. Therefore, at the publisher's request we have minimized the use of Pāli terms in this work. When a Pāli source term first appears in translation, the original Pāli word is provided immediately following it in parentheses. After a Pāli term has been introduced, it is occasionally reiterated alongside its English translation as a means of indicating that Ajahn Buddhadāsa often left such terms untranslated in his

Thai discourses, and as a way of helping readers become more familiar with source terminology. Certain terms are either so central to understanding the teachings (e.g. *dukkha*) or lack a good equivalent (e.g. *vedanā* and *samādhi*) that we use the original Pāli term more often. The Pāli terms used herein are discussed in the glossary, where they are explained in keeping with Ajahn Buddhadāsa's understanding.

The suttas passages that begin each chapter have few if any Pāli terms. For readability we have used all English terms even when some of them are problematic (see Glossary). This is also the case with additional passages from Ajahn Buddhadāsa's *From His Own Lips* series. These translations from the Pāli via Thai are found in *Companion to Under the Bodhi Tree* (Liberation Park Press). These additional readings are recommended on a chapter by chapter basis in the "Guide to Source Texts" that follows the final chapter. As multiple translations are now available, such as those by Bhikkhu Bodhi and published by Wisdom and online repositories such as Sutta Central and Access to Insight, I've chosen to be less strict in my renderings from Ajahn Buddhadāsa's Thai in order to bring out nuances that "more orthodox" translations may obscure. Such alternative translations are referenced throughout and readers are encouraged to compare the various translations in order to better understand how an ancient language finds its way into modern English.

Acknowledgments

Two old friends from Suan Mokkh helped get this project going: Sister Wendy McCrae transcribed the original oral translations and Sam Settle (then Sujitto Bhikkhu) provided early editing. Since then, Jonathan Watts has championed this manuscript more than anyone and kindly nudged me toward its conclusion. He also transcribed the chapters on existence and helped with the organization of the chapters. His patient encouragement has been much appreciated.

Viriyanando, an even older Dhamma buddy from Suan Mokkh, and Lise McKean, a more recent Dhamma friend, read later drafts of the manuscripts and offered valuable advice. The participants in classes in Oak Park and Chicago, Illinois, and Viroqua and Madison, Wisconsin, asked helpful questions, challenged certain wordings, and gave me chances to try the chapters out.

Jo Marie Thompson, my life-partner through the later stages of the project, provided the emotional support that got me though some personal hang-ups and blockages, and a year of successful cancer treatment. Without her multifaceted aid, this book may never have reached completion. She also did the last round of proof reads.

Finally, I hope that students of Buddha-Dhamma will find this teaching inspiring, provocative, and insightful as we cultivate the right understanding that guides the noble path of suffering's quenching.

Santikaro

1 ❇ Buddhism Is Natural Truth

Kālāmas, you ought to question, you ought to wonder, your doubts have arisen concerning things you should question. Come, Kālāmas,

do not accept (or reject[10]) something as true merely because of oral tradition;

do not accept (or reject) something as true merely because of customary practice;

do not accept (or reject) something as true merely because it is widely rumored;

do not accept (or reject) something as true merely because of scriptural citation;

do not accept (or reject) something as true merely because of logical inference;

do not accept (or reject) something as true merely because of reasoned deduction;

do not accept (or reject) something as true merely because of thinking according to appearances;

do not accept (or reject) something as true merely because it holds up to (or goes against) one's views;

do not accept (or reject) something as true merely because the speaker appears (or does not appear) credible;

do not accept (or reject) something as true merely because the speaker is (or is not) one's teacher.

Kālāmas, whenever you yourselves know that these things are unwholesome, these things are harmful, these things are criticized by the wise, and when practiced according to their own standard these things bring suffering and have no benefit, then you ought to abandon such things.

Kālāmas, how do you regard the following: When greed arises in someone does it arise for their benefit or not? "Not for any benefit." When that person is greedy, when greed dominates, when greed overwhelms the heart, he may kill, steal, commit adultery, lie, and encourage others to behave in such ways, which are actions leading to suffering and are without benefit for a long time, is that not right? "That is true."

How do you regard the following: When hatred arises in someone does it arise for their benefit or not? "Not for any benefit." When that person is hateful, when hatred dominates, when hatred overwhelms the heart, she may kill, steal, commit adultery, lie, and encourage others to behave in such ways, which are actions leading to suffering and are without benefit for a long time, is that not right? "That is true."

How do you regard the following: When delusion arises in someone does it arise for their benefit or not? "Not for any benefit." When that person is delusory, when delusion dominates, when delusion overwhelms the heart, he may kill, steal, commit adultery, lie, and encourage others to behave in such ways, which are actions leading to suffering and are without benefit for a long time, is that not right? "That is true."

How do you regard the following: Are these things wholesome or unwholesome? "They are unwholesome." Are they harmful or not harmful? "They are harmful." Do the wise censure or praise them? "The wise censure them." After one practices according to their standards do they lead to suffering and are of no benefit, or the opposite? "After one practices according to their standards they lead to suffering and are of no benefit."

[The Buddha repeats the ten bases for unwise acceptance and rejection again.]

Kālāmas, whenever you yourselves know that these things are unwholesome, are harmful, are censured by the wise, and when practiced according to their own standard bring suffering and have no benefit, then you ought to abandon these things.

[The Buddha repeats the ten bases again and then asks the same questions about non-greed, non-hatred, and non-delusion, which the Kālāmas answer appropriately.]

Kālāmas, whenever you yourselves know that these things are wholesome, are harmless, are praised by the wise, and when practiced according to their own standard bring happiness and are beneficial, then you ought to dwell with these things.[11]

We are here to investigate something of central importance to our lives. I can think of no better way to begin than to be clear about the meaning of the word "Buddhism" (*buddha-sāsanā*). Later in this book, we will consider other important terms and concepts, including one that is at the very core of Buddhist teaching. So please relax your preconceptions about Buddhism, as well as religion in general, in order to explore with a fresh mind. We will begin by clarifying what kind of religion Buddhism is. In subsequent chapters, we will probe deeper into the core of Buddhism—the law of conditionality (*idappaccayatā*).[12]

What Kind of "Ism" is Buddhism?

The world is full of "-isms," each of them with their different meanings. Among them, the meaning of the suffix *-ism* changes, transforms, and bounces all over the map. Specifically, "-isms" such as communism, socialism, materialism, and consumerism are fundamentally different from the "-ism" of Buddhism. Since those kinds of "-isms" might prejudice us, we should try to understand what the "-ism" of Buddhism means.

Although Buddhism is also an "-ism," it differs in a crucial respect from all the other "-isms" of the world. All those other "-isms" are theories and ideologies created by human beings. They are made up of ideas, opinions, beliefs, theories, and structures concocted by people. Conversely, the "-ism" of Buddhism is not dependent on or created by human beings in any way. Buddhism is something natural; it exists naturally in nature. At its heart, it is natural law that has been discovered by the Buddha because it has always been available to discovery. Thus, real Buddhism is in no way man-made.

Inseparable from nature, being the truth of nature, Buddhism is in itself free and independent. It depends only on its own reality, which it itself is. Consider the words "fact," "truth," and "law." Facts or truths exist naturally, in line with the laws of nature. That is what Buddhism is: it exists naturally, in line with the laws of nature. A human being discovered this truth of nature and then showed people how to understand it, so that they could apply it in their everyday lives. Every aspect of this process of discovery and transmission is natural and unfolds according to natural laws. This reality and the way to understanding it are all there is to Buddhism.

Any who care to look can discover this law for themselves. For this reason, true Buddhism is unique among all other "-isms" in that it is not exclusive or monopolistic. It does not assume any exclusive authority to itself, nor is it dependent on any other authority. It remains intellectually free and spiritually independent as a natural truth to be discovered, studied, and explored by any who care to look.

Originally, Buddhism was not called "Buddhism" or "*buddha-sāsanā*." And even when the term *sāsanā* was applied to the Buddha's teachings, it wasn't used in the way that it is frequently used nowadays to mean "religion."[13] The Buddha's disciples did not call it "Buddhism," "the Buddhist religion," or anything like that. The Buddha initially spoke of his teachings as *brahmacariya*—a way of life that is sublime, excellent, and able to solve all human problems. This supreme way of life later came to be called "sāsanā," which has in turn become associated with the English word "religion," creating misunderstanding. The Buddha did not talk about sāsanā, as Asians do now, to mean "a religion." If we treat Buddhism in terms of religion, our discussion is likely to become sloppy, complicated, and confusing. Instead, to keep things simple and clear, think of Buddhism in terms of "truth," "facts," and "laws of nature." These truths or laws are the foundation of the Buddha's teaching. He rediscovered and then revealed them to us. Now we must understand and apply these truths so that we can live free from problems.

Buddhism does not depend on or assume any external authority whatsoever. It is neither exclusive nor possessive. Being Buddhist is a matter of living a sublime way of life, the *brahmacariya*, wherein one explores the law of nature and lives in harmony with it. It is not a matter of external identity or affiliation. Therefore, you need not convert or register yourself as a Buddhist in order to study and practice Buddhism. You can follow whatever religion pleases you or follow no religion at all, and still study and practice Buddhism. It is simply a matter of how you live your life. Any who are willing to approach, learn, investigate, practice, and live according to natural truth can experience this. Buddhism is available to everyone and is not exclusive in any way.

Another way to understand Buddhism is by thinking about the word *buddha*, which means "to awaken from sleep" or "to be awake." We should reflect on the difference between ordinary sleep and ordinary wakefulness. Here, however, "to be awake" means more than simply being awake in an ordinary sense; it means not going through life in a sleepy, befuddled way. To do so requires that we see things as they really are, that we see the genuine truth of things. Our practice as Buddhists, then, is to wake up, to use that awakening to see everything in the light of truth, and to live accordingly. Once awakened, we know: we see and experience all things as they actually are. Through knowing, we blossom into the fullness of life—clear, calm, and clean. This is how we understand "Buddha" in Thailand, as the Awakened One, the Knowing One, and the Blossomed One. The Buddha's awakening is symbolized by the lotus that rises above muddy pond waters and fully opens to the sun. This is what Buddha and Buddhism are all about.

We may also consider the word "religion" here, but let's be careful that our understanding is not superficial. The Latin roots of this word tell us that religion is a system of life and practice that binds humanity to the highest reality or to "the supreme." Christians and other theists might say that their way of practice ties humanity to God, but in Buddhism the highest reality does not have to be God. So we prefer to speak of "the supreme" or the highest reality (*paramadhamma*), as these are more inclusive terms. In our case, "the supreme" specifically refers to that condition, state, or reality in which all problems end and there is no suffering.

We Buddhists call this supreme reality *nibbāna* (Pāli) or *nirvāṇa* (Sanskrit). Nibbāna is the end of all suffering and misery, of everything that burns and scorches us. Nibbāna is the coolness of life, the quenching of the fires of suffering (*dukkha*) that burn us. This is the supreme reality in Buddhism: the supreme truth that can be realized. So, where other religions speak of God as that highest reality to which religion binds us, we Buddhists speak of the supreme reality in which all dukkha ends.

Some claim that there is no God in Buddhism. Don't mind them. Know that Buddhists have their own kind of God, but understand it differently than how the old pre-Buddhist gods or the monotheistic Gods of the West are understood. It's neither correct nor fair to describe Buddhism as atheistic, which is a rather narrow-minded point of view. It's just that Buddhists have a much different kind of God than the kind most people understand. The Buddhist God is nonpersonal. It doesn't have the anthropomorphic characteristics, such as consciousness and personal feelings, that many people attribute to God.

Nevertheless, you must not allow such trivial points of debate to interfere with your study, make it difficult for you to practice, or make it impossible for you to get along with people of other religious persuasions. In the end, issues such as whether or not there is a God are not really that important.

We should not allow them to become obstacles or to create divisions. Such things are often just a matter of language, so it's best not to let them get in the way of understanding. Putting an end to suffering and solving our problems is what really matters. Awakening, release, and blossoming into the fullness of life is good enough to accomplish this. We shouldn't let minor questions get in the way of this freedom.

Further, you needn't worry about whether you can believe another religion and still practice Buddhism. Nor do you need to worry that you must believe something in order to practice Buddhism. Please let go of such apprehensions and fears. Please also let go of any opposition or hatred that you might feel toward Buddhism or any religion. Give up any notion you might have about the impossibility of various religions meeting and cooperating with one another. It isn't true that we cannot develop mutual understanding. We can get along perfectly if we all help find ways to end suffering. Each religion contributes its own methods and practices for putting an end to dukkha, it's just a matter of which works best in whichever situation and for whichever people.

We have the right to choose for ourselves which religion we will practice from among all the religions of the world. As human beings, we can test for ourselves as many teachings and practices as we like. If one genuinely frees us from suffering, we will be able to affirm, accept, and follow it; we will believe it with the firmest confidence. This is our right and freedom within the laws of nature. If you wish to look into Buddhism, you must understand this point from the start.

Faith, Energy, and Wisdom in Religious Practice

Discussions of religion inevitably bring us to consider another problematic concept—that of faith. There are generally two kinds of faith. One is the kind of faith that comes from knowledge, intelligence, and wisdom. It is a product of correct understanding and wisdom. The other kind is the blind faith that is mere belief and comes before or instead of any real understanding. Both kinds of faith may be necessary. Those who are unable to understand directly, such as young children, may rely on blind faith. Those who are mature and intelligent enough to understand what is happening in life now, who are able to investigate suffering in their own lives, have no need for such blind faith. We need a faith that comes with wisdom. In Buddhism, such faith is called *saddhā*, and arises from a clear awareness of suffering. If you can understand the difference between blind faith and saddhā, the word "faith" won't cause any problems for you.

Some may prefer the word "confidence" to "faith." Confidence implies a certainty, a conviction, that can only come from wisdom. If we lack direct knowledge and understanding, real certainty is impossible. True faith must follow from wisdom. The kind of blind faith that merely believes what it is told without reason or direct experience is a false certainty. We must know how to tell the difference between these two.

To be true saddhā, true faith, as Buddhists conceive of it, it must be a confidence accompanied by energy (*viriya*) and wisdom (*paññā*). From the Buddhist perspective, all three of these factors—faith, energy, and wisdom—must be present in order for us to practice whatever religion we follow. We cannot get by as religious people if we are lacking any one of them. Energy refers to the effort we put into that which we believe. We must back up our faith with effort and perseverance. Wisdom refers to the knowledge and intelligence that oversee and regulate faith, energy, and other factors so that they proceed correctly.[14] It is natural that different religions place more or less emphasis on these three aspects, favoring one above the others in their practice. Some religions lay much greater stress on faith and belief, some emphasize energy and perseverance, and others focus mainly on developing understanding and wisdom. Buddhism falls within the group of religions that emphasize wisdom and take experiential understanding as their central principle. This is reflected in the fact that the religion has named itself after Buddha—that which is awake, knowing, and fully blossomed. This discerning, guiding, and balancing element is given prominence in Buddhism. Despite the fact that Buddhism places great emphasis on wisdom, we should understand that problems with our religious practice will arise if we neglect to cultivate faith and energy alongside it. The qualities of faith and energy are still vitally important to our religious practice.

When faith is exalted as the most important principle, for example, we must ask ourselves from where the energy to follow it through will come. Will we have enough wisdom to govern our beliefs and views, to rein them in should they go awry? Sometimes, when we have too much faith, we don't have enough energy and effort to make it meaningful. We may even hear from those that emphasize faith over all else that we only need to believe, and that effort is unnecessary. Some even say that practicing pure faith is a way to eliminate suffering. Whether or not that works, I don't know. I haven't followed that approach.

Although effort and wisdom may be underemphasized in "faith-based religions," they cannot be ignored altogether, whatever some adherents claim. Similarly, other religions that focus almost solely on motivation, mental effort, meditative power, and energy as their means of getting rid of suffering, shouldn't abandon faith and wisdom altogether. Of course, it is only natural that we are drawn to a form of religion that has a particular emphasis appropriate to our needs and situation. Those in life situations that require great faith will need sufficient faith, those in situations that require great energy will need sufficient energy, and those in situations that require great intelligence will need sufficient intelligence. You must know well enough to discern which cases require faith, which require energy, and which require wisdom. Such knowledge provides you the tools to free yourself from suffering.

Understanding this will allow us to draw upon all the religions, not let particular emphases distract us, and eventually transcend them all. We need not bother to critique them as right or wrong, good or bad, although we may be wary of overly simplified claims. They all have their place and value. Seeing that the background and development of unique individuals and cultures leads to reliance on different religious factors in accordance with the times and circumstances in which they grow, we also see that we have no reason to begrudge people what they need. We have no need to say our way is right and that others are wrong, or that ours is good and others are bad. Such judgments are unnecessary. We can accept that all three approaches to religious practice—faith-dominant, effort-dominant, and wisdom-dominant—are valid. We should not judge other religions as wrong, while considering ourselves alone to have the right religion. Please reflect on this.

The important thing to remember is that we must employ all three factors in our lives. Faith, energy, and wisdom have necessary roles to play in everyone's lives. There is no reason to disparage any of them or any religion based primarily on one or the other. We should manage all three factors skillfully according to the different challenges and problems that face us in life. So, let's accept that sometimes faith is most needed, sometimes energy, and sometimes wisdom, depending on our proclivities and the circumstances in which we find ourselves. If we understand the differences among religions in this way, we lose any inclination we might have had to argue about which approach is best or right.

2 ⁂ Independently Investigating Causes and Conditions

Friends, there are these three sectarian tenets that however they are considered, evaluated, and critiqued by the learned ones, no matter how much they are turned and spun, these tenets will lead to inaction regarding what is wholesome.

What sort of sectarian tenets are these three? The three are

1. Certain groups of wanderers and priests hold and teach the view that "all persons who experience pleasure, pain, and neither-pleasure-nor-pain do so because of previous actions."
2. Certain groups of wanderers and priests hold and teach the view that "all persons who experience pleasure, pain, and neither-pleasure-nor-pain, do so because of God's creative power."
3. Certain groups of wanderers and priests hold and teach the view that "all persons who experience pleasure, pain, and neither-pleasure-nor-pain, do so for no reason whatsoever."

Friends, I have approached and questioned groups of wanderers and priests who hold and teach such sectarian tenets . . . I said to them, "If that is the case, those who kill beings . . . steal . . . misbehave sexually . . . speak falsely . . . provoke discord . . . speak crudely . . . speak frivolously . . . are greedy of heart . . . harbor ill-will . . . have perverted tenets, must do so because of actions previously acted . . . or because of God's creative power . . . or for no reason whatsoever. When actions done previously or God's creative power or no reason whatsoever is taken as the primary issue, those individuals will have no desire and will make no effort regarding things that ought and ought not to be done. When appropriate acts are not accomplished and inappropriate acts are not abandoned with sincerity, these people who lack mindfulness to guard themselves have nothing by which to honestly call themselves samaṇa (wandering seekers of truth)."

Friends, this is how I rebuked with Dhamma the wanderers and priests who held such sectarian tenets.[15]

Having considered religion in general, we will focus specifically on Buddhism, which emphasizes wisdom as the predominant factor in spiritual practice. Its name—Buddha-Sāsanā or Buddhism—already clearly announces what it is about. *Buddha* means to know, to awaken, and to blossom into the fullness of human potential. While faith is not made the primary factor, it still has a significant role, as does effort. The Buddha is the wise person who uses wisdom in solving problems. The Dhamma is the wisdom system pointed out by the Buddha for solving those problems. The Sangha are those who practice accordingly, following this wisdom system in order to solve their problems, that is, to end suffering. So in Buddhism there is the wise being, the system of wisdom itself, and the practice of this wisdom system. In this way, Buddha, Dhamma, and Sangha—the Triple Gem of Buddhism—are all intimately connected with wisdom (*paññā*).

The Path of Wise Self-Reliance

With faith, there must always be an object that one believes in, whether a person or a thing. If one has faith, it is faith in something. Thus, faith implies dependence on something outside oneself. When it comes to energy and effort, however, we do things for ourselves. One cannot rely on anyone else; energy is one's own responsibility. Even more so, wisdom is a matter of self-reliance because self-knowledge and understanding must be direct and intimate; nobody can know our own reality for us. We cannot rely on anyone or anything external, though they may be of great help to us along the way. Thus, with energy and wisdom one can only rely on oneself, although faith may rely on others. So it is that Buddhism teaches a self-reliance that goes beyond faith in things outside oneself.

Self-reliance has a synonym: reliance on Dhamma. Self-reliance means to depend on the Dhamma that arises from one's own effort. Self-reliance is reliance on this Dhamma performed by oneself, for oneself, through oneself, in and of oneself. This is what we mean by self-reliance. It is not some sort of egoistic self-striving. If there is a God that can truly help or save us, it is the God of Dhammic duty and self-reliance. In other words, the true, correct Dhamma practiced with wisdom is the God that saves. In this way, even followers of Buddhism, who rely on wisdom, have a God of salvation. In other words, wisdom and the Dhamma that arises from wisdom is the God of Buddhism. This wisdom clearly understands natural law and the natural duty that follows from it.

On this path of self-reliance, the basic questions we ask are: Where does the problem come from? From where do happiness and suffering arise? In Buddhism, we hold that happiness and suffering do not come from a personal god, nor do they arise from the "old karma" of past lives, nor are they a matter of fate. Rather, we hold that happiness and suffering depend upon whether we act rightly or wrongly regarding the natural law of conditionality (*idappaccayatā*), the flow of and interrelatedness among causes and conditions. While the details of conditionality will be considered in a later chapter, here you should know that the wisdom that understands conditionality is essential. This wisdom allows us to see the duty of the moment and practice correctly regarding conditionality so that dukkha (suffering, distress) does not occur and problems do not arise. Please understand the true sources of happiness and suffering. They do not come about through old karma, an anthropomorphic god, fate, or luck. The reality is very simple. Happiness and suffering are the results of correct and incorrect action regarding conditionality. This natural fact can only be known through wisdom.

Deepening investigation leads to the wisdom that understands how dukkha happens and from what it arises. An important question to consider is whether dukkha happens constantly or intermittently. We will discover that it occurs when there is mistaken action, action in conflict with the law of conditionality. Suffering does not occur all the time; it is not a continuous phenomenon, as some think. Thus, we have an opportunity to prevent it from arising. With the wisdom that understands this, we will be able to prevent distress and solve the problems associated with it. Because dukhha occurs intermittently, there are times when our duty is to protect against new suffering arising. There are other times when our duty is to get free of the suffering that has already arisen. Both require the wisdom that understands the law of nature.

Investigating Causes and Conditions

It is important to understand that the principle of conditionality (*idappaccayatā*) is central in Buddhism. Everything that happens has causes and conditions, proceeds according to causes and conditions, and leads to results in line with those causes and conditions.[16] Buddhism focuses on these causes and conditions, especially whether we act rightly or wrongly regarding the law of conditionality. We do not consider a personal god or actions in past lives to be the causes of problems in our lives.[17] Rather, the causes and conditions are right here in the lack of wisdom and the foolishness that acts in conflict with the law of conditionality. This is the source of suffering. Understanding this, there is enough wisdom to act correctly in line with the law of conditionality. Then, dukkha cannot happen. We are able to deal with suffering through wisdom concerning causality.

The principle of conditionality requires careful scrutiny so that we understand it correctly. Everything happens through its causes and conditions; thus, we must address the causes and conditions, not the effects and results. In Thai, there is a saying that, though it is rather crude, may help you understand this vital point: "Do not scrape shit with a short stick." When cleaning up animal dung or the old-style toilets, you're likely to get a mess on yourself if you use a short stick. So use a long stick. This means that when there is a problem, do not just go poking around with a little stick that merely rearranges the effects. Use a long stick; find out what the causes and conditions are and address them. This is much more likely to be successful.

"Scraping shit with a short stick" is understood by ordinary Thais to mean something that will not get the job done properly. If we merely mess around with results, we never get anywhere. We stay in crisis management mode all the time. The point is to find out the causes and conditions. If there is a fire, you can never put out the fire without finding what is causing it. Do not just fight the fire impetuously; find out what is causing it and address that. The Buddhist way of putting out a fire is to remove the fuel. In this religion of understanding causes, conditions, and their effects, find out what the causes and conditions are, then remove them and you will obtain the results you are seeking. This is another essential principle of Buddhism.

There is something I have heard that illustrates the same point, though I cannot verify whether it is true or not. People say that if one takes a long stick to poke, annoy, and hassle a puppy, the puppy will bite the end of the stick. If one takes the same stick to poke, annoy, and hassle a lion, the lion will not bite the stick, it will bite whoever is holding the stick. The lion has an intelligence that the puppy lacks. The lion understands the cause of its problem, while the puppy just reacts.

So which are we going to be in life? Are we going to be puppies or lions? When problems come, will we react impetuously or will we go to the source of the problem? One of these is a rather foolish approach and one is the approach of wisdom. The approach of the lion is that of the Buddha—the Awakened, Wise, Knowing One. So we follow the same principle of going to the sources of problems and eliminating them. This is the method that we learn by taking up the Buddha's way of practice.

Natural Evolution of Truth and Duty

Buddhism takes an evolutionary approach. Buddhism holds that the world and everything in it evolves through various causes and conditions. Understanding how this natural evolution flows through our lives is at the heart of Buddhism. Conversely, creationist religions believe that the world was created by a Creator God. Today, we have the freedom to choose whichever approach satisfies us, whichever quenches dukkha. Buddhist evolutionary understanding follows the law of nature and uses it to investigate how suffering arises. Studying the law of nature, learning how distress and misery occur, we can then learn how to live without them. Buddhism sees this as a natural evolution beyond dukkha. Rather than focusing on a creation story, we focus on that reality in which no suffering can be found, which is the core issue.

When we see these evolutionary principles through our own reasoning and are satisfied with them, then we can understand the law of evolution[18] as God without sacrificing anything. When we take natural law as our fundamental principle, we will have four basic categories within nature that we can study and investigate in order to understand what nature is all about. The first category to be studied is nature itself; the second is the law of nature (conditionality); the third is duty according to that law of nature; and the fourth is the results of living in that way, the fruits of following natural duty according to the law of nature. So we study, investigate, and practice with nature, the law of nature, natural duty, and the natural results that come with doing that duty correctly. If we investigate all four of these aspects of nature, we will fully understand nature.

The word *dhamma*, in Buddhism (*dharma* in Sanskrit), correlates with all four categories of nature: nature itself, natural law, natural duty, and natural fruits. Of these four meanings of dhamma, "duty" is perhaps the most ancient. This meaning of dhamma is most important and ought not to be brushed off, as so often happens nowadays. Dhamma simply means "duty," which is the duty that follows from the law of nature and must be carried out in line with the law of nature. This is the core meaning of the word *dhamma* and the essence of Buddhism.

Unlike pre-Buddhist understandings, we understand this duty in terms of natural law rather than as God-given or man-made. We follow such duty according to the authority of wisdom rather than external or coercive authorities. Understand "duty to the law of nature" correctly and you will be able to carry out your duty, and duties, wisely. The sublime way of life or brahmacariya is exactly the same as this duty in line with the law of nature. If you practice according to the law of nature until you are able to quench all distress and pain, then you have practiced the supreme duty as understood in Buddhism. This practice is the essence of Buddhism.

The Buddha's Natural Scientific Method

In seeing everything as happening through conditionality and then proceeding and functioning according to the power of causes and conditions, Buddhism uses the same basic principle as science. If something is truly scientific, it uses the approach of searching out causes and conditions in order to solve problems at the level of their basic causes or manage things through their causes and conditions. However, if we take a philosophical approach in these matters, such as the approach of logic and inductive reasoning alone, we merely create a hypothesis, interpret data to fit it, and then argue for its rightness. In Buddhism, rather than taking a hypothetical approach, we take the more direct and pragmatic scientific method of searching out the causes and conditions of a problem. Once we find the relevant causes and conditions, we can deal with them appropriately and solve the problem or get the results that we seek. In this way, Buddhism is more a pragmatic science than a philosophy, more a methodology than theory or theology.

Now, let us consider the order or process that we must practice. First, we must begin by learning what we need to practice. Second, we act upon what we have learned; we must test it by putting it into practice. Third, we receive the results appropriate to the actions and thus can evaluate how correct our practice has been. So, there are three interlocking steps: learning, acting upon that learning, and finding out what the results are. All three of these stages take place upon a foundation of natural causality. What is the reason for learning this? What is the conditionality for knowing its truth? What is the reasoning for practicing a certain way? What are we looking for and what kind of effect do we expect to occur? What is the reasoning behind our practice and the conditionality that it follows? What results actually happen? For what reasons? None of this occurs without causes and conditions. Every effect has its causes and conditions. Understanding and reasoning about practice in terms of natural causality is fundamental to Buddhism. This process requires wisdom. We must learn, we must try these things out, and we must carefully observe what the results are. This principle is the heart of practicing Buddhism.

Spiritual Freedom and Intelligent Independence

The next fundamental principle is that of freedom or independence. Let's be clear right away that Buddhism is a religion of freedom. There is no pressure, coercion, or obligation to believe or do anything. As a religion of intelligence and wisdom, Buddhism is not a dogmatic system and does not accept any dogmas unquestioningly. Authoritative dogmas are out of keeping with the spirit of Buddhism. There is freedom to think, to investigate, to research, and to experience each for oneself. If there is any pressure to believe, or if there is any dogma, that is not Buddhism. The Buddha himself made this clear in a discourse known as the Kālāma Sutta, named after the Kālāma people of a district named Kesaputta.[19] In this discourse, the Buddha points out the importance of independence in thought, study, understanding, practice, and receiving the benefits of practice. All must be completely free. If not, it is not Buddhism.

In Buddhism, you are not required to believe something, even if our prophet or founder said it. This is the kind of freedom advocated in Buddhism. You do not have to place blind faith in its teachings. Instead, listen carefully and think about these teachings before believing. Do they make sense? What results will they bring? Will they end dukkha? If you can see for yourself that these teachings will end suffering, give them a try. Test them out and see what the actual results are. If the practice of these teachings genuinely quenches distress, then you can believe in them. This is the essence of the Kālāma Sutta and a clear example of how Buddhism is a religion of freedom. What other religion has the courage to say we need not believe something said by our own founder and teacher?

In the Kālāma Sutta, the Buddha advised not to accept something merely because it is a tradition passed down through generations; nor because everybody is talking about it; nor because it is written down in scriptures. Do not believe something merely because it is logical; nor because it was arrived at through methods of philosophical or metaphysical speculation; nor because it corresponds with common sense. Do not believe something just because it agrees with your own opinions; nor because the speaker has impressive credentials, a charming voice, or friendly appearance; nor even because the speaker is your teacher, your guru, or the founder of your religion. The Buddha taught that none of these are sufficient reasons for belief. Instead, something is worthy of belief when it has been investigated thoroughly and through direct experience. This is the kind of independence the Buddha recommended in the Kālāma Sutta as a fundamental tenet of Buddhist practice.[20]

We should use this standard even with children. Instead of using a switch to threaten them if they do not do as we say, we help them apply natural reasoning: "If you behave like this, what will be the results? If you do that, what will happen? Look carefully at the results and choose what is best." With children, we should not use coercion, nor should we use rewards and bribes. Such means are incorrect. We need not force or trick children into believing what we want. Instead, we can teach them to think for themselves: Which way is correct? Which way leads to the proper benefits? Children are capable of deciding for themselves what is proper. The Kālāma Sutta also applies to them.

Unfortunately, religious conservatives in Thailand (as well as most other places) disagree. These authorities claim the Kālāma Sutta does not apply to people today, children or adults. They claim people are not educated enough or are too foolish, and that it is necessary to trick, convince, or bribe them to believe. Fearing that people will not have the wisdom to choose correctly for themselves is not the Buddhist way. Rather, we should do whatever we can to enable people to choose wisely and independently.

Let's offer the highest level of spiritual freedom to everyone willing to listen, think, and investigate through their own practice. Buddhism is a religion that offers such freedom in thought, practice, and wisdom. This does not mean the kind of selfish independence that blindly does whatever one wants. Rather, this is about investigating carefully and having the freedom to think things through, to try them out, and then to believe based on that personal experience. This is the freedom Buddhism holds as fundamental and that is always necessary in our study, practice, and realization.

3 ❊ Training in Direct Experience of Freedom

Friends, depending on eyes and forms, eye-consciousness arises. The meeting together of these three is contact. With contact as condition, feeling arises, which is sometimes pleasant, sometimes painful, and sometimes neither painful nor pleasant.

When someone experiences pleasant feeling, he delights, relishes, and indulges in it. The tendency toward lust naturally accumulates for such a person. When someone experiences painful feeling, he sorrows, worries, laments, despairs, and is deluded regarding it. The tendency toward aversion naturally accumulates for such a person. When someone experiences a feeling neither painful nor pleasant, he does not understand in accordance with reality the causes for this feeling, the cessation of this feeling, the delicious charm of this feeling, the penalty from this feeling, and the skillful means of escape from this feeling. The tendency toward ignorance naturally accumulates for such a person.

Friends, such a person cannot abandon the tendency toward lust arising in reaction to pleasant feeling, cannot diminish the tendency toward aversion arising in reaction to painful feeling, and cannot remove the tendency toward ignorance arising in reaction to neither-painful-nor-pleasant feeling. Unable to abandon ignorance, he cannot cause true knowledge to arise. That he could make an end of suffering here and now is not possible.

[The identical wording is applied to the other sense media as well as the consciousnesses, contacts, and feelings that arise depending upon them.][21]

Naturally, changes have occurred during the more than two thousand years since the Buddha first taught. In the religion based on that teaching, there have been inaccurate transmissions due to faulty memorization, misguided corrections, and additions. This requires freedom for us in examining and interpreting Buddhism, including the Tipiṭaka—the Three Baskets, the main body of Buddhist scriptures—let alone the later commentaries, opinions, and interpretations that have accumulated since the Buddha's time. We need not accept the Pāli texts, commentaries, and traditional interpretations of Buddhism until we have investigated them thoroughly and proven them in our own practical experience. Consequently, there is no need to worry that something has been lost or mistaken due to the centuries of time that have passed, or for whatever other reason, if we adhere to the fundamental principle of skillful independence in studying Buddhism.[22]

Spiritually Empirical Science

As we stated from the beginning, we will study Buddhism scientifically, that is, as a spiritual science. When we speak of spiritual science, we mean that we must study and learn through our own spiritual experience rather than from scriptures and texts. In Buddhism, we practice spiritual science by observing and investigating suffering as it actually occurs in our hearts and minds (*citta*).[23] We search out the causes and conditions of that dukkha and learn how to remove them in order to be free of all suffering, misery, and distress. In this way, there is direct spiritual experience of these matters, not mere hypotheses and theories. When we approach Buddhism as spiritual science, we will not have any problems regarding the accuracy of the scriptures, worries about mistakes and inaccuracies that may have crept in over the centuries, or whatever other doubts might arise. These will not trouble us, because we will be able to verify Buddha-Dhamma for ourselves, in our inner spiritual experience.

Nor need we worry over considerations of the various environmental and cultural factors. When we take Buddhism as a spiritual science, we need not be overly interested in such matters, to the degree that they become distractions.[24] Quite a few Westerner scholars of Buddhism focus on India, and on its history, geography, politics, philosophy, and the like. They go too far with unnecessary things like comparative psychology before they get around to actually studying Buddhism itself. Do not waste time on nonessentials. Instead, focus on direct spiritual experience. I'd like to say that even the Buddha's life story is unnecessary. In the Buddha's time, nobody studied the details of his life as is done nowadays.

What of the popular books about Buddhism in China, Buddhism in Tibet, Buddhism in Burma, Buddhism in Sri Lanka, Buddhism in Thailand,

and the like? None of them are essential or necessary, either, because they do not really concern Buddhism itself. Such books are about the cultural trappings, the outer crust that has been added by the cultures of the various countries where Buddhism has flourished. You need not study such crusts and rinds; put them away for now. Simply focus your study on the basic facts of suffering as found within one's own heart and look there for the way out of distress. Direct spiritual experience of dukkha is the only lesson you need to know.

Training through Experience within Oneself

We can learn all we need to know within ourselves, through our own spiritual experience. The method for doing so is called *sikkhā*, which means "to see oneself" (*ikkhā* is "look" or "see" and *sa* is "oneself"). The deeper meaning of this Pāli term is to look into oneself, to observe oneself within oneself, until seeing oneself and knowing oneself as one actually is. Please do not confuse this with the modern Thai understanding of *sikkhā* as education or study, which is more about books, schools, and other externals. Proper Buddhist study or *sikkhā* is to look into oneself, see oneself, and know oneself. Once again, the only authority is our own direct spiritual experience, where we learn from the suffering and problems within. In this way, we truly study Buddhism.

For this reason, we need not concern ourselves with external revelation, such as from God. In Buddhism, we do not believe or maintain that Dhamma has been revealed to us by God. There is no need to cite or refer to divinity, to rely on divine authority, or to depend on divine revelation.

Instead, study Buddhism directly within dukkha itself. Explore it like a surgeon investigating a wound.[25] The surgeon cuts into the wound to find out what is wrong, in order to cure the illness correctly according to its cause. Once finding the cause of the wound, he removes it and solves the problem. We can take this surgeon's approach to life and Buddhism. Whenever there is a problem, cut into its core and look for the cause of the problem. Seeing the problem clearly, we will understand its opposite, the state of well-being that is free of the problem. Then remove the cause and experience the well-being that remains. This is called "studying like a surgeon."

Sikkhā in Buddhism must include practice (*paṭipatti*, lit. "traveling the path"). The usual kind of study or learning is not sufficient. Our study must be applied through direct practice within life itself so that it leads to spiritual experience. Think carefully about what one has learned, then try it out, test it, and put it into practice in real life. This is where one really learns Buddhism, through actual practice. Schools, books, and classrooms are not necessary for the study of Buddhism, although they have their uses. Even the Tipiṭaka is unnecessary. In the Buddha's time, none of these existed, yet his followers were able to practice successfully. They did not rely on any of the later developments that are considered so important today. For the original disciples, study was practice. They directly confronted the problems of life and learned to solve those problems with guidance from the Buddha. Solving the problems of life is the practical meaning of study and learning.

Knowledge and Wisdom as Direct Realization

Now it is time to say something about knowledge and wisdom, which in the Pāli language are called *ñāṇa* and *paññā*. While knowledge has many levels, we can summarize three basic levels of knowledge. The first level is the learned knowledge (*suta-maya-paññā*) that comes from books, listening to others, and schools. We may call it third-hand knowledge. The second level is the reflective knowledge (*cinta-maya-paññā*) that comes from thought and pondering, from reflecting and reasoning about what we have heard or learned. We can investigate with all the tools of thought and logic available to us, especially when they are guided by the four noble truths. This is a higher level of knowledge that might be called understanding. This secondhand knowledge is more certain and useful than mere book learning.

Finally, the third and highest level of knowledge is the realization that comes from spiritual cultivation (*bhāvanā-maya-paññā*). While learned knowledge comes from listening to the words of others and reading books, and reflective knowledge comes from thought, reflection, and reasoning, the realization that comes from spiritual cultivation comes from immediate spiritual experience. The realization arising from direct experience is much different from the previous two levels. It alone can be considered firsthand or direct knowledge. Understanding Buddhism requires the third level of direct spiritual realization regarding whatever one seeks to know. Please recognize that knowledge has these three levels; improve your understanding of knowledge so that you practice to fulfill all three levels.

Nowadays, what passes for education in this world merely involves the first kind of knowledge, and sometimes the second. Consequently, all the schools and universities in the world, all the great institutions of higher education and the libraries filled with millions of volumes of books, can never bring us to the heart of Buddhist understanding. We can study all we like, take copious notes, even write our own books, but it is just the study of records and texts. We need to understand that such learning is not our purpose. Instead, we can employ the scientific reasoning that investigates dukkha and its causes so that we can remove the fundamental causes of that distress. In the end, this must lead to direct realization. To merely think about suffering, its causes, and its end will never solve the dilemma of dukkha. We must see and experience it directly within our own hearts. Nobody can learn this in our stead and such realization cannot be taught. We must investigate and discover for ourselves if it is to be realization that comes from spiritual cultivation, the realization that leads to awakening. Realization and awakening come from this. Please improve your understanding of how to study. Whatever is most important must be learned in this way.

Do not be dependent on external conditions. Your spiritual well-being should not rely upon external factors. Instead, let it rest upon internal foundations. The real classroom is within oneself; the most voluminous library is within oneself. It is not necessary to read whole libraries with millions of books, thousands of books, or even hundreds of books. A few dozen well-chosen books are plenty, if they support a system of internal study and direct spiritual experience. This is where true learning takes place.

Because you think you need external help, whether from books, teachings, or gurus, you have come here from Europe, America, Australia, and various parts of Asia to study Buddhism. Though well-intentioned, your effort may be misguided. You should know that the most you can do externally is to learn the method of discovering Buddhism; you'll never find Buddhism itself through such externals, whether here or anywhere else in Asia. Instead, just sit still. Sit down and open your studies internally. If you've come here to learn about Buddhism, then learn the methodology of sitting down and studying Buddhism from within. We call this *sandiṭṭhiko*, seeing Dhamma for oneself, knowing Dhamma within oneself. This is the only valid school and library for learning Buddhism. You cannot learn Buddhism itself from anybody but yourself. Other people can at most help you understand the method of study and practice. So please understand what we mean by learning within.

The Prisons of Positivity and Negativity

In short, we study *citta* (mind, heart, consciousness). You might call it psychology, but it is not the psychology commonly studied in the world today. Most of modern psychology is for the sake of personal advantage and profit. Psychological cleverness can give an advantage in competition, marketing, and profiteering, which often are the main purpose of learning psychology today. While clinical and therapeutic psychologies are of some benefit to people, they are not the primary applications and at best rearrange the ego-structure rather than dissolve it.

Buddhist psychology is another matter altogether. It seeks to liberate mind from attachments and thus liberate it from dukkha. This is the kind of psychology that can be used with Buddhism. Please do not confuse it with the ordinary worldly psychology that is more about personal advantage and selfishness.[26] We do not study mind for the sake of worldly advantage but solely to help mind free itself from all problems. Later, once it is free, other suitable benefits can follow.

In Buddhism, mind's salvation is the purpose of psychology; it is about freeing mind from imprisonment. Mind is entrapped in a most profound prison of its own making, the prison of infatuation with positive and negative. Buddhist psychology aims to liberate mind from this prison of the problems and bondage regarding positivity and negativity.[27] When minds are deceived by the positivity and negativity of this world, they cling to and are trapped by them. Positivity and negativity are the prisons of mind; infatuated bondage to them turns our minds into their prisoner. For a psychology to be Buddhist requires that it understand this spiritual prison and help our minds escape.

When we are prisoners of positivity, we have a positive ego. When we cling to something as positive, a positive kind of ego is born and we are caught in a positive prison. When we cling to something as negative, a negative kind of ego is born and we are caught in a negative prison. Look well! Positivity is prison and negativity is prison. In this respect, there is no difference. Both lead to clinging and bondage to whatever we regard as being positive or negative, which creates problems and distress, so we call them prisons. Please avoid these prisons, both the positive ones and the negative ones, no matter how attractive or repulsive they may appear.

When we feel positive, when we have a positive self, we pull things to ourselves, we gather them in. When we feel negative, when we have a negative self, we push things away, we try to get rid of them. Our lives are pulling and pushing, pushing and pulling, all the time. Is this enjoyable? Is it really fun? Does a life of constant push and pull make you happy? Or is it unbearable? Please consider how it is actually more difficult and troublesome than anything else. Consider seeking a life that is free rather than a life of push and pull. With this objective your study of Buddhism will be easy and rapid.

Gladness and happiness are not at all restful. They are extremely busy, stressful, and dynamic. Sadness is painful; it is not restful either. It is also quite busy. Neither gladness nor sadness is restful or peaceful. Both keep mind busy, excited, and spinning around. True spiritual rest requires being above happiness and suffering, above positivity and negativity, and beyond good and evil. If we seek peace, we must lift mind above positivity and negativity. This is the objective of our study and practice.

The Push, Pull, and Spin of Defilements

We must intelligently understand the things known as *kilesa* (defilements, reactive emotions). Positive feelings cause positive defilements such as lust (*rāga*) and greed (*lobha*). Negative feelings cause negative defilements such as hatred (*dosa*) and anger (*kodha*). Liking leads to positive defilements that pull and attract; disliking leads to negative defilements that push and repel. These negative and positive defilements are bad enough, yet there is still a third kind of defilement that is confused and foolish about positive and negative. This defilement of foolishness cannot distinguish, figure out, or decide what is positive and what is negative. It runs around in circles. Positive defilements pull toward, negative defilements push away, and neither-positive-nor-negative defilements run in confused circles. These wear us out almost to death, leaving no opportunity to rest and find peace. Please understand these things called defilements very well.

You ought to know that there are many terms for distinguishing the defilements. We can classify dozens, hundreds, even thousands of them. If we want to specify them in detail, we can do so beyond counting. However, if we want to be concise, we can more simply categorize them within these three basic kinds or types: the defilements that attract, the defilements that repel, and the defilements that circle around. Positive defilements make us want and pull in so we live under the power of liking and needing. Negative defilements make us hate and push away so we live under the power of disliking and hatred.

The third kind of defilement, the sort that is neither positive nor negative, makes us doubtful and uncertain. This word "doubt" is very important.[28] It concerns truth and our inability to see things as they are. Buddhism seeks to eradicate doubt because it causes confusion and disturbs us terribly. Doubt is so disturbing it keeps us from sleeping at night. When there is not any positive or negative, it wonders whether something is positive or negative. It creates confusion out of neutrality. This third type of defilement is called delusion (*moha*). Please understand these three categories of defilements. Though their variations are many, all are found within our own hearts. By eliminating doubt, we can be free of all these kinds of defilements. All the thousands of defilements and reactive emotions—every kind of bad mood or bad temper—are included in these three terms: greed, hatred, and delusion.

Please observe this thing called "doubt" in depth; it prevents us from stopping desire and craving. When there is doubting mind, it is impossible to stop wanting and desiring. Whenever there is desire and craving, there is defilement and suffering. When we doubt we do not know whether something is good or bad, beneficial or harmful, right or wrong, sufficient or inadequate. So we will always be uncertain about it and full of desire. Even millionaires with their piles of money still wonder whether they have enough: "Will it ever be enough?" Doubt is the most disturbing thing. Anyone able to eliminate doubt will be a saint, an Arahant. With no doubt, one is above positivity and negativity. If still beneath the distorting influence of this binary pair, one will not be able to give up doubt. You ought to declare doubt as your Enemy Number One. Eliminating doubt will require knowledge, intelligence, wisdom, and a high level of realization. There the matter ends. One realizes the highest coolness, Nibbāna.

4 ✻ Beyond Positive and Negative

Gain and loss, disrepute and prestige,
blame and praise, happiness and suffering—
These are the common human conditions,
transitory, unstable, and subject to change.
The wise, ever mindful, know these dhammas,
seeing them as subject to change.
Pleasant experiences do not excite such a mind;
unpleasant experiences do not irritate such a mind,
There is no decay of virtue due to grasping at
or repulsion from these conditions.
The wise one, knowing the path, realizes
Nibbāna free of passion and sorrow.
Such a one has found the end of becoming.[29]

Our study leads us to see the reality and truth of all things. When we see things (dhammas, natures, phenomena) as they actually are they cannot deceive us or lie to us, whether with positivity or negativity. Whenever we speak of truth it can never be positive or negative. Now, however, most of us are deluded by positivity and negativity, and may construe truth to be positive. Concepts of positive and negative occur repeatedly, turning up as good and bad, as right and wrong, or as similar dichotomies, which have no real value or meaning. Happiness and sadness are equally worthless and delusory, as are profit and loss, and all the other oppositional pairs. They merely delude, trick, and mislead us. Heaven and hell are the worst of all; they reek of positive and negative. As they entrap us in suffering, we have no real need for them. Our purpose is to be above all meaning of positive and negative. Our aim is this freedom of mind independent of all the delusive, nefarious oppositional pairs.

Duality's Fundamental Dilemma

This point was well understood by the Hebrew teachers who compiled the Old Testament. In the third chapter of the Book of Genesis, God warns our ancestors Adam and Eve not to eat the fruit of the Tree of the Knowledge of Good and Evil.[30] Once that fruit is eaten, we attach to good and evil, consequently revolving, spinning, and recycling in that good and evil, which is dukkha. Wise people have known this for millennia. Not being enslaved by the meaning of good and evil is the heart of Buddhism. If you know this, you will know everything you need to know and will escape from the tyranny and misery of all influences of good and evil, of positive and negative, and of heaven and hell. This takes you beyond dukkha, which is the sole purpose of our study and practice.

All our difficulties concerning this matter follow from our original ancestors consuming the fruit of attaching to good and evil. Ever since, this has been the original sin, the universal sin within humanity. Each and every one of us attaches to good and evil, to positivity and negativity. Our difficulties occur because of this fundamental problem, which we have been living with since we were born. Although freeing ourselves from positive and negative is immensely troublesome, our path is to be beyond them. This is the heart of Buddhism, living above and beyond all influences of positivity and negativity with utmost certainty.

Now we may understand how clinging to positive and negative is a problem, causes misery, and creates suffering, but we are still unable to free ourselves from the power of positive and negative. For example, we may realize that love is problematic, especially with how it is often spoken of in confused ways. Though it troubles and torments us over and over again, we are unable to extricate ourselves from its power.[31] More obviously, we know that anger and hatred are painful and worthless, but we cannot get free of their power, either. We bounce back and forth between liking and disliking, loving and hating, trapped by the delusions of positivity and negativity. We are spiritual ping-pong balls, unable to find peace, trapped in endless cycles of heaven and hell.

Living with this spiritual dilemma is hell in this very life. Positivity and negativity, liking and disliking—in other words, good and evil—are our fundamental problem. These two are the basic conditions for all our problems. Whenever we fall for positive or negative, selfishness is born. If we do not like, are dissatisfied with, despise, or hate something, we want to get rid of it, even destroy it or kill someone. If we like, approve of, or prefer something, we want it, must have it, seek to possess it, and compete with others for it. When something is positive, it leads to liking and wanting, and being selfish about getting it. When something is negative, it leads to disliking, anger, and hating, and being selfish about getting rid of or destroying it. Whether through liking or disliking, loving or hating, there is always a problem. They cause infatuation, anger, fear, excitement, confusion, worry about what hasn't happened yet, and longing after what has passed away.

Our lives and world are full of these problems, both individually and collectively. We are full up with such selfishness and the harm it does to ourselves and others. All this egoism and violence is because we are imprisoned by positivity and negativity. Please study life until you have the capacity to live beyond positive and negative.

We might call this "new life," at least for those who are unfamiliar with it. In fact, it is not really new at all. It just appears new to those who have not heard of or experienced it. Actually, it is the original life that sages and saints have realized all along. It merely seems new to those still trapped in the old, stale life of positivity and negativity. We study for the sake of new life above, beyond, and free of all positive and negative.

Highest Unconcoctable Level of Knowledge

The highest Dhamma, the supreme Dhamma to be known and realized, is called unconcoctability (*atammayatā*). I suppose this is a strange word for you; it is unlikely that you've heard of it before. Although it appears in the Tipiṭaka, nobody ever talks about unconcoctability or teaches it. Nonetheless, this is the most important Dhamma. Unconcoctability is very powerful because it means that neither positive nor negative can be concocted. With *atammayatā* (unconcoctability) mind is in a state or condition that nothing can affect or concoct. We call this "unconcoctability." There is nothing taken or regarded as positive or negative such that it can affect, condition, or concoct thoughts, moods, and reactions in mind. If doubt is finished, there is no concocting. If doubt remains there will be continual concocting via positive and negative and there will not be unconcoctability, the state of being that is so free that positive and negative can never affect or concoct. Usually, there is this condition or that situation concocting, spicing, decorating, and spinning us round. Please aim for the highest freedom wherein positive and negative cannot concoct and stir up mind. That is unconcoctability.

We have checked through the dictionaries of Buddhism that have been published in the West and none of them seem to say anything about unconcoctability (*atammayatā*). This is really quite surprising, because in the scriptures this word has an important place. That the Western scholars who compiled these dictionaries have left out this important word shows that their understanding of Buddhism was deficient in this respect. Please do not make the same mistake of overlooking this word unconcoctability and its supreme meaning, which leads us to the highest realization. The state of unconcoctability is the state of mind in which nothing can concoct or create messes of positivity or negativity. With this as your objective, you will meet the new life that is most excellent and peaceful.

When there is unconcoctability as both insight and realization, when life is above all influence of positive and negative, concepts of self and soul cannot arise. Feelings of positive and negative cannot occur in a mind that is unconcoctable. Thoughts of I and mine, he and she, hers and his, cannot happen with unconcoctability. Currently, lacking unconcoctability, we must live with all the problems and distress that come with self and ego, with I and mine, with he and hers. Suffering occurs due to these concepts of self, because we believe we are separate individuals and then this individualism grows into selfishness. Such selfishness inevitably causes suffering in life. Yet we only become selfish because we do not see unconcoctability.

When you lack understanding of unconcoctability (*atammayatā*) and cannot live with a mind free of positive and negative influences, you may travel around the world however many times you wish without ever finding a place to rest. So please consider the "resting place of struggling souls"—unconcoctability. Our lives are constantly embattled and struggling. Desperately searching for a place of peace, they never succeed in finding one. But as soon as you discover unconcoctability here and now, you will be able to find rest and peace in *atammayatā* .

Do not think of *atammayatā* as something negative or lacking in something important; unconcoctability is beyond positivity and negativity. It is emptiness—reality empty and free of self. This is the resting place of the soul that has struggled without let up, afflicted by disturbance, conflict, and distress. Mind will be free, beyond concocting by positive and negative, beyond all ego and selfishness, unaffected by all things that once disturbed, hurt, and annoyed. This is the essence or heart of Buddhism, so please give this word your special attention: unconcoctability.

Salvation from Positive and Negative in Emptiness

To speak of salvation, of being united with God, is to speak in positive terms. In Buddhism, we speak of liberation (*vimutti*) from all things so that they can never cause distress and misery. Vimutti is neither positive nor negative. True liberation is beyond all meaning of positive and negative. This is our highest aim, to be above all influence of positive and negative.

Please lift your understanding beyond positive and negative. This must be called empty and free (*waang* in Thai). Observe how emptiness (*suññatā*) has no dimensions; something without dimensions cannot be positive or negative. Thus, emptiness has nothing to do with positive and negative. Mind that is void and realizes emptiness does not attach to positive or negative. We take this emptiness to be the supreme liberation, according to its meaning in Buddhism.

Finding the right translation for the Pāli word *suññatā* is difficult. Even "emptiness" cannot capture the meaning completely. Still, it is necessary to use these words on a preliminary basis until you discover the full meaning for yourselves. Then you can find the best translation for these words. Whatever the translation, emptiness or voidness has no dimensions or aspects that could be positive or negative. That is freedom on the highest level.

Coolness Never Bites

Having considered emptiness, we come to that which is called *nibbāna* in Pāli and *nirvāṇa* in Sanskrit. Nibbāna is the *summum bonum* of Buddhism. Ordinary people, when hearing the word Nibbāna, take it to be something positive. People are always taking things one way or the other, either as positive or negative, then clinging to them. Imputing positivity to Nibbāna is wrong, misrepresents Nibbāna, and makes it something other than Nibbāna. True Nibbāna is free of positive and negative; it has nothing to do with them. Please remember that Nibbāna is completely empty and free of positive and negative, is the supreme liberation, and contains unconcoctability to the fullest.

Please be very careful speaking of Nibbāna as "the utmost goodness," you might confuse it with something positive. It is important for you to understand the word Nibbāna correctly. It must be beyond goodness and beyond utmost goodness if it is to be truly void and the real Nibbāna. It is completely beyond even the highest good, but there is not any way to speak of that or describe it. In speaking with ordinary people, the proverbial man in the street, we need to use words like goodness and happiness. Thus, we might say that the utmost goodness is beyond all forms of goodness. This understanding of Nibbāna can lead to genuine freedom, that is, realizing Nibbāna.

When we feel good, it bites. When we feel bad, it bites. They may bite in different ways, but they are equally painful, difficult, and tortuous. The better it feels, the more seductive it is and the more there is clinging to that goodness. The more clinging, the more it bites and the more suffering there is. Whenever there is clinging to something, it bites. Mind is stirred up again, resulting in pain, distress, and misery. Do not cling to bad or good; then they cannot bite. Beyond good and bad there is no biting. The absence of all biting, whether by positivity or negativity, is called Nibbāna in Buddhism. Nibbāna is the state that is absolutely, perfectly, and totally free of all attachment. In Nibbāna, there is no clinging to good or bad, to I and mine, or to anything.

This word Nibbāna means "coolness." You may have been mistakenly told that Nibbāna means death or is about death. If you understood it that way, you might think that death is desirable, and perhaps contemplate suicide. But that is wrong, absolutely wrong. Nobody can realize Nibbāna through suicide. It is crazy to think that suicide can lead to Nibbāna. Nibbāna does not mean death, it means coolness, the kind of coolness that need not die, that is beyond death. Rather, this supreme coolness is discovered when life is no longer bitten by positivity and negativity. Please understand this most important word correctly.

Nibbāna literally means "coolness." When dead, there is no opportunity to be cool in this way. If cool temporarily, it is temporary Nibbāna. If cool always, it is eternal Nibbāna. Cool, here, means the absence of heat, that is, nothing burns mind and causes dukkha. In other words, it is not being bitten by positive and negative. This is not about death; death is just another kind of heat. When negative and positive bite mind, mind becomes hot and suffers. Nibbāna is the absence of any heat that would bite mind. We call it coolness, which is Nibbāna. It is realized through unconcoctability. With unconcoctability, nothing can bite mind because *atammayatā* prevents anything positive or negative from affecting mind. Please be interested in Nibbāna. With correct understanding of it, you will correctly understand the goal of life and will have a map that shows you how to walk the path of life correctly. I cannot sufficiently stress the importance of this.

Positive bites, is hot, and brings suffering. Negative bites, is hot, and brings suffering. The essence of this matter is clinging (*upādāna* or attachment). Whether clinging to good or clinging to evil, whether clinging to positive or clinging to negative, clinging is the central issue. If no attachment, there is no good or evil. Clinging sprouts from ignorance (*avijjā*), from not understanding things as they truly are. When there is no ignorance, there is no attachment, and thus no good or evil. Then we discover coolness, where the influence of positive and negative cannot seize us. Please understand Nibbāna in this way.

Above the World, within the World

Although this matter is something very profound, we can still teach it to children by helping them to see the things that bite them every day. We must point these out to children one by one, because there are so many things that bite them, increasing as they get older. Start with love, perhaps: have them observe how selfish love bites. Demanding and needy love also bites pretty badly. Second, try hatred: how is it hot and how does it bite? Third, consider anger: how does anger bite? Help children to observe hatred and anger. Then there is fear: how does fear bite so there is no space, no possibility of rest or peace? Fifth, excitement: there is no calmness when we are excited; how does that bite? Sixth, worry and anxiety concerning things that have not happened yet: how do they bite? Seventh, longing after or regretting the past: when we remain stuck on things that are gone, how does that bite? Eight, envy: how does it bite and who does it bite first? Does it bite the envious person first or does it bite the envied person first? Obviously it first bites the person who is envious. Lastly, jealousy: in Thai there are two kinds of jealousy. The more general kind of jealousy is possessive of things and the more specific, intense kind is possessive of sexual things, specifically one's lover, spouse, or partner. When either form of jealousy or possessiveness occurs, how does it bite? Show children how to observe these forms of biting in themselves and around them. In the process, you will understand the biting better, too.

Although there are many more, these examples are sufficient for our needs. Whenever one of these occurs, it is not cool, it is hot, and it bites. When none of these occur, how cool will life be? This approach can be used to help children understand what Nibbāna is about. Although Nibbāna is the most profound thing that we can know in life, we can still explain it so that children can understand.

Everything in the world is ready to take a positive or negative meaning. Whenever there is attachment to a positive or negative meaning, it burns and there is suffering in those forms we have just named, such as love, hatred, anger, and fear. The world only gives meanings as positive and negative. Being beyond the influence of positive and negative is called, in Buddhism, "living above the world" (*lokuttara*). We can be above the world even though our body is in the world. Transcending the world like this, being above all positive and negative influences even while the body remains in it, is Nibbāna. Nibbāna means being above and beyond the influence of all things of the world.

These words are quite strange, are they not? "Above the world while in the world" probably sounds most bizarre. When the influence or power of the world, whether positive or negative, cannot do anything to us, that is being "above the world while in the world." Please listen carefully: "in the world but above the world" or "in the world as if above the world."

Being beyond the world but still within the world may seem illogical, but it is not. This is the most correct understanding once we know how to uplift mind beyond the influence of all positive and negative. Then we will be above the world yet living within it.

This is what I like to call new life. It is new for those who have never heard of it or understood it before. In fact, people have known about this way of living for thousands of years. Until we know it for ourselves, however, it may sound strange and appears to be something new. Whether you think of it as new life or new way of life, may you all meet with success in coming into contact with Buddhism and discovering new life.

5 ❋ The Natural Law of Conditionality

Friends, the world is thoroughly understood by the Tathāgata;[32] the Tathāgata has removed himself from the world. The origin of the world is thoroughly understood by the Tathāgata; the Tathāgata has completely abandoned the world's origin. The quenching of the world is thoroughly understood by the Tathāgata; the Tathāgata has realized the world's quenching. The practice leading to the quenching of the world is thoroughly understood by the Tathāgata; the Tathāgata has cultivated the path leading to the world's quenching.

Anything in the world with its devas, māras, and brahmas,[33] that the myriad beings—including wanderers and priests, devas and humans—have seen, heard, smelled, tasted, touched, known, reached, searched, or visited with mind, that is thoroughly understood by the Tathāgata; thus he is called "Tathāgata."[34]

In the first chapter, we explained that Buddhism does not believe or accept that happiness and suffering arise as the fruits of old actions committed in previous lives or that they are ordained by God. Rather, happiness and suffering depend on whether one acts correctly or incorrectly regarding the law of dependent co-arising (*paṭiccasamuppāda*). For this reason, the remainder of this book will focus on dependent co-arising.

When speaking generally about any kind of phenomena whatsoever, whether mental or physical, animate or inanimate, having to do with human beings or not, we use the word conditionality (*idappaccayatā*). The law of conditionality is broad and general. When speaking specifically about sentient beings that experience feelings of happiness and suffering, we use the word dependent co-arising (*paṭiccasamuppāda*). It applies to things with a mental life, to the inner world of consciousness, and precisely refers to how suffering arises in sentient beings. Fundamentally, both terms refer to the same principle and law, but differ in how we apply and observe that law.

The Law of Arising

When speaking according to Buddhist principles, we do not use the word "create," nor do we have the word "creator." Instead, we speak of arising and causing to happen with no anthropomorphic implications of intention or will behind it. If anyone were to ask "who created the world?" the question would not make sense in Buddhist terms. Buddhism cannot respond to such a question because it has not been asked properly. However, if the question is phrased "how does the world come to be?" or "how does the world arise?" the Buddhist response is straightforward; the world comes about through the law of conditionality: because this exists, this arises; through the arising of this, this happens.[35]

If one believes that the earth is a fragment that broke off from the sun, this means that the earth's existence depends on the sun. If one considers it in other terms, such as it was formed out of nebulae, stellar gases, or whatever, it all still comes down to everything happening through the law of conditionality. Something had to exist in order for other things to arise from it; and that thing arose from other things. We refer to this broad, general understanding of dependence on causes and conditions as "conditionality" (*idappaccayatā*). The world happened because of conditionality, without any meaning or implication of a creator; nonetheless, *idappaccayatā* brought the world into being. Please understand conditionality in these terms.

When we believe that the earth comes from the sun, this means it came with the law of conditionality. Naturally, people will ask from what the sun comes. We reply that the sun came from one thing or another according to the same law of conditionality. No matter how far one traces things backward, everything comes from and depends on conditionality. Once there is this world, things arise in it due to conditionality. Water, bacteria, plants, animals, and human beings appeared on this planet through conditionality. This law applies to everything; it is universal: this arose due to this, which arose due to that, and so on endlessly. Observe how everything that has occurred was born or has happened because of something else. This continues on into the future. No matter how far we might go back into the past or forward into the future, everything can be traced to conditionality—this arises due to that. This is the fundamental law to be investigated.

Law of Nature as God

If some of you still have affection for the word "God," you might be interested to know that we have a word in Thai with essentially the same meaning. It even sounds pretty much the same, just a little shorter. Shorten the way you pronounce God and you'll get *gōt*.[36] Thai *gōt* means "law." If the vowel is lengthened, it becomes God.

God, for us, equals the law of all nature that when wisely practiced fully quenches all dukkha. This law of nature performs the functions of creating the world; of sustaining and preserving the world; and of destroying the world. It has all the attributes that are usually associated with God (for example, in Vedantic thought). The law of nature has those attributes that usually signify the power of God and, in fact, has all the power of God. You can follow this God if you like.

If it were necessary for Buddhism to have some sort of God, we could say that conditionality is the God of Buddhism. However, we must be clear that conditionality is an *impersonal* God rather than a personal God. Many people believe that Buddhism does not have a God, but they do not understand that there is another kind of God different from what they normally consider God to be. In Buddhism, we have an impersonal God, the law of conditionality. This law of conditionality can be considered the Buddhist God. Ordinarily, Buddhists do not speak in such terms and it is not really necessary to do so. Most Buddhists simply say that there is no God in Buddhism and instead affirm that there is the law of conditionality. We affirm that everything arises by means of the law of conditionality.

Universal Law and Suffering

To make it easy to understand and keep straight, please settle on this straightforward distinction: when speaking in general, universal terms about anything whatsoever, use conditionality, the universal law of nature; but when speaking specifically about sentient beings and their experiences, especially when it comes to suffering, use dependent co-arising or *paṭiccasamuppāda*. Whether they be plants, animals, or human, their bodies, all the physical and material aspects of their lives and world, arise and carry on according to the law of conditionality. But the experiential aspects that occur in their minds, especially the feelings of happiness, pain, pleasure, and misery, happen through the law of dependent co-arising.[37] This is true for human beings, animals, and even plants, supposing plants, too, have consciousness and sensitivity to experience dukkha.

To clarify the matter further, in each of us the aspect that is body—the material or physical parts—come from conditionality. The feelings that are suffering, painful, or stressful—which are mental phenomena—arise from the law known as dependent co-arising. A human being can be seen as having these two aspects. All of the material, physical aspects arise and happen due to the law of conditionality. On the other hand, mental feelings of happiness and suffering are a matter of the law of dependent co-arising.

Regrettably, these two words quite often are mixed up and used interchangeably. Generally, Buddhists do not make a clear distinction between conditionality and dependent co-arising. For example, I have read Buddhist writers who say that the sun arises because of dependent co-arising or dependent co-origination. That is not correct; they should say it happens through the law of conditionality. They should only use dependent co-arising about matters of mind, especially those concerning suffering, its arising, and its quenching. The confusion, though, is common even here in Thailand. This is unnecessary, as it is quite easy to make a clear distinction between conditionality and dependent co-arising.[38] Please be confident with their correct usage.

Just Happiness and Suffering Arising, Carrying On, and Passing Away

In Buddhism, when asked where joy and suffering come from, we answer that they arise from the impersonal God, the law of conditionality, and specifically from *paṭiccasamuppāda*. There may be others who understand that suffering and joy come from a personal God, but that does not have any meaning for us. For us, the law of conditionality is the impersonal God that makes everything happen. So we do not accept that happiness and suffering arise because they are determined by a personal God (God understood as a being, entity, or person). To understand, you must know how to distinguish the impersonal God of Buddhism from a personal God. If we understand this point properly, we will be able to continue our discussion.

The Pāli term corresponding to "personal God" is *issara*. The Buddha explicitly states that happiness and suffering do not occur because of the personal God. Further, neither happiness nor suffering arise from or happen because of old karma in so-called past lives, as some people assert. He also stressed that they are not without causes and conditions. Happiness and suffering are not a matter of blind luck or coincidence. They occur due to causes and conditions, that is, the law of dependent co-arising, which is the same basic law as conditionality, but applied to the experiences that living beings feel as either happiness or suffering. Consequently, if we wish to learn about happiness and suffering, we must learn the law of dependent co-arising.

If asked, "what is conditionality?" we will answer that it is the law that makes all things arise, carry on, and cease. Everything arises through the law of conditionality; everything proceeds, changes, and carries on through the law of conditionality; and everything ends or ceases through the law of conditionality. Happiness and suffering arise, continue to change, and then pass away the same as everything else. Whether material things or the stuff of experience, the characteristics of arising, continuing, and ceasing are always occurring due to conditionality.

It is necessary to observe and see—that is, contemplate—the symptoms of arising, continuing, and ceasing that ordinarily manifest according to the law of conditionality. We can describe all of this as the stream of becoming, but never in terms of creating or creation. There is no creator—a person or agent that creates—involved. Yet there is arising, continuing, and passing away, arising, carrying on, and ceasing, over and over again. This is the nature of all things, without any need for words like creator, creating, or creation, however popular they may be. There is just the process of becoming, which is what conditionality is all about. These are the conditions of all things within this world. All things arise, continue, and pass away through conditionality. If you understand these three aspects of the process of becoming, you will understand conditionality.

God Arose from Conditionality

We have the privilege to say that in India before the Buddha appeared the words conditionality and dependent co-arising did not exist. Instead, most people at the time believed that a God or gods caused things to happen.

Others denied that there was any causality at all. Such were two of the opposing views of the time; none spoke of conditionality or dependent co-arising. The Buddha was the first to use these two words. There were those who said everything happens because of God; there were those who said there is no cause, reason, or sense behind things; and there were those who preached radical materialism. Since none of these groups knew about conditionality and dependent co-arising, we can safely say that these words were not heard in the world until the Buddha arose.

To take this distinction further, if the question arises concerning where God comes from and how God continues, we can say quite simply that the personal God comes from and happens according to the law of conditionality. The impersonal God, however, is the only exception to this law. Everything comes about through conditionality, except for the impersonal God, which does not occur through conditionality because it is the impersonal God, the Law of Nature, itself. To make this subtler distinction, beyond the simpler one above, is also necessary.

Later, people were able to observe action and reaction, that is, karma, the fruits of karma, and the law of karma, all of which they attributed to God. For them, God oversees and governs karma and the fruits of karma. They did not consider action and the results of action to be simply the workings of conditionality. Such an understanding of karmic law is not the same as conditionality. Only when seen in terms of causes and conditions—that this is called "action," this is called "result," and they are mutually conditioned by each other, is karmic law the same as conditionality. The karma that is simply conditionality does not require an entity above and beyond conditionality itself.

Often, those who believe in a personal God have a way of speaking that is unfair, untruthful, and manipulates reality to their advantage. They claim that God created the law of conditionality. We Buddhists respond that it is the other way around: the law of conditionality created God. The point is not to win an argument or convert others but to fairly understand the various teachings, even those we do not agree with. We can respect others' understanding without fighting. So let us be polite about such differences. Please contemplate this carefully and come to your own understanding: did God create the law of conditionality or did the law of conditionality create God?

You might examine this question from the perspective that God is a human conception and that a process of development led to this conception appearing in our world. Our long-ago ancestors conceived of mysterious powers and sacred forces at work in the world. Eventually, this led to the idea of the most sacred power, which they called "God." If you consider this carefully, you can see that God is merely a conception that occurred in minds of human beings at a certain stage of their evolution. Then, you will see immediately how God comes from the law of conditionality.

In ancient times, early humans began to think and name things. Their thinking evolved until they conceived that within everything there is mind, consciousness, or spirit. The kind of thinking that modern people labeled animism appeared in minds of those ancients. They further believed that this consciousness or spirit had great power and was central to how things happened. They recognized an ability to control various things. Behind these smaller spirits or consciousnesses were bigger ones (gods) that had power over the smaller ones. Finally, this line of thinking led to belief in one all-powerful mind, soul, or spirit. They called this omnipotent mind or power God. This is how the concept of God arose through and from conditionality, just like everything else. This, at least, is how Buddhism sees the matter.

Buddhism holds that everything, including God, comes from the law of conditionality. Conditionality governs everything without implying a governing consciousness, intentionality, or agency. Thus, we speak of it as *gōt* or law. Only this law can create God. You have the freedom to investigate whether or not this is true. You are completely free to agree or disagree, and to believe whatever you wish. Think about this yourself, investigate it yourself, and come to your own conclusions. If you believe as Buddhism believes, you will see that the law of conditionality has given rise to material things, conscious things, all things—even the concept of God.

6 ✻ Conquering Ignorance, Selfishness, and Superstition

"The inner tangle and the outer tangle,
these people are entangled in a tangle.
So I ask of you Gotama,
who can disentangle this tangle?"
One established in virtue, deeply knowing,
developing mind and wisdom,
a cultivator ardent and sagacious:
she can disentangle this tangle.
Those for whom lust and hatred,
along with ignorance have been dispelled,
the arahants with impulses ended:
for them the tangle is disentangled.
Where both name and form
stop without the least remainder,
also impingement and perception of form:
it is here this tangle is cut.[39]

Having discussed the broad principles of conditionality as the impersonal God and law of nature in the previous chapter, let us now take a look at ourselves, at our side of things. The concept of ourselves that we might speak of as "self" or "soul" is also a product arising from the law of conditionality. This law of conditionality creates the concepts of *attā*, self, soul, or ego—however we wish to name it. They arise out of causes and conditions; they do not exist on their own. Consequently, concepts such as *attā*, self, ego, and soul cannot co-exist with insight into the law of conditionality. They are in opposition to it; we cannot have both insight and delusion together. If one sees conditionality, such concepts of self and soul disappear. If one still believes in and clings to such concepts, one has not understood the law of conditionality. Thus, we have the teaching of not-self (*anattā*). Everything happens through the law of conditionality, without there being any self-existing ego or soul.

Do Not Scoff at Not-Self

Some people, perhaps most people, will think this business of not-self is crazy or stupid. The lack of self, or *attā*, is bewildering to them because they insist on having a good self or special self or supreme self. People think they just have to have a self. We say to them that there is no such self to be found and understanding not-self is the most important way to keep suffering from occurring in this life, so that life will not bite its owner. Whenever the concept of self appears, life bites its owner. Living without self is to be free of all problems and above all dukkha. Understanding not-self is crucial.

Suffering, the condition of self-torment, comes from mind having a concept of self, that is, clinging to self. This mental or spiritual clinging is like carrying a heavy weight or burden. Whenever the hands and arms must carry a heavy load they become tired and may even ache with the weight. When the burden is carried by mind rather than the hands and is nothing other than self or *attā* it creates distress. It burdens itself by clinging to self, to ego-me. And just as we can set down physical loads, mind can relieve itself of the burden of *attā*, self, ego, and I.

This dukkha of carrying burdens has both positive and negative aspects. Please do not think that the positive side cannot be a burden. The positive aspects are as burdensome as the negative aspects. They're opposites yet equally weighty. We can cling in both negative and positive ways; either way bites its owner. Sometimes, the positive can trick us into clinging even more strongly than the negative. We like the positive without knowing that it is a heavier load. Sometimes the pain and misery due to the positive is even greater than that due to the negative. They're both burdens, but the positive tricks us into clinging more. Suffering and torment arise most of all because we've fallen in love with things we cling to as positive.

Clinging to Self Is the Biggest Burden

You must see that there is nothing heavier than clinging to the concept of self. Wherever there is self, there is burdensomeness and nothing is more of a load than self. Even worse, once the self concept occurs, selfishness follows. The heaviness spreads to others; it takes advantage of, harms, and abuses others. Consequently, the burden is shifted to the world. Selfishness is the heaviest burden carried by the world. Clinging to self leads to selfishness, which further leads to the competition, conflict, and fighting that fill and torment the world.

Please look and consider carefully. You can see for yourself that selfishness is running the whole world. Our entire universe is being dominated by selfishness. Selfishness tries to force the world to go according to its desires, so we can say that all the problems and crises of this world are due to selfishness: economic problems, political crises, exploitation of women and children, environmental degradation, crime, and all the rest. There is not one crisis that does not have selfishness at the bottom of it. If we wish to remove this selfishness and the problems it causes, we must remove the foolishness and misunderstanding of self. How to do so is our topic of study here.

To understand more easily, we might compare our current situation with ten thousand or even a hundred thousand years ago when our forest dwelling ancestors still went about naked. Back then, selfishness was minimal because people did not have the things to desire that we do today. With few things to desire their desires and selfishnesses were few. As the forest people developed little by little over the centuries and millennia, selfishness increased in line with material development. Arriving at the huge material development of the modern era, life is full of selfishness. Nowadays, selfishness is everywhere. This pressing problem is that the more we are selfish, the more we behave in ways that harm and exploit ourselves and others. Is not this ridiculous? Our very self-interest, self-centeredness, and over-concern with ourselves afflict ourselves and others. Such selfishness rules the world.

The modern world has developed education to very high levels and has spread modern education everywhere. Many of us are highly educated after many years in school. Despite all its power, the weakness of modern education is that it does not or cannot do much to limit or lessen selfishness. In fact, modern education often supports and strengthens selfishness in subtle, profound, and complex ways. Such selfishness and selfish education prevents there being any real peace in the world.

Nowadays we have levels of material and technological development that are beyond words. We have electricity, televisions, computers, cars, airplanes, and many other things our ancestors never could have dreamed of.

Why, then, do we not have peace in our world? With all our modern developments, why do we have so many crises instead—crises that appear to be increasing and getting worse? Our ancestors in the forests did not even need clothes to wear and did not have the problems modern humanity has now. We have increasing selfishness according to how modern education shapes us. We need to find a way to solve this situation and to understand how it came to be. Get rid of selfishness and peace will appear.

What is both amusing and pitiful is that we are so proud of our development and evolution. Yet we have all kinds of problems that we should not have because of all the selfishness. Our ancestors did not have problems with drugs, pollution, and nuclear weapons. With what, really, are we developing? To a large extent, we are developing with crises created by selfishness and with the clinging to self that creates selfishness. Thus we are assailed by insecurities and fears. Until we can develop unselfishly and peacefully there is not much for us to be proud of.

The Spirits Are Laughing at Us

Why do not we think for a minute whether those people in the forests would be laughing at our situation today? They lacked all these modern problems that trouble us so—pollution, addictive drugs, ever-increasing mental illnesses—but we have them all. They did not and we do. If they could see us now, they would be laughing at the ridiculous condition in which we find ourselves.

Look at the world nowadays. It is time to recognize our mistakes and the imbalances of modern development that is too focused on material goods. We are killing each other more than ever. People are committing suicide in greater numbers. Abortion is increasing. We must build more prisons and mental hospitals. The militaries and police forces continually expand, along with the globalized arms trade. Our ancestors the forest people did not know any of these things. We should be ashamed by them. If they could see us, how much they must be laughing!

If we did not have all these problems we might consider ourselves more advanced than they. They were not civilized and developed like this, yet we are the ones with all these problems and they would be laughing. We are in this predicament because of selfishness. Selfishness depends on the sense of having a self, believing in the concept of self or individual. To correctly eliminate this sense of self and let go of the self-concept, we have the teaching of not-self. The purpose of not-self is a life governed by mindful wisdom and free of ego-me. Buddhism aims at this realization and a life that does not need ego-me, and is consequently free of selfishness and all its attendant problems and dukkha.

We Thais have a saying: *phii huarau*, which means, "the spirits are laughing." *Phii* are the spirits of the trees, rivers, mountains, earth, sky, and everything else of importance in nature. Talking about these spirits comes naturally to Thai peoples. Do European cultures have a concept like this? The spirits are laughing at the foolishness of humanity. Whether spirits, angels, or whatever, they cannot help laughing at the delusions of we humans as we do so many wrong and destructive things that cause great distress to ourselves. Or maybe they would be weeping out of compassion.

Phii huarau means the same as if our ancient ancestors could see our modern developments and laughed at the ridiculousness of our dilemmas, but those ancestors are gone. The spirits, though, are still here, all around us, and they are laughing at the foolishness of people doing so much wrong, so much harm, such that our lives are full of problems and the world is full of crises.

If we were a little bit ashamed and embarrassed by the spirits mocking us, we wouldn't do so many foolish and harmful things. We wouldn't act so wrongly and there would be more peace in the world. If only we were a little bit ashamed of ourselves being mocked by the spirits.

Ignorance Regarding Conditionality

In Buddhism, we have a specific word for the condition of not knowing or not understanding conditionality and not-self. This word is *avijjā*, usually translated as "ignorance," which refers specifically to not knowing that which ought to be known. It does not refer to a lack of common sense or a lack of knowledge in academic areas, arcane trivia, or superabundant data. Ignorance does not understand conditionality, which, of course, is what ought to be known.

Ignorance, especially ignorance regarding conditionality, is the basis and support for superstitious concepts, beliefs, and practices.[40] We speak of these as superstitious because they are unreasonable, have little basis in reality, and do not actually accomplish what they purport to do. They follow the feelings and emotions of people who do not understand conditionality. All the foolish, silly, and distasteful things we consider superstitious come from ignorance, not knowing and understanding conditionality. This means that superstition and selfishness go together quite easily.

Our ancient ancestors were animistic in their experience and sensibility toward daily life. They saw sacred spirits in all kinds of things, such as, trees, rocks, rivers, stars, the sun, and the moon. They took those spirits to be causal, as central to how things transpired. They worshipped these spirits in order to curry their favor. As their understanding developed, they conceived of gods that were more powerful versions of those individual spirits. This line of belief eventually developed into the belief in one supremely powerful God. So they worshipped, prayed to, and pleaded for help and protection from this highest God.

In Buddhism, such beliefs are considered superstition because those people did not know about the law of conditionality. Animism occurred because people did not understand the law of conditionality. If people understood conditionality, they would stop believing such things. Mental and spiritual civilization ought to follow this trend, from not understanding the law of conditionality, to beginning to understand it, and finally understanding it thoroughly. Then we will be able to understand all things correctly, that is, how they all are subject to the law of conditionality.

Sacred and Holy Confusion

Next, let us consider something that in Thai is called the "highest sacred" or "highest holiness."[41] When people do not understand conditionality, they will attribute the highest sacredness or most holy power to a God, to an Original Cause, or a Creator. If they are particularly foolish, they will attribute the most sacred to things they do not understand, such as the sun and moon, or seemingly mysterious forces of nature. In such cases, "sacred" just means the things people do not understand.

Once we people understand conditionality, we will see that there are not any truly sacred things. There is simply the law of conditionality that governs and controls everything. In other words, the law of conditionality is the most sacred, holy thing in the entire universe. This is quite unlike the primitive peoples of long ago, who considered all kinds of things to be sacred or holy: sacred trees, holy mountains, sacred rivers, sacred elephants, even holy monkeys. Everything becomes sacred, and they worship all of them through their ignorance of conditionality.[42] That is the penalty and danger of not knowing conditionality.

On my visit to India many years ago, there were still small shrines with the image of sacred cows and the image of Hanuman the monkey god at modern hospitals that we visited. When we asked what these images were for, we were told they were for the patients to worship and pray to in order to be cured and recover quickly. Even in railroad stations and modern hospitals, these holy objects can still be found. In the sacred bathing areas, there were images of Hanuman to be worshiped as people bathed. These superstitious objects and beliefs are still influential, even in the supposedly modern, progressive world. Look carefully, you will see that many modern people still do not know the law of conditionality.

Many superstitious beliefs and practices remain in the world because people remain ignorant of the law of conditionality. For example, some of you may think that the number 13 has some special power or influence. As soon as you know the law of conditionality, the number 13 will have no meaning. Is not it strange that so many superstitions still operate in this modern, scientific world? They still manage to compete with science. Please get to know conditionality deeply and thoroughly.

Superstitions have existed for tens of thousands of years. They go back to our forest dwelling ancestors who did not know the law of conditionality. Their animism and their superstitious ideas developed and—now, tens of thousands of years later—still exist because people do not understand conditionality. Because of our fears arising out of ignorance, we cling to superstitions. Why is it necessary to break a bottle of champagne when launching a new ship? What is the reason for this? Because we do not know conditionality, even in the age of science. I beg you to study conditionality—up to and including dependent co-arising—because it can actually solve these problems. In seeing conditionality you will also realize not-self.

The Antidote for Ignorance and Superstition

Now we will examine and study the essence of conditionality and paṭicca-samuppāda more clearly and directly. The basic formula for conditionality is as follows:

> Because this exists, there is this.
> Due to the arising of this, this arises.
> Because this does not exist, this does not exist.
> Due to the quenching of this, this quenches.[43]

That is all there is to the formula of conditionality.

You can see for yourself that this is lawful, timeless, unbounded, and unlimited. You can use it with everything at any time. There is nothing that does not happen in these ways. Everything arises, establishes itself, proceeds, and ends according to the law of conditionality. Try to prove it wrong. Use any computer you want, but there is just no way that this law can be wrong. You simply cannot find an exception to this rule that everything arises, happens, changes, and ceases due to causes and conditions.

Everything, in fact, is not-self. To put something above or outside this law is superstition. Wise practice recognizes and lives by this law; it accepts that nothing can be found to be an independent, lasting self (*attā*).

7 ❋ Dependent Co-arising: Birth into Suffering

What are the concoctings? There are these three kinds of concocting (*saṅkhāra*): bodily concocting, verbal concocting, and mental concocting. Friends, these are called "concocting."[44]

Friends, why do people call them "concoctings" (*saṅkhāra*)?

Because of the activity of concocting into "something" this activity is called "*saṅkhāra*." And what does this activity concoct into something concocted? It concocts form into "form," it concocts feeling into "feeling," it concocts perception into "perception," it concocts concoctings into "concocting," and it concocts consciousness into "consciousness." Because of this activity of concocting into "something" this very activity is called *saṅkhāra* ("concoctings").[45]

Now we will focus on the law of dependent co-arising (*paṭiccasamuppāda*). Unlike the general law of conditionality, this more specific law is solely a matter of sentient beings and their conscious experience. Dependent co-arising begins with ignorance (*avijjā*) concerning the law of conditionality.[46] Lacking knowledge of what ought to be known, there arises *saṅkhāra*, or the power to concoct various things into existence. Conditions have power because of this ignorance. Ignorance brings about the power of conditioning.

The Power of Concocting

Saṅkhāra is an important Pāli term that means "to put together, to make complete, and to make ready." In its verb form, we can translate it as "concocting, conditioning, or fabricating." The equivalent noun forms are concoctor and concoction, conditioner and condition, and fabricator and fabrication. Through the power of this concocting, there is consciousness (*viññāṇa*). This means that the naturally existing consciousness-element (*viññāṇa-dhātu*) is conditioned or concocted into the sense-consciousness that experiences things—objects—through the six senses. In other words, the basic potential of mind is made to act as the consciousness that cognizes things—the very things or objects concocted by ignorance—by means of eyes, ears, nose, tongue, body, and mind. Consciousness-element takes the form of sense-consciousness through the power of concocting.

Through the power of this consciousness, because there is such consciousness, there arises mind-body (*nāmarūpa*). Although mind and body can be spoken of as two things, here it is one thing, namely, mind-body. If there is just form (*rūpa*) or body without consciousness, there can be no mind-body. Consciousness makes it possible for there to be mind-body, that is, a living being, what we conventionally refer to as a person or a being. Consciousness gives rise to mind-body, in our non-personal terminology. Do not forget that this is mind-body conditioned by ignorance.

Once mind-body arises as an ignorantly active structure, the sense organs (*saḷāyatana*) arise in that mind-body. The sense organs are the media that allow us to experience the world: eyes, ears, nose, tongue, body, and mind. Because there is mind-body, the six sense organs exist and function. In Dhamma terms, one sense organ arises and functions at a time, depending on how sense-consciousness has been concocted. Previous to this moment, the senses exist in a dormant or merely physical way.[47]

With an active sense organ there is contact (*phassa*). The sense organs make it possible for the external sense objects of the world—sights, sounds, odors, flavors, touches, and mental phenomena—to make contact, that is, make a meaningful impression on mind. Based upon what has just arisen, the interaction of sense organ and sense object is called "contact." Another name for contact is sense experience. So we say that through the sense media, there is contact or experience, and experience means it is conscious and felt, not merely a physical impingement.

Craving Reacts to Feeling

Next, because there is contact there is *vedanā* (commonly translated feeling[48]). Without the senses, there is no contact. Without contact, we wouldn't feel or know anything; nothing would exist, not even the world. Through contact, through these six ways of experiencing things in the world, there is *vedanā*, which refers to the feelings of pleasure, pain, and neither-pleasure-nor-pain that occur with contact. Because *vedanā* depends on contact which depends on the senses and mind-body—all of which are concocted by ignorance—the feeling here is foolish. Because it all starts with a lack of understanding, which continues to influence these things as they arise, the feelings that occur are consequently shot through with ignorance.

Due to *vedanā* there is craving (*taṇhā*). Ignorant vedanā leads to ignorant desire or craving. *Taṇhā* refers only to foolish, ignorant desires. If a desire or want is intelligent and wise, we do not speak of it as craving. If the word desire is used by itself, it must be understood as foolish desire. Wise, intelligent want (*chanda*), wise aspiration (*sammāsankappa*), is not the same as desire. Foolish *vedanā* conditions foolish desire and craving.

Let us look at this in more detail. If the *vedanā* occurs positively, the craving will carry on positively. If the *vedanā* occurs negatively, the craving will carry on negatively. Whether it feels positive or negative, the result is always craving, wanting things foolishly, ignorantly, in ways that are not truly beneficial.

Here, craving leads to clinging or attachment (*upādāna*). As craving becomes more intense, it gives rise to clinging. This is a most important word; I hope you take it to heart—clinging, which is the conception of self. Without clinging, it is as if nothing exists and there is no dukkha. With clinging, anything can be grasped as "mine." Attachment clings in two primary ways: the first clings to things as "self," as "me," as "soul"; the second clings to things as "of self" or "belonging to self," as "related to self," as "mine." This is what is meant by attachment, and clinging. It happens because of craving.

A crucial thing to observe here is that clinging, whether to me or mine, is merely a concept that just now has arisen. A mere moment ago it did not exist. Ordinarily, mind does not cling to things this way. The fundamental nature of mind sees clearly and does not cling. Prior to clinging, ego-me did not exist. Whenever there is clinging, the concepts of me and mine are born here and now by means of craving. It is as if I did not exist until the concept of self or soul is born. Then I exist, though only as a concept, which means it is born internally, in mind, and not as something physically existing in the world. This is the essence of clinging. Do not go looking for it outside, you will find it right here inside when craving causes attachment.[49]

Once attachment is born, it causes the arising of what we call existence (*bhava*). Through the concepts of self and related-to-self (*upādāna*), the concept of existence or becoming occurs. Once there is some form of clinging, there is a basis for the existence of something. Whatever is clung to as "I" now exists as somebody in someplace. Existence can also mean "realm of existence," so there is both a being and an environmental realm of being that are created internally, further rigidifying the separation between inner and outer.

With becoming, what we call birth (*jāti*) follows. With existence or becoming as condition, there is birth. Even though it was previously just clinging to a concept, the self or ego has grown, developed, and become more intense until a complete sense of ego or self-centered "me" is born. This is called birth. An easy way to understand this development is to compare it with the development of the human fetus. Upādāna parallels conception of the embryo, which develops into a fetus. Existence parallels the developing, maturing fetus in the womb. It grows until it is sufficiently complete to be born. Jāti parallels the birth of the newborn infant. The "I" or self, too, is conceived, matures, and is born as fully matured me and mine. This is the natural sequence of clinging, becoming, and birth. Due to upādāna there is existence and due to existence there is jāti. You will have many opportunities to observe this birth process each day.

Birth needs to be understood correctly. In dependent co-arising, birth is a mental or spiritual kind of birth, not the physical or biological birth that happens from our mothers' wombs once in a lifetime. Rather, it happens mentally or spiritually every time there is craving. Whenever there is craving, through clinging, existence, and birth, the conception of the "I" grows into existence and the birth of ego follows. The sense of I and my that begins with clinging grows until it is so big that something is born. Then our inner life is dominated by this ego and that which belongs to ego. It is like the birth of a spirit or ghost, so we call it spiritual birth.

This different kind of birth is extremely important as all sorts of problems are connected with it. Unlike physical birth from the mother's womb, this kind of birth happens many times each day—dozens of times, perhaps hundreds or thousands of times—depending on how many times there is craving. Every time there is craving, there will be a birth each time.

Please remember the meaning of birth; it is essential for a profound understanding of Buddha-Dhamma. This spiritual birth is something most people never hear about, never study, and seldom understand. Yet it recurs many times each day and is of great importance in our spiritual life. Always remember that this is a spiritual birth within mind. Do not mistake it for the regular physical kind of birth.

Literal, physical birth from the mother's womb happens just once in a lifetime. It is not a problem now. The mental birth that comes from craving and clinging happens many times in a single day and continues endlessly. Thus we can say that whenever there is craving, this spiritual birth will occur every time.

The Process of Ego Birth and the Arising of Suffering

This is called "being born out of craving." We could just as well say that we are "born through clinging" or "born from becoming" or "born in ignorance," since they all are involved. Usually, though, we speak of "being born from craving." A special term for craving is *ponobhavika*, which means "leading toward another birth." Every time there is craving, there will be this kind of birth. Regrettably, many Buddhists are not interested in this kind of birth anymore, do not pay attention to it, and are not able to end suffering.

Practice observing yourself: Has craving arisen yet? Is craving present or not? Once craving is born, clinging arises and self is born immediately. How does that happen in you? How do you feel when it does? Once craving creates birth, there is wandering and searching for a place to be born. The birth of ego-me is called birth. Each day, this happens dozens, hundreds, perhaps thousands of times. Can you recognize such birth in the various circumstances of your life?

The crucial insight is that every birth is dukkha—every time, without exception. Whenever there is this kind of birth, there is the birth of ego, which is the locus of every sort of problem. With ego-birth all the problems of life come to be. Such birth creates a heavy burden that entails all the problems and burdens of life. So it is quite natural to say that birth is suffering. However, this is not something to be learned primarily from books or from listening to other people. It is a fact we must learn within ourselves by observing how such birth and distress occur within ourselves. Conversely, because we do not know this and have not learned this fact, we keep on being born. The various forms of ego continue being born over and over again. Consequently, we fall into dukkha repeatedly and cannot prevent suffering from arising. When birth is the condition, all the different forms of dukkha occur, such as getting old, dying, and experiencing all sorts of fear and sorrow. All of these only occur with birth as the underlying condition. This is how the Buddha put it:

> What arises is only suffering arising, what quenches is only suffering quenching.[50]

Another secret that nobody seems to notice is that as soon as the ego is born and exists, it is the basis for taking all naturally existing things as "mine." All things that occur naturally are grabbed up and accumulated by the ego. Thus, birth, growing old, getting sick, and dying—which are just natural phenomena—are claimed by the ego. They are identified with in such a way that it becomes my birth, my growing old, my getting sick, and my death. In this way dukkha arises on top of birth, aging, death, and the like.

All natural activities, such as those that naturally occur in body and mind, are taken as "mine." Physical pain, sadness, sorrow, and despair are just naturally occurring things. When birth has occurred, they are all taken to be "mine," and so become the basis of "my suffering." Consequently, they are transformed from natural phenomena into problems.

Being separated from things we love, having to live and experience things we do not like, and being unable to get the things we desire are the most ordinary of experiences. When they are taken as "mine," they are dukkha. We can summarize this: "all forms of suffering are born from clinging to I and mine."

Even more concise is the formula: "the birth of ego is the birth of suffering." Every time!

This is something to be experienced in our own hearts or minds. We must mindfully feel, study, and learn Dhamma within ourselves. It cannot be learned and understood merely by reading books or by going to school. We must look within ourselves and observe what is happening within our own minds until we see clearly what craving is, what clinging is, what existence is, and what birth is. We must see all the stages of egoistic development within our own experience.

This is the heart of studying dependent co-arising. It happens in all of us, every day, throughout our lives, for as long as we still lack true knowledge. Most of you will have plenty of opportunity to explore it by looking deeply into your own inner experience.

8 ❋ Dimensions and Streams of Dependent Co-arising

Depending on eyes and form, eye-consciousness arises. The meeting together of these three phenomena is contact. With contact as condition, there is feeling; with feeling as condition, there is craving; with craving as condition, there is clinging; with clinging as condition, there is becoming; with becoming as condition, there is birth; with birth as condition, old age and death, sorrow, grief, pain, lamentation, and despair arise completely. The dependent co-arising of the entire mass of dukkha happens in just this way.

Depending on ears and sound, ear-consciousness arises. . . . *and so on . . .*

Depending on nose and odor, nose-consciousness arises. . . . *and so on . . .*

Depending on tongue and flavor, tongue-consciousness arises. . . . *and so on . . .*

Depending on body and physical sensation, body-consciousness arises. . . . *and so on . . .*

Depending on mind (*mano*) and an "idea" (*dhammāramaṇa*), mind-consciousness arises. The meeting together of these three phenomena is contact. With contact as condition, there is feeling; with feeling as condition, there is craving; with craving as condition, there is clinging; with clinging as condition, there is becoming; with becoming as condition, there is birth; with birth as condition, old age and death, sorrow, grief, pain, lamentation, and despair arise completely. The dependent co-arising of the entire mass of dukkha happens in just this way.

[It so happened that a monk was standing and listening to the Buddha (as he recited the above passage). When he noticed the monk standing there, the Buddha asked him,]

Monk, did you hear this recitation of Dhamma?

"Yes, Venerable Sir, I did."

Monk, you ought to take this recitation of Dhamma to heart. You ought to learn this recitation of Dhamma. You ought to remember this recitation of

Dhamma. This recitation of Dhamma is most beneficial. It is the beginning of the spiritual life (*adibrahmacariya*).[51]

Two Types of Contact

Now, we should look with more detail and clarity at how this stream of dependent co-arising appears in our lives each and every day. The best way to begin this practical study is by paying careful attention to the inner sense media (*āyatana*, connectors), that is, eyes, ears, nose, tongue, body, and mind (functioning as a sense door). These are paired with the six outer sense media (also *āyatana*), that is, the forms, sounds, smells, flavors, physical sensations, and mental experiences that corresponded with the six sense doors. When an inner connector and an outer connector interact, sense consciousness (*viññāṇa*) arises. There are six kinds of consciousness: eye-consciousness, ear-consciousness, and so on through mind-consciousness. When these three things—inner connector, outer connector, and sense consciousness—arise and function together, it is called sense contact or sense impression (*phassa*). Altogether, there are six avenues of contact and this is where we begin our study.

For example, when eyes and a visual form interact, eye-consciousness arises. There is seeing, which means that eye-consciousness has arisen. When the eye, the form, and eye-consciousness come together and function within the same action, we call this activity "eye-contact," which is the experience of seeing something through the media of the eyes. It involves the simultaneous functioning of the three elements just described. The other senses are bases for parallel forms of contact.

Sense contact has two levels. The first level is external, the primarily physical contact between the inner and outer media, for instance, the eyes and a visual form. We can see the form and shape, the color, the dimensions, and other physical aspects of the visual object. This can be called "contact by the eye" and this kind of sense contact amounts to "mere contact." It is simply the basic sense experience of a sentient being within a sensual world. Next is the mental level or aspect of contact. Mind-consciousness arises on the basis of the physical contact and knows the meaning or value of that contact: that something with a certain shape, color, and size is called "flower," "feces," or whatever the case may be. Contact has these two levels: the external or physical level, and the internal or mental level.

These two stages of contact occur throughout our daily lives. The first is merely the natural encounter of the nervous system with the shape, color, physical dimensions, and other qualities of a visual form (and similarly with the other senses). Next, mind-consciousness (*manoviññāṇa*) makes its contact and knows that the meaning of this whole experienced thing is "flower," "feces," "woman," "man," or whatever. Both levels are called contact. Together they make up sense contact, which is the moment-to-moment basis of our daily experience.[52]

As with eyes, there is the same combination of factors constituting contact via ears, nose, tongue, body, and mind-sense. Contact has two levels in each case. As for the sixth sense, the mind-sense, an example of mere contact is the arising of a memory, while naming it is the second level of contact.

Foolish Contact Leads to Clinging

When there is sense contact without mindfulness and wisdom, the contact takes place within ignorance, that is, under the power of non-understanding or misunderstanding. Contact occurring through ignorance is foolish contact. The lack of mindfulness and wisdom allows ignorance to take over the experience, which makes it "ignorant contact."[53]

Contact or sense impression is the necessary condition for *vedanā* (feeling, if it must be translated). When, because of ignorance—the lack of wisdom—the contact is foolish, the *vedanā* will also be foolish. Ignorant contact leads to ignorant feeling. Foolish *vedanā* comes from foolish contact. Such foolish contact is the predominant situation of our lives because we have never studied and understood what is taking place here. We naively take the basic sense activity for granted, as givens, as real, without investigating more deeply. Contact gives rise to *vedanā* and the vast majority of contacts and feelings that arise through our sense doors are foolish.

Vedanā leads to craving (*taṇhā*). When feeling is foolish, it inevitably concocts foolish desire, which is the meaning of craving. The kind of wanting that operates in ignorance is taṇhā. When our desire or need is ignorant, it further leads to clinging, that is, foolish attachment. When desire is foolish it leads to foolish attachment or clinging. Please examine this well, as it is an important point. Craving, which is inherently foolish and fixated, conditions or causes clinging, which is equally foolish and stuck.

When contact is foolish it brings up foolish *vedanā*. Foolish feeling brings up foolish wanting (craving is inherently foolish), which in turn brings up foolish attachment (clinging is also inherently foolish). It is one stupid thing after another. This ignorant conditioning of foolishness is an essential matter to be observed if one is to understand dependent co-arising clearly.

Therefore, the ego—the self and what belongs to self—is a product of ignorance. The arising of self comes out of this flow of foolishness. Please give this your utmost attention and interest. It is vitally important. The ego—me and mine—is just a product of foolishness.

The Development of I and Mine

Here we have the existence of the foolish ego. The concept of self, the sense of an independently existing ego, has firmly established itself in mind. This is existence (*bhava*, becoming). It develops into the fully developed sense of ego known as birth, in which the feeling of "I am" is fully born. This too is a product of foolishness. Once the concept of I is established in mind, the ego is born complete as ego-me. When there is this deluded ego, it takes everything that comes into contact with this foolish mind—whether through eyes, ears, nose, tongue, body, or mind—as being mine. Because of the ignorant ego, the whole world is taken to be mine, putting a tremendous load on one's head. With the whole world stuck on its head, the ego is greatly burdened and full of problems. This is the flow of dependent co-arising that has reached its end and torments life with inestimable distress.

Does this flow of dependent co-arising occur in your daily life? If you do not see it happening within your own life, you cannot understand dependent co-arising at all. Once you begin to see this flow in your normal everyday experiences, you will begin to understand what dependent co-arising is and the effect it has in our lives from day to day, hour to hour. This is something to be observed directly within your own personal, inner experience.

When you observe dependent co-arising and really see it working in your own experiences, when you see this directly and clearly, you will know that it is true. You will understand what the Buddha said about dukkha, that it is not a result of old actions (karma) in past lives nor is it caused by God. You will understand that suffering only occurs because of ignorance and mistaken reactivity within the flow of dependent co-arising throughout our everyday lives. Please look carefully until you are able to see this truth personally and directly.

Two Kinds of Language

We ought to understand that there are two kinds, meanings, or levels of language, whether spoken or written. The first level is that spoken by ordinary folks, the language of relative truth, which we call people language. The wise speak a different language, the language of ultimate truth (*paramattha-dhamma*, supreme, ultimate meaning), which we call Dhamma language. People language is spoken by ordinary folks; Dhamma language is spoken by those who understand the Dhamma. The language of relative truth speaks in terms of I and you, selves and people, so we call it people language or personal language. The way of speaking based on the truth of not-self is Dhamma language. Every word can be understood in both languages. This is crucially true regarding dependent co-arising, especially with terms like birth, death, rebirth, and transmigration. One meaning is that of people language and the other is of Dhamma language. We should be aware of this so that we can understand words correctly on both levels of truth.

Buddha gives us a clear example of both kinds of language. Most people think of a certain human being when they hear the word *buddha*. They think of a historical figure that lived about 2,600 years ago, of a flesh and blood body that walked and talked then. That is the people's language understanding of Buddha. Some people think of *buddha* as the statues that Buddhists install in their temples and shrines, which is the Buddha of children's language. In Dhamma language, *buddha* refers to the seeing of Dhamma and the embodiment of that wisdom, as in the words: "What benefit is there in seeing this body? Vakkali, whoever sees Dhamma, sees me. Whoever sees me, sees Dhamma."[54] This saying cannot be understood intelligibly if one does not know Dhamma language. The same is true with many of the terms of dependent co-arising.

Understanding dependent co-arising allows us to understand Dhamma language and speak in Dhamma language. Through understanding dependent co-arising, we can speak the truth that is really true. When we speak in people language, we speak truths that are not really true, but that we must say in accord with the knowledge of unlearned, ignorant people who do not know the truth. From examining life carefully in our study of dependent co-arising, it becomes possible to see deeper truth and then speak Dhamma language in the terms of that truth.

Two Kinds of Transmigration

For example, take the term transmigration. In the Upanishads,[55] transmigration means that there is a self or soul that transmigrates through physical births, that reincarnates into the wombs of mothers, grows up, and dies, only to reincarnate into another womb, grow up again, and die, over and over again. Here, transmigration refers primarily to the physical births and deaths through which the being or entity passes.

In Dhamma language, there is also rebirth and transmigration, that is, the rebirth and transmigration of the illusive self. Clinging within the flow of dependent co-arising gives rise to becoming and the birth of the illusory self, which is inherently delusive. Once it dies, as long as ignorance remains, further clinging in terms of self will occur. With each spin of dependent co-arising there is another birth. When dependent co-arising happens again, there is another birth. Birth happens over and over again, connected by dependent co-arising (though not by any *attā*, independent self, or soul), because ignorance remains. The ignorance of one deluded birth is left over to influence the next. Connected by ignorance there is the transmigration of this self that does not actually exist as a self; it is just a feeling or notion in mind. This recycling of self concocted by ignorance is the true meaning of transmigration according to dependent co-arising.

Be careful. Words have these two levels of meaning, especially religious terms. If we do not understand that there are two possible meanings, everything will become confused and we will not understand what the Buddha is teaching. Dependent co-arising helps us a great deal in understanding Dhamma language and speaking accordingly. It allows us to distinguish between relative truth and supreme truth, between personal language and Dhamma language. When we understand this distinction between the two kinds of language, we can keep things clear. People may talk about rebirth and transmigration in ordinary, literal terms. We can speak about them in terms of dependent co-arising, which is truer. We need not be trapped in the truths of a more limited understanding.

Two Kinds of Rebirth

Now, let us consider a word of great importance in traditional Buddhism—rebirth—which always elicits many questions, some emotion, and not a little confusion. Is there rebirth or not? We must say that there is, there certainly is rebirth, but is it in terms of people language and relative truth or Dhamma language and ultimate truth? Rebirth in people language is a physical rebirth as taught before the Buddha, such as in the Upanishads. Obviously, there is physical birth; we can see it happening all around us. They say, too, that there is reincarnation and they are welcome to that belief, as well. Rebirth in Buddhism, in Dhamma language, is the reappearance of the concept of self. With each clinging to self there is a new birth or "rebirth." In other words, with each spin of dependent co-arising there is a new birth (just as there are new moments of contact, feeling, craving, and so on). Each occurrence of dependent co-arising is a new birth of the illusive self, which is never exactly the same old thing. Still, it feels like a rebirth of something very familiar just the same.

Actually, this kind of rebirth is not of anything real, but it feels real and thus causes numerous problems. When we see the truth that this kind of rebirth is illusory, then dukkha ceases and there are no problems. In short, if there is rebirth in Buddhism it is the birth of dependent co-arising, a kind of spiritual birth, which happens in mind. The people language understanding is of a physical birth; please do not mix up the two.

It is wearisome that so many books on Buddhism have chapters on "Karma and Rebirth" that explain rebirth in the old physical terms. In other words, though these writers are writing on behalf of Buddhism they explain rebirth in non-Buddhist terms. They inevitably bring in some version of a self or being that is reborn, which contradicts the fundamental Buddhist principle of not-self. I have seen many of these books and chapters; it is appalling how often the writers get it wrong. If they write about "Rebirth in Buddhism," they should explain the re-occurrence of the illusive self as in dependent co-arising.

So if you are wondering about rebirth, please look carefully whether it is rebirth of a physical kind or rebirth of a spiritual kind that you are considering. Buddhism teaches the spiritual kind that occurs within the stream of dependent co-arising. Others teach the physical birth, which is their pleasure and still has ethical value. We should preserve it for the sake of ethics, for encouraging people to do good. The spiritual kind of rebirth must be preserved for the sake of ultimate truth (*paramatthadhamma*). In this language, rebirth is the concept of "I" being reborn in mind. Actually nothing is reborn, but the thought of "I" is familiar and feels like rebirth.

Reflection and Experience in Terms of Dhamma

This is how to reflect on the question as to whether there is rebirth or not. If we cannot see the difference between these two ways of understanding the word rebirth, it is impossible to understand the Buddha's teaching, and that lack of understanding makes it impossible to be free of suffering.

If you happen to be wondering "am I going to be reborn or not?" or "will there be rebirth for me?" the question, response, and truth depend on the kind of rebirth you are wondering about. Is it the physical rebirth of people language or the spiritual rebirth of Dhamma language? Is it rebirth in conventional terms or ultimate terms? If we are considering the rebirth of Dhamma language, you need not ask anyone else. Just look around and look inside, you will see rebirth of the illusive self happening within dependent co-arising over and over. You can see this directly, personally, in each occurrence of dependent co-arising. Then you can answer for yourself, "Yes, I have this kind of rebirth."

As for the physical rebirth of people language, there is no way you can know, see, or experience that for yourself. How can you see here and now whether you will be physically reborn or not? On the other hand, the rebirth of Dhamma language can be experienced directly and seen clearly. Every time ignorance, craving, and clinging give birth to the illusive self we can see it internally. We can know personally when there is such spiritual rebirth. We cannot see the people language kind of rebirth for ourselves and can only believe what others tell us. In that case, one does not have one's own truth. You rely on someone else's authority. Please resolve this question by looking into your own mind.

Why Worry?

Actually, there is no real need to worry about whether there is physical birth or not. That is not the problem; suffering does not happen because of physical birth. Suffering occurs because of the rebirth described in Dhamma language of dependent co-arising. Dukkha occurs because of this kind of rebirth, which is the kind of rebirth to avoid.

You can relax about the other understanding of rebirth because you cannot see it for yourself, it is not subjectively experiencable, it does not cause distress, and you are not around to suffer from it. Just let it be; it has its value in terms of morality. Let children and those with little knowledge believe in it. If they believe it, perhaps they will be motivated to do good and will lead moral lives. This kind of rebirth is good, it has its value; however, it is not the real truth. It is just relative truth, not ultimate truth. Still, it is worth keeping for its moral value.

The kind of rebirth that is personally subjective, that we can see for ourselves, is described as *sandiṭṭhiko*—to be seen personally by those who practice. We have the sort of rebirth that we can see clearly and truly for ourselves without needing to believe someone else, and which is the first of the virtues of Dhamma. We have rebirth every time that dependent co-arising occurs in our hearts. Every cycle of dependent co-arising in our mind is a rebirth. This is the genuine rebirth as explained in the language of ultimate truth.

There are many of them. Each day, rebirth occurs many times. Some people are especially talented and experience a rebirth every second. When eyes see a visual form there is a rebirth. When ears hear a sound there is a rebirth. When the nose smells an odor there is a rebirth. When the tongue tastes a flavor there is a rebirth. Mind having memories and thoughts are more rebirths. Rebirth can happen quite often, if one is really creative.

If we understand dependent co-arising thoroughly, we can regulate its stream and rebirth will stop. When rebirth stops, that is Nibbāna. Well-rounded and profound understanding of dependent co-arising solves the dilemma of rebirth and thus ends suffering in and by ourselves.

9 ❋ Dependent Co-arising for Children

Sakka, King of the Gods, asked the Buddha: "Venerable Sir, what is the cause, what is the condition, that prevents certain kinds of beings in this world from thoroughly cooling right here; and what is the cause, what is the condition, that enables certain kinds of beings in this world to thoroughly cool right here?"[56]

King of the Gods, there are forms cognizable by eyes, forms that are pleasing, attractive, satisfying, delightful, bases for desire, establishments of lust. If a cultivator takes pleasure in, indulges in, and is infatuated with such forms, while he takes pleasure in, indulges in, and is infatuated with form, the consciousness on which craving for that form depends occurs for him. That consciousness is clinging.[57] King of the Gods, the cultivator with clinging does not thoroughly cool.

[Identical wording is used regarding the other sense media—sounds heard by the ears, odors smelled by the nose, flavors tasted by the tongue, and physical sensations felt by the body—differing only in terms of the relevant sense door. We will continue with the sixth sense.]

King of the Gods, there are phenomena cognizable by mind, phenomena that are pleasing, attractive, satisfying, delightful, bases for desire, establishments of lust. If a cultivator takes pleasure in, indulges in, and is infatuated with such phenomena, while she takes pleasure in, indulges in, and is infatuated with a phenomenon, the consciousness on which craving for that phenomenon depends occurs for her. That consciousness is clinging. King of the Gods, the cultivator with clinging does not thoroughly cool.

King of the Gods, this is the cause, this is the condition that prevents certain kinds of beings in this world from thoroughly cooling right here.

[the inverse]

King of the Gods, there are forms cognizable by eyes, forms that are pleasing, attractive, satisfying, delightful, bases for desire, establishments of lust. If a cultivator does not take pleasure in, does not indulge in, and is not infatuated with such forms, while he does not take pleasure in, does not indulge in, and is not infatuated with form, the consciousness on which craving for that form depends does not occur for him. The consciousness that would be clinging does not happen in him. King of the Gods, the cultivator without clinging thoroughly cools.

[Identical wording is used regarding the other sense media differing only in terms of the relevant sense doors.]

King of the Gods, there are phenomena cognizable by mind, phenomena that are pleasing, attractive, satisfying, delightful, bases for desire, establishments of lust. If a cultivator does not take pleasure in, does not indulge in, and is not infatuated with such phenomena, while she does not take pleasure in, does not indulge in, and is not infatuated with a phenomenon, the consciousness on which craving for that phenomenon depends does not occur for her. The consciousness that would be clinging does not happen in her. King of the Gods, the cultivator without clinging thoroughly cools.

King of the Gods, this is the cause, this is the condition that allows certain kinds of beings in this world to thoroughly cool right here.[58]

Just as there are two levels of conditionality (*idappaccayatā*) or dependent co-arising (*paṭiccasamuppāda*), the ordinary physical level and the more profound, refined mental level, there are also two corresponding levels of mindfulness.

To explain the first level, we can explain to our children how there is the sun in the sky and water upon this earth. The sun gives off light that warms and evaporates the water. The evaporated water rises into the sky and collects in clouds. Eventually, rain falls from the clouds. If you get caught in the rain, you get wet and may catch a cold. If that turns into a fever, you must go to the doctor to cure the fever.

Or, as another example, the rain wets the ground making it slippery. Because the ground is slippery, you slip and fall down. You crack your head, have a wound, and it aches. You go to the doctor to have it treated. These various things depend on each other one after the other until bearing fruit. Collectively, we call this the "stream of dependently co-arising conditionality."

If one has sufficient mindfulness, one need not get caught in the rain and catch a cold. Or, if one must go out, with sufficient mindfulness one need not slip on the wet ground to the point of falling. Because one is mindful, there is no need to get hurt or catch cold. These are material examples of being mindful regarding conditionality and dependent co-arising.

Next, we may teach our children concerning higher matters of heart and mind. We can tell them that they have eyes, ears, nose, tongue, body, and a mind that can feel and think. We teach them to know these things well enough; these facts are not so hard as to be beyond the capacity of children to learn and understand.

Start with Seeing and Hearing

Further, we point out that in this world there are visual forms, sounds, odors, tastes, touches, and thoughts that stimulate their eyes, ears, nose, tongue, body, and mind. When a form stimulates your eyes, that form is seen and the seeing is called eye-consciousness. Tell them to observe how eye-consciousness just happened when there was stimulation between eyes and a form. Before that, it hadn't happened. Now, there is seeing. When the light waves stimulate the optical nerves, those nerves feel and know it. It is the visual pathways of the nervous system that see the form, not "I see the form."

Children can observe for themselves that if there are merely the visual pathways of the nervous system seeing the form the results are much different than "me seeing the form." Only the latter is dangerous and harmful. If there is just the experience of the nervous system interacting with light waves, there is not much meaning to it and therefore not much to cling to. So, one does not feel "I see the form." There, the meaning is much stronger and nasty because it is foolish enough to make everything about ego-me and the visual form is taken to be positive or negative.

When a sound stimulates the ears, help children to understand that the sound waves have struck the ears, not "I heard a sound," which is very different. Merely experience that a sound has been heard and consider how to deal with it, if necessary, or leave it alone if nothing needs to be done about it. There is no need for a crazy ego-me to get upset, be angry, hate, love, be afraid, or whatever.

When an odor stimulates the nerves of the nose, the nervous system is aware of that odor. There is no need for "I smell an odor." When a flavor stimulates the nerves of the tongue, such as when eating food, the nervous system in the tongue is simply aware of that flavor, rather than "I taste this flavor." For example, if the tongue does not feel the flavor is palatable, it can be improved with seasonings to make it delicious. However, if "I am not feeling deliciousness," the cook will be blamed and cursed. Can you see the big difference?

When something touches the skin or body, the nervous system is aware of that touch sensation and deals with it accordingly. If it feels like "I am touched," the results are feelings of positive and negative, which create difficulties and trouble. The difference between merely experiencing and reacting with ego-me are much different.

When the mental system thinks, let it be the just the mental system thinking, nothing more. Do not let it turn into, "I think," which is much different. Please help our children to understand these six things in this way. Show them the important difference between the way of experiencing that gives birth to the egoistic concept of self and the way of experiencing where nobody needs to be born. Then, whatever needs doing is done without any birth.

How Experience Gets Inside Us

Further, we may have children study how the eyes are inside and the visual forms are outside. When the two interact, a third thing occurs, namely, eye-consciousness. When these three things work together, that is, when a form is seen through eye-consciousness, we call it contact. When there is contact, the next reaction to emerge is feeling (*vedanā*). Since we were in the womb, we've lacked the necessary intelligence and wisdom to understand these experiences. Basically, we've been ignorant most of our lives. When feeling stimulates our foolishness, we feel that some things are positive, and so fall in love with them, and that some things are negative, so we hate them. Feeling can be turned into these two kinds of meanings.

When there is such foolish feeling, desire follows—specifically, foolish desire. The desire is concocted according to the power of the feeling: reacting to positive feelings with wanting to get or have, delighting in, or becoming infatuated, and reacting to negative feelings with annoyance, anger, resentment, and hatred. We call these foolish desire because they simply react according to the influence of feeling. They are not wise wants based in genuine understanding. Ordinarily, the ignorant wants, foolish desires, and craving are what occur.

If we are mindful, truly intelligent, and wise, we will have intelligent wants. We can call these aspirations, which is an entirely different matter than foolish desire or craving.[59] We are ignorant from the time we were in our mothers' wombs, lacking in mindfulness and wisdom, so we carry on with foolish wants; it is rare for there to be wise wants. Be very careful about this.

When the feeling of desire is strong and intense, another reaction occurs. The conception of "I desire" is concocted. "I the desirer" is created out of desire. This requires subtler study. When desire strengthens and becomes intense, the further reaction occurs of feeling "I am the one who desires." The conception of self arises here particularly. Have the children notice the ego-me desiring something. This conception of self is called clinging. When the feeling of clinging occurs in mind, there is the starting point of existence, of becoming, and existence takes root in mind.

When becoming continues and carries on to its full extent, there is birth, the emergence of a fully formed ego-me. Please consider this carefully. This is birth out of ignorance and clinging, that is, a mental kind of birth, not birth from a physical womb. This kind of birth is very important; it involves and creates many problems. Birth from the womb is not a problem.

The birth of ego-me is called ignorant birth. When born this way, one is ignorant, foolish. It is like a deceptive-ghost (*pii-laug* in Thai) being born. This is taken to be me, ego, my self. Everything is appropriated as mine. Birth from the womb becomes mine, aging becomes mine, illness is mine, and death is mine. Happiness and sorrow are mine. All this me and mine means the Fool has been born through the power of ignorance, which is a mental form of birth.

There are many opportunities for this kind of birth: sometimes born through the eyes, sometimes born through the ears, sometimes born through the nose or tongue, sometimes born through the skin and body, and sometimes born through mind. In a single day, there are dozens, hundreds, even thousands of births.

From our mother's womb, we are born only once. From the womb of ignorance, craving, and self-centered defilement, we are born hundreds of times a day. Before we physically die, we are born hundreds of thousands of times and spiritually die every time. The difference between these two kinds of birth is huge.

If the parents are not too lost, they can get their children to understand dependent co-arising as described above. The children might understand a material example of conditionality, such as, rain falling and making the pavement slippery, someone falling and cracking his head open, and so on. Then they might just be able to understand the inner, mental concocting of dependent co-arising, too.

Mindfulness Is the Answer

The preceding will enable children to understand that mindfulness (*sati*)[60] can stop material aspects of dependent co-arising. There is no need for them to catch cold or to fall and crack open their skulls. Further, they will be able to understand that mindfulness can stop the flow of dependent co-arising in the moment of contact. If we are mindful and have sufficient wisdom in that moment, the stream of dependent co-arising will stop or will change its course in a direction that does not create suffering. This means that mindfulness can stop the flow of dependent co-arising both in its material and mental aspects. Mindfulness, then, is crucial and essential.

If they have genuine intelligence, that is, mindful wisdom, there will be mindfulness in the first instance. For example, when eyes see a form there is clear seeing that eyes see a form and no one is fooled into thinking "ego-me sees something." When ears hear a sound, there is just hearing the sound by the ears, not by "me hearing." With the nose smelling odors and the tongue savoring flavors there is mindfulness from the very beginning rather than ego-me.

It is much better to be mindful in the moment of contact than to try to catch up later. When mindfulness is right on time, there is understanding of what contact is and how it functions in the coming together of eyes, form, and eye-consciousness (or any other combination of inner sense media, outer sense media, and sense consciousness). Thus, they'll have intelligent contact. With intelligent contact, there is intelligent feeling; feeling is not foolish, it is not deceived by positivity or negativity. Consequently, craving and clinging do not arise. When mindfulness is immediately present at contact, it regulates the stream of dependent co-arising correctly. In other words, it is not careless. So it stops right there. Mindfulness blocks or stops the flow of dependent co-arising, the stream of dukkha, in this way.

Here, our problem is that the ordinary mindfulness with which we are born is insufficient for the task. It is not enough to stop the flow of dependent co-arising, especially in the moment of contact. Consequently, we must develop mindfulness to a higher level; we must practice being mindful through the approach known as "mindfulness with breathing in and out" (*ānāpānasati*) as you are learning and practicing at the International Dharma Hermitage.[61] To practice having mindfulness means training a higher than usual level of it, as well as training related factors such as wisdom, clear comprehension (*sampajañña*), and collected stability of mind (*samādhi*). Training mindfulness brings many benefits, most of all, when it is sufficient, that it can stop the flow of dependent co-arising's stream.

When we speak of "being mindful," we mean mindfulness that is sufficient, complete, not lacking in any essentials, and quick enough to do the job. "Having mindfulness" must mean this level and not partial or half-baked mindfulness. One who has fully developed mindfulness is called "Arahant," one worthy through having stopped the flow of dependent co-arising for good.

The essence of mindfulness is the highest speed of wisdom that arrives exactly when needed. That swiftness of wisdom appearing in time is the core meaning of mindfulness (*sati*). If it is not quick enough to stop dependent co-arising from concocting, it cannot be called mindfulness. *Sati* has the same root as *sara,* or arrow. At the time this usage of the term *sati* developed, it seems the fastest thing known to people was the arrow, so its speed was used to represent mindfulness. Nowadays, we'd compare *sati* with a bullet or the speed of light, which would give us a different name altogether. In short, the quickness of attention that can prevent nasty circumstances from occurring is the meaning of mindfulness.

You can experience for yourselves without needing to believe anyone else that having a lot of knowledge but being unable to apply it in time is useless. Such knowledge is equivalent to nothing. Mindfulness is the in-time speed that makes knowledge useful. This has tremendous benefits. It allows knowledge to be in-time with the circumstances that are arising. This eliminates any problems, which is the primary benefit of mindfulness. It makes knowledge and understanding useful. Without mindfulness, understanding is too slow to be useful.

Doing without a Doer

The predawn walk from the retreat center across the highway to here is an opportunity to practice walking with the highest Dhamma, which is to walk without a walker. Walk step by step without needing somebody to do the walking. This is the highest Dhamma in Buddhism, which enables any activity or movement to be done without there needing to be an "I" or ego-me to do it. Body simply walks under the control of the nervous system and consciousness. No self, ego, or "me" is required. This is a lesson we hope you will study here. With this kind of practice every moment is a lesson and everywhere is our school.

You can carry this over into all the activities of your life. Just do them without a doer. Take, for example, eating food. Eat without an eater; then there will not be any of the problems associated with eating. Do whatever needs doing, do it with mindfulness and a ready active wisdom, so that the feeling of an ego-me who acts does not arise. We can train doing everything without an ego-me, actor, or doer.

In life there are six basic activities: seeing, hearing, smelling, tasting, touching, and thinking. When watching or seeing a visual form with the eyes, let it be eyes and nervous system that see. There is no need for the ego-me to see. When hearing sounds by the ear, it is not necessary for an ego-me to be the hearer. In smelling odors through the nose, the nervous system functions naturally without any ego-me. In tasting flavors through the tongue, there is no need for an ego-me or self that tastes or experiences those flavors, just a naturally functioning nervous system. The experiencing of physical touches or sensations through the skin and body do not require an ego-me either. Even thinking can happen with mind free of ego-me. Do not think with ego-me, a thinker, or a person who thinks; that only causes trouble and distress. This is the essence of Buddhism: seeing, hearing, smelling, tasting, touching, and thinking without an ego-me as seer, hearer, smeller, taster, toucher, or thinker.

This is the meaning of the Buddhist teaching gathered under the word not-self—*anattā*, selflessness. This teaching is unique among the religions of the world. You will not find such a direct expression of not-self anywhere else. Please try to understand not-self: in our life and experience, no lasting, independent, or permanent self or essence can be found. When this is realized, there is no ego-me to be a locus of suffering. Then you will know, understand, and realize the whole of Buddhism.

10 ❈ Three Existences Are the Basis of Self

Friends, how does dukkha originate?

Depending on eyes and form, eye-consciousness arises. The meeting together of these three is eye-contact. With contact as condition, there is feeling; with feeling as condition there is craving. This is the origin of dukkha.

Friends, how is dukkha disestablished?

Depending on eyes and form, eye-consciousness arises. The meeting together of these three is eye-contact. With contact as condition, there is feeling; with feeling as condition there is craving. Through the fading away and remainderless quenching of craving, clinging quenches. Through the quenching of clinging, becoming quenches. Through the quenching of becoming, birth quenches. Through the quenching of birth, aging and death, sorrow, grief, pain, lamentation, and despair quench thoroughly. The quenching of the entire mass of dukkha occurs in just this way. This is the disestablishment of dukkha.

[Identical wording is used for the remaining sense doors, their outer media, and corresponding forms of consciousness.][62]

In this chapter and the next we will discuss the arising of the sense of a separate self, of egoism, and of the selfishness that follows. To clarify certain aspects of this we will examine what is called existence, the existence of self. Later, we will examine how existence relates to dependent co-arising (*paṭiccasamuppāda*).

Existence Is the Abode of Self

Bhava is somewhat difficult to translate into English. It is usually translated as existence; however, the meaning of this word *bhava* is broader than any single English word. Its meaning includes "to become," out of which emerges "to exist," and a "state of being" that arises out of existence. First, there is becoming, then there is existing, and finally there is a state of being of life. These three terms—becoming, existence, and state of being—together are called *bhava*. They are the basis for the solidification of the concepts "self" and "of self" that appear with clinging. There is nothing more worthy of your study.

Existence does not refer, really, to physical or material existence. Rather, it refers to mental existence or spiritual existence. *Becoming, existing,* and *state of being* refer to mental or spiritual experience. It might be easier for you to understand and observe if we speak of the spiritual abode: the being, the having, the existing, or the place of being for what's called self. Mind, under the influence of ignorance, creates a place to exist and this then is where self exists. This existence is a tricky, deceptive thought. Although it does not refer to anything actually real, it is powerful and gives rise to all sorts of problems. Though merely an illusion concocted by mind, this deceptive thought nonetheless leads to selfishness and many problems. Therefore, it is important to understand what existence is—first becoming, then existing, and finally a state of being. These together are existence.

In Buddhism, and probably even before, three kinds of existence have been distinguished. First is existing with or within sexuality or sensuality (*kāma*). Second is existing with or within form (*rūpa*), pure form not mixed up with sexuality and sensuality. Third is existing with or within that which is without form, formless (*arūpa*). These may be difficult to understand, especially the last, but your study of them will be well rewarded. Knowing these three kinds of existence—sexual, material, and non-material—is most valuable. Sensuality, solely form, and formless are the meaning of and basis for different kinds of existence.

Many Existences Right Here in This Life

Let us use a simple example to illustrate—a housewife.[63] For an hour, she is busy with her partner in the bedroom; in this hour she is involved with sexuality, romance, and sensuality. The next hour, she is busy with her child and has nothing to do with the stuff of the last hour. Or she is occupied with money, jewelry, wealth, and other possessions. In this second hour, she is busy with and interested only in form, solely with material things, without any sexual or sensual aspects. In the third hour, she is not the least interested in the above things; she's interested only in goodness, merit, and wholesomeness. She is busy with doing good, charity, earning merit, and developing virtue in order to progress toward Nibbāna. There is sexual stuff, then there is formish[64] (material) stuff, and there is also formless (non-material) stuff. These are easy to understand examples of the three kinds of existence: sensual existence (*kāmabhava*), formish existence (*rūpabhava*), and formless existence (*arūpabhava*). Try to understand these examples and you will be able to understand existence correctly and thoroughly.

These examples illustrate how all three kinds of existence can occur in just this body, right here, within a few hours, not to mention a few days or a lifetime. In, however, the orthodox or traditional teaching on existence, found in both traditional Theravāda and Mahāyāna Buddhism, but not necessarily correct or original Buddhism, these existences are shunted off to other places. Sexual existences are located in other worlds full of sensuality. Formish existences are located in yet other worlds, especially the worlds of the Brahma gods of pure form. And formless existences are located in other kinds of worlds, those of the formless Brahma gods. For those who follow such interpretations, existence means realms, worlds, and dimensions outside the sensual human realm. This traditional approach was taught before the Buddha's awakening. When Buddhism came along, it sought to teach about this life in this body and thus found new meanings in the terms, meanings that can be found right here in this body's lifetime; there is no need to die to shift to another existence. As the Buddha told Rohitassa the Deva's son,

> I do not speak of any world's end in which beings are not born, do not age, do not die, do not pass away, and do not reappear, that somebody might see and might reach such a world's end by going there. In this fathom-long perceptive and conscious body we specify the world, the origin of the world, the thorough quenching of the world, and the path leading to the world's quenching.[65]

The traditional teaching requires one to die in order to go to or experience other existences, with biologically human birth considered a kind of sensual existence. What kind of problem is solved when one has gone somewhere else? How can those other worlds be relevant to our problems here? Now we are here, are we not? In one day all three kinds of existence can be experienced here. If one is really talented, they can be experienced in an hour or even minutes. Please understand how mind exists in these different ways. We all cycle through these three existences, right here in this body. If your understanding of this is correct, you will be able to solve the problems associated with the various kinds of existence.

What is even sillier about the traditional existence beliefs are claims that the sensual existences last on the order of one hundred years; that lifespans in the worlds of the Brahma gods of pure form are in the range of tens of thousands of years; and that the existences of the formless Brahma gods last for hundreds of thousands of years. Perhaps these explanations are intended metaphorically, but many people seem to take them quite literally. If one only changes existence every ten or hundred thousand years, of what value or use to us is any of that information? Setting aside metaphysical debates over whether such realms really exist, what relevance do they have for our own lives? That stuff cannot be changed. We cannot do anything with them; they are totally out of our control. Why bother with such beliefs?

In Buddhism proper, becomings and existences are dynamic and change much more often than in the traditional scheme, sometimes every few minutes. In an hour one might experience many existences. You will see that they're changing all the time, which calls for appropriate understanding.

Problems with Existence

Each kind of existence has its problems for us; we suffer from the various becomings and existences in particular ways. Sensual existence creates certain problems, formish existence creates its particular problems, and formless existence creates other unique problems. This means it is necessary to manage the stuff of existence.

Let us consider the example of our housewife's husband. He is involved with his wife and sexual matters for a while. Then, he is involved with their children, the house, family finances, or the like for a time. And at other times he is involved with doing good, charity work, virtue, and honor. Each kind of existence might change after just minutes for both him and her, as well as the rest of us. If we are unable to manage these experiences, they will be full of problems. They will become difficulties, burdens, and torments full of suffering.

Our housewife and husband have one set of problems concerning sexual activities, partners, and related struggles to get what they desire. Regarding their children, house, possessions, finances, jewelry, and investments they have another set of problems to weigh down their hearts and burden their minds. Even when they are interested in virtue, honor, reputation, integrity, spirituality, and other formless, intangible things there are problems. Each kind of existence has its attendant problems and struggles. Whether sexual, formish, or formless, every kind of existence is troublesome and leads to dukkha, because with existence there is birth, and with birth there is suffering. Becomings and existences bring about the birth of ego-me and thereby dukkha. As long as there is becoming and existence of self, ego-me will be born into suffering. Whatever style of existence, it is the place where self is born to have problems and suffer.

The question that naturally follows is how can we be free of the problems originating from sensual, formish, and formless existence? To return to the example of our housewife and husband, how can they live without distress concerning sensual, romantic, and sexual matters? How can they live without distress concerning children, money, possessions, and other material stuff? How can they live without distress concerning virtue, honor, and reputation? It is impossible that they could have nothing to do with any of these; they are all necessary aspects of life. If these matters are thoroughly understood, our couple will be beyond the problems of the three kinds of existence. The end of existence is the end of problems and suffering. So please try to understand these three categories of existence.

Of course, the problems do not exist for our housewife and househusband alone. We all have the same challenges. Thus, partners like this wife and husband must be the best of friends for each other, correct and fitting friends, in order to face all these challenges together so their lives are free of the problems of existence. For such reasons, please examine the details of these three styles of existence and understand them well.

This is a good point to mention that marriage ought to be a way for two people to solve the problems of the three existences together. It is not about increasing their problems concerning sex, as so often happens. Marriage should not exacerbate the problems that individuals already have, whether concerning finances, status, or whatever. In a world of fools, marriage exists to bring more problems; it increases troubles until people go crazy. In a world of intelligent people, marriage is a means of helping each other resolve challenges, of combining strengths, experience, and intelligence to solve the problems of life rather than increase them.

Both partners may have the right understanding that enables them to get rid of the three kinds of problems that trouble them concerning sensual existence, formish existence, and formless existence. If we examine them and have true understanding, they will not cause us any trouble. Nobody, however, seems at all interested in the last two. Perhaps they appear too distant or too profound. Even with the basic one of sexuality, few people can actually manage it or get it right. So this life keeps biting its owner, that is, is full of repetitive dukkha. Perhaps it is time to understand these three kinds of existence.

The Lessons of Existence

We must pass through the experience of these three existences as lessons that test us in life, and we must pass these tests in order to graduate to nibbāna, the quenching of suffering and ending of problems. Nibbāna is the ultimate purpose of life, that which is beyond and above these three existences and their troubles. The same holds even for other religions. Christians, for instance, must learn the lessons of these three kinds of existence to enter the kingdom of God. To live with the highest reality or truth we must pass these three lessons. So please study these three existences as lessons that need to be studied and passed in order to realize the supreme potential in life.

Sensual Existence

The first kind of existence is sexual-sensual becoming and existence, the first of these lessons through which we must pass. This kind of existence cannot be avoided because nature has arranged things so that we inevitably experience sexuality in order for us to reproduce and avoid extinction. Reproduction in itself is not much fun. Reproduction is difficult, inconvenient, painful, troublesome, and stressful. But nature is clever to add *kāma* into the mix as bait or bribe so that we will reproduce. It hires or tricks us to reproduce with sensuality as the wages or payoff. Without the pleasure of sex, who would bother with the trouble? Because of sensuality we put up with the hassles and hard work of reproduction. So this is the basis of life; without it life would not continue. Thus, sensuality, the conditions for sensuality, the sources of sensuality—sex and sexuality—are integral aspects of our lives. You can see the truth of this for yourselves.

Modern psychologists, most of all Freud, have emphasized the central importance of sexuality or *kāma*. A newborn infant even before knowing anything about sex still has sexual feelings that it experiences. For example, a child experiences pleasure when urinating and defecating. Both give a feeling with sexual meaning, a savoriness, satisfaction, or pleasure when the lump of feces or stream of urine passes. Once we are old enough to directly engage in sexual activities, sensuality is more intense and direct. Sensuality is experienced and consumed from the beginning of life and becomes a difficult problem that dogs us throughout life. We need to understand the problem of sensuality in order to regulate it so that we are not enslaved to it.

One approach is to raise one's purpose to a higher level of sex for the sake of reproduction rather than merely for sensuality. Please note that reproduction and sex are two different things. Sensuality is the most infatuating and deceitful thing, just a flash of insanity. Still, it can trick us into complete abject indulgence. Really, it is merely the wages nature pays out for us to reproduce and continue the species, whether humans or other animals. We all must reproduce, which is different than merely engaging in or indulging in sensuality.

The dilemma is easy enough to understand but are we smart enough to deal with it? Will we hire ourselves out to reproduce or not? If our minds are sufficiently lofty that we do not indulge in sensuality, are not tricked by sensuality, are not enslaved by sensuality, and do not eat the wages of sensuality, it is possible to reproduce purely. That would go beyond sensuality and enter the realm of form. On this level, there is no indulging in and infatuation with sensuality. Here our minds merely reproduce as needed and dwell in formish existence. This illustrates how to successfully pass the first lesson and test, namely, sensual existence (*kāmabhava*).

Formish Existence and Formless Existence

Once we are married, are househusbands and housewives, the responsibilities and burdens of house, possessions, and finances occur. Our interest in and excitement with *kāma* weakens somewhat. The urgency of *rūpa* and formish existence—formishness and formish existence—insinuate themselves as we get older. As we continue to age, we think more often about death and what comes after. Then, experiences of nonmateriality and nonmaterial existence infiltrate, lessening the feelings of sensuality and form. We have all three kinds of existence in our lives. We must make each of them correct in order to speak of emancipation in a complete way, which is to be released from all three kinds. This is the purpose of investigating existence and related matters.

The above description concerns ordinary people. We may also consider those who are above and more noble than the ordinary run of things: renouncers, hermits, rishis, and other contemplatives. Some of them meditate using forms or material objects as the basis of *samādhi* (inner collectedness and unity of mind). *Samādhi* dependent on things with form, including the so-called absorptions in form (*rūpajhāna*), is deeply satisfying and joyful. Thus, these experiences are the highest levels of formish existence, because these existences are based in the most refined material forms.

Other hermits and contemplatives have taken formless objects as the basis of their meditation and been successful at even more refined levels of *samādhi*, with correspondingly subtler satisfaction and joy. Nevertheless, these are still formless existences, though of the highest kind. While these advanced meditators experience the highest levels of *rūpa* and *arūpa*, they remain caught within existence and are not fully emancipated. These most refined existences are suffering so long as there is clinging to such formish existence and formless existence. Such contemplatives suffer just like ordinary people, though in more refined terms. Even the Brahma gods within their Brahma worlds suffer due to clinging to those existences. Whatever existence one falls into, even the best of existences, there is burdensome dukkha.

Ready to Fall

Another useful word is *avacara* (wandering), which means to be ready to fall into something, that is, the habit of falling into one direction or another. If a person is of the habit of being ready to fall into sensuality, that is considered to be sensual wandering (*kāmāvacara*). If a person is of the habit of being ready to fall into form, that is considered to be formish wandering (*rūpāvacara*). If a person is of the habit of being ready to be beyond form, with non-material and intangible experiences, that is considered to be formless wandering (*arūpāvacara*). Nonetheless, these three wanderings are embodied right here in this world; we need not go into other worlds. They are a way to describe the general habit or tendency of a person. In fact we are falling into all three, they change regularly, but we categorize people according to their strongest predilection, whether their habits tend primarily toward sexual-sensual existence, formish existence, or formless existence. This depends on each person's mental habit and which of the different states of being one falls into most readily.

All the kinds of existence are difficult. Right now, each of us ought to examine ourselves and know ourselves in terms of the kind of existence we most incline toward. Most commonly it will be sensual-sexual existence, especially when we are young; it is quite difficult to dwell primarily in formish and formless existence. Still, it is inevitable that we experience formish and formless existence more often as we age and gain life experience. Please study these through meditation and Dhamma practice. Will you strive to study and investigate these different states of existence so that you can regulate them and triumph over them? This is the most important thing to understand for a peaceful life.

What does it take to regulate and be released from such existences? Essentially, a thorough understanding of dependent co-arising and a well-developed practice of mindfulness with breathing in and out (*ānāpānasati*) are required. That is what it takes to cope with sensual, formish, and formless existence, so that none of them arise as problems. In a later chapter, we'll discuss mindfulness with breathing as a response to dependent co-arising for the sake of the highest emancipation in life.

11 ❋ Heavens and Hells

Friends, there are these three causes for the occurrence of actions (karma). What are these three? The three are greed as a cause of actions, hatred as a cause of actions, and delusion as a cause of actions.

Any action that someone has carried out with greed, occurring with greed as its cause, and having greed as its origin—that action bears fruit within the aggregates that are the basis for his individuality. In whichever individuality that action bears fruit, he experiences that karmic fruit within that very individuality, either immediately, a moment later, or some later time.[66]

[The exact same description is applied to hatred and delusion, word for word.]

Friends, this is comparable with plant seeds that have not broken, rotted, or been destroyed by wind and sun, that have been chosen for their soundness, carefully stored, and planted by someone in a well-prepared plot with good top soil. Further, the rain falls according to the season. Those seeds will sprout, develop, and thrive most certainly. In the same way, any action that someone has carried out with greed . . . hatred . . . delusion, occurring with greed . . . hatred . . . delusion as its cause, and having greed . . . hatred . . . delusion as its origin—that action bears fruit within the aggregates that are the basis for his individuality. In whichever individuality that action bears fruit, he experiences that karmic fruit within that very individuality, either immediately, a moment later, or some later time.

These are the three causes for the occurrence of actions.

Friends, there are these three further causes for the occurrence of actions (karma). What are these three? The three are non-greed as a cause of actions, non-hatred as a cause of actions, and non-delusion as a cause of actions.

Any action that someone has carried out with non-greed, occurring with non-greed as its cause, and having non-greed as its origin—being free of greed in this way, that action has been abandoned by him, been uprooted, been made like a palm with its growth removed, become nothing, so that It won't arise again.

[The exact same description is applied to non-hatred and non-delusion, word for word.]

Friends, this is comparable with plant seeds that have not broken, rotted, or been destroyed by wind and sun, that have been chosen for their soundness, and carefully stored. However, someone burns them until only ashes remain, then tosses them into a scattering wind or sprinkles them into a fast flowing river. Certainly, those seeds are as if uprooted, been made like a palm with its growth removed, become nothing, so that they won't sprout ever again.

In the same way, any action that someone has carried out with non-greed . . . non-hatred . . . non-delusion, occurring with non-greed . . . non-hatred . . . non-delusion as its cause, and having non-greed . . . non-hatred . . . non-delusion as its origin—being free of greed . . . hatred . . . delusion in this way, those actions have been abandoned by him, been uprooted, been made like a palm with its growth removed, become nothing, so they won't arise again.

These are the three causes for the occurrence of actions (kamma).

Any karma that the actor sees as born
from greed, hatred, or delusion,
once done, whether small or great,
that karma will bear fruit to be
experienced within this individuality.

No other basis can be found.
Therefore, the practitioner
who clearly understands greed, hatred, and delusion,
summons true knowledge and thereby
abandons all evil, unwholesome actions.[67]

We've discussed existence and examined its consequences. Not only is existence an important teaching in its own right; existence is also a prominent mode (*ākāra*) within dependent co-arising (*paṭiccasamuppāda*), falling between clinging and birth. So now we will look at existence within the stream of dependent co-arising.

The Dependent Co-arising of Existence

This stream of dependent co-arising has taken us to existence, to becoming and existence, where we exist in one way or another—I am this, I am that—where we consider ourselves to be a man or a woman, a German or a Thai, or whatever we think we may be, according to the process of dependent co-arising. Any kind of "I am this" or "I am that" is existence. Once there is existence, then the role is played to the hilt. With existence, there is the one, the person, who exists in that particular way. There are the different kinds of existence, and then there is the one who plays that role, who is born into that role and acts it out fully. The birth of this person in the role it must play is called *jāti* (birth), which is the result of existence.

In every cycle of dependent co-arising, there is existence and birth. Every time this flow takes us in, there is existence and birth. Physical birth out of our mother's womb is not the problem; we need not make problems with being born physically. The problems do not start until there is spiritual birth. Because of ignorance and through clinging an ego-me is born. In the Dhamma way of speaking, we include suffering with birth. The two are inseparable. As soon as ego-me is born, there is some form of distress or suffering. Birth is stressful, painful, and troublesome. Of course, we mean spiritual not physical birth.

Whether the cycle of dependent co-arising is dependent on eyes, ears, nose, tongue, body, or the mind-door, each cycle will include becoming and birth. Once there is birth, there is the big fat ego playing this role or that. That ego is heavy and suffers. Whatever the form of existence, and whatever sense experience it is based on, there appears the birth of this "I am," the ego, playing its act, getting into trouble. This is something that requires special attention because we have been overlooking this for all of our lives. We have not been paying any attention to existence and to this birth of ego-me. This habit continues to churn along with almost everyone ignoring it. The time has now come to start paying attention to it, to understand it, and to find a way to get away from this endless spinning around in circles of dukkha.

An easy way to understand this is to reflect in terms of heaven or paradise (*sagga*). There is heaven even here in this world, in this life; and there is heaven in other worlds, wherever those may be. Let us consider the heavens of this world first. Whenever sexuality or sensuality is fulfilled and satisfied, that is paradise, a sexual or sensual heaven, a delicious kind of sensual existence. When we are thoroughly, perfectly happy with material things, that too is heaven, a kind of formish existence. When we are fulfilled and happy due to honor, fame, power, influence, and other immaterial things, that is a formless existence kind of heaven. Each of these heavens can be found here in this life.

If, however, we speak more traditionally and take the conservative, orthodox view based on the commentaries written long after the Buddha, the heavens are other worlds (*paraloka*). The heavenly worlds filled with sensual pleasures are sensual existence. The higher worlds full of joys based in fine material things, such as form-based *samādhi*, are heavens of formish existence. The highest levels of paradise come from developing *samādhi* until one is born as a Brahma god.[68] In this scheme, sensuality is rather lower, form is superior, and formless is the highest. Yet, even the heavens of other worlds are still suffering because they are still existence.

The heavens of this world are dukkha. The heavens of other worlds that we cannot see but have heard about are suffering. Every heaven is stressful and burdensome. On the other hand, the Arahants, the Worthy Ones, are beyond all worlds and have transcended the various heavens. One must be beyond the heavens of sensual existence, formish existence, and formless existence to be Arahant, the highest kind of person. It is necessary to be above heaven in all its meanings in order to be totally free, liberated from dukkha.

All Heavens Bite

Let us come back to the heavens of this world; they're easier to understand, more relevant, and can be seen clearly. Take a look at your friends, especially those who are young. Their heavens here are often in sexuality. They will invest anything, spend all their money, to fulfill their sexual joys. So they dwell mainly in such sensual existence. Even this heaven of theirs bites them. Because of it they undergo all sorts of difficulties, expenses, conflicts, competitions, and jealousy. Sexual heavens, so common in this world, consume many of our friends.

Once their sexual searches lead to consummation in marriage, a higher or more refined level of heaven is found. With marriage there are children, a home, possessions, and wealth. These are heavens of formish existence. No matter how difficult it is to maintain these heavens, no matter how much people have, they cling to these heavens and suffer, unless there is sufficient Dhamma understanding. Most people do not have enough Dhamma, so these heavens bite their owners. The heavens of formish existence gnaw and devour; they even drive some people mad.

Climbing higher, people find the heavens of purely mental matters. Enjoying and delighting in great fame and prestigious awards such as Nobel Prizes are heavens of formless existence. These chew and chomp. Seduced into clinging to these exalted pleasures their hearts are heavy with jealousy and possessiveness, with fighting to preserve their existences. So the formless paradises also bite their owner. Whatever kind of heaven it may be—sexual, formish, or formless—each and every kind of existence turns and bites. Observe the existences of life around us and you will understand existence well. There is not any kind of existence that is free of suffering.

The existences connected with sex and sensuality have the usual problems, difficulties, jealousies, and conflicts with which you are familiar. The existences connected with simple materiality—with form, money, jewels, and possessions—have the problems and stress of the hard work and struggle to obtain, protect, and increase them. The existences connected with things having no form—matters like power, prestige, honor, reputation, virtue, and vice—all have their problems and difficulties. They all involve a lot of effort, concern, worry, and time. One can see that all three kinds of existence are fraught with trouble, cause problems, and bring distress.

Please take your study to the level that sees how every level of heaven and every kind of existence contains the devouring reactions known as defilements (*kilesa*). Each level has its corresponding defilement and all of them wound. There are things that bite, that inflict aches and pain, on every level of heaven and in every kind of existence. One cannot escape pain even in the highest heaven.

A common summary of dependent co-arising illustrates the role of defilements. This version of dependent co-arising contains three basic elements: defilement, action, and fruit.[69] Egoistic reactions lead to karma, which bears fruit (*vipāka*) and often provokes more reaction and karma. All three of these aspects—defilement, action, and fruits of action—are found in the standard sequence of dependent co-arising. We find defilement in ignorance, craving, and clinging. We find action in concocting, contact, and existence. Finally, we find the fruits of action in consciousness, mind-body, sense media, feeling, birth, and all the forms of dukkha. This further emphasizes the burdensomeness of existence and its actions that give birth to suffering.

This weightiness is the burden of life, which depends on existence. Whenever there is existence there is going to be distress because of the afflictive defilement. Nothing can spare us from this fact. It is what all the existences have in common. Even the smallest existence, the smallest particle, will involve suffering. The Buddha compared it with excrement. A tiny bit of excrement still stinks. Even if it is so small you cannot see where it is, it still stinks. As soon as the name existence comes up, there is dukkha.

Is there any need to doubt that all existences create birth and distress, a heavy burden upon life, a life that bites its owner? This requires our understanding as it is our fundamental problem. It highlights the suffering of dependent co-arising and requires our most special observation.

The Biting Beasts of Existence

We'd like to mention ten clear, straightforward examples of things that bite and cause dukkha in every kind of heaven, existence, and birth. Please consider them carefully.

Fondness: You can find liking, preferences, and fondness in all the different kinds of heavens and different levels of existence. You all know what love and infatuation is; you have loved and been loved. So you ought to know the biting of fondness.

Anger: When something appears positive, we love it. When something appears negative, we get angry and then anger bites. You have all been angry before; you know how anger bites.

Hate: We hate without any reason, full of unreasonable hatred because of ignorance and stupidity. We hate until we are unable to stand anything, full of annoyance and ill-will. You have hated before; you know how whatever we hate bites us.

Fear: We have foolish irrational fears about practically anything. We fear illness, fear poverty, fear having our reputations destroyed, and fear things we have never seen. Wealthy people commit suicide when faced with fear of their wealth wasting away. All kinds of foolish fear bite our hearts and gnaw our minds.

Excitement: We like things to stimulate and excite our minds. The Caucasians who travel in Asia are wandering about looking for excitement and adventure. At home they require sports and strange entertainments to excite them. We fill our homes with curious and interesting things that stimulate our minds. There is no end to such bouncing of the heart and its lack of peace.

Hope: Overly concerned with the future, we foolishly hope because of craving. Everyone builds castles in the sky with their dreams and hopes for the future. These gnaw the heart, too.

Longing: Dwelling in and clinging to the past, we miss things that are lost, faded, or diminished, especially things we have loved in the past. We cannot help longing after them, so they bite our hearts.

Envy: Without reason, we envy someone for being better looking than us, having more money, or having whatever we might think makes them better off. This burns us the most. Envy stabs and pierces us, while the person we envy knows nothing about it. The odious comparisons of envy devour the heart.

Jealousy: Jealousy is a kind of possessiveness or stinginess—having and not wanting to share. This small-mindedness will not give or share. It is afraid that others will request things of us; it is trapped in its pettiness. Ordinary jealousy rankles and curdles within us.

Sexual jealousy: In Thai, we speak of a special and powerful form of jealousy called *heung*, which specifically refers to sexual jealousy. Being jealous regarding one's sexual partner, husband, wife, or lover is extremely strong. People often kill because of this.

In everyday life, here in this world, these ten products of dependent co-arising bite us repeatedly. You will find all ten of them biting and chewing in the heavens, let alone the hellish existences. Every kind of existence, every existence without any exception, has these ten things to bite us. So we say that wherever there is existence, right there is suffering. Even the heavenly and divine levels of existence bite. How could ordinary humans escape getting bitten? Existence is unbearable.

Existence in Dependent Co-arising

We are reflecting on the consequences of the stream of dependent co-arising foolishly concocting to the level or extent of existence, being, and having, which arises from clinging. When there is clinging, there is existence, the sense that "I am this," "I am like that." One arranges oneself to be "like this" or "like that," as either sensual existence, formish existence, or formless existence. One of these existences fills our mind and then expresses itself fully as birth. It is born according to its intentions, motivations, and desires. Now there is an ego-being existing in some kind of existence: a sensual being in sensual existence, a formish being in formish existence, or a formless being in formless existence. Each of these beings is full of egoistic clinging. Every one of them is a being experiencing its appropriate dukkha.

In every cycle of dependent co-arising there is always existence and ego-birth. In a single day, however many cycles occur—whether based on eyes, ears, nose, tongue, body, or mind-sense—there are that many existences and births. For most of us, there are too many to count and observe carefully. For a start, then, notice that with each experience of suffering there has been a spin of dependent co-arising. Recognize existence and its nasty fruits, namely, that existence brings distress and burdens. Life bites its owner because there is an ego-me born into one existence or another. Most people overlook these facts completely. From now on, please be interested and please pay attention. Your life depends on it.

The flow of dependent co-arising is just the flow of life. Please contemplate your life experience until you understand how the flow of life is the flow of dependent co-arising. If you understand dependent co-arising you will see these facts clearly, directly, and thoroughly.

12 ❋ Damming the Streams of Suffering

Friends, any group of wanderers or priests when regarding things[70] tends to regard self as existing in various ways. All of those wanderers or priests regard the five clinging-together aggregates collectively or one or another of the five clinging-together aggregates as being self.

What are the clinging-together aggregates? In this world, worldlings who have not paid attention, who have not seen noble ones, are not intelligent regarding the noble ones' Dhamma, and have not received the Dhamma advice of the noble ones, and who have not seen true gentlemen, are not intelligent regarding the Dhamma of true gentlemen, and have not received the Dhamma advice of true gentlemen: (1) tend to regard form as being self, or regard self as having form, or regard form as being in self, or regard self as being in form; (2) tend to regard feeling as being self, or regard self as having feeling, or regard feeling as being in self, or regard self as being in feeling; (3) tend to regard perception as being self, or regard self as having perception, or regard perception as being in self, or regard self as being in perception; (4) tend to regard thought as being self, or regard self as having thought, or regard thought as being in self, or regard self as being in thought; and (5) tend to regard consciousness as being self, or regard self as having consciousness, or regard consciousness as being in self, or regard self as being in consciousness.

So it is that the regarding of self occurs, and so such thicksters also take possession of things regarded as self with "I am."

When one takes possession with "I am," the descent of the five faculties occurs, namely the eye-faculty, ear-faculty, nose-faculty, tongue-faculty, and body-faculty.

There is mind (as a sense door), there are phenomena (as objects of experience), and there is the ignorance-element.

When the untrained worlding experiences the feelings arising through ignorant contact, there is appropriation with "I am," with "this is me," with "I will be," with "I will not be," with "I will have form," with "I will not have form," with "I will have perception," with "I will not have perception," or with "I will neither have perception nor be without perception."

The five faculties remain established amidst these appropriations. However, in the case that ignorance is something naturally abandoned by noble well-trained disciples, right knowing arises. With the arising of right knowing through the complete vomiting up of ignorance by that noble disciple, there is no appropriation with "I am," nor with "this is me," nor with "I will be," nor with "I will not be," nor with "I will have form," nor with "I will not have form," nor with "I will have perception," nor with "I will not have perception," nor with "I will neither have perception nor be without perception" in the noble disciple.[71]

Having explored how dependent co-arising (*paṭiccasamuppāda*) brings about becoming, birth, and suffering, we now face the question, "How do we prevent the arising of suffering?" When ignorance perpetuates dependent co-arising, we suffer. When we live correctly in terms of dependent co-arising we do not suffer. The question, then, is how can we manage or live with this dependent co-arising in order to prevent the arising of foolishness and distress?

We speak of damming or blocking the flow of dependent co-arising, just like we might dam or stop a current of water. In fact, this is a matter of governing or mastering the flow so that it is within our control. Our duty, then, is to regulate (*kuabkum* in Thai) the flow of interdependently unfolding experience correctly so that dukkha does not occur.

The most central and essential factor in mastering the flow of dependent co-arising is mindfulness (*sati*). Specifically, this mindfulness is developed through the practice of mindfulness with breathing (*ānāpānasati*) that you have come here to learn and train. Starting with the breath as a basis for mindfulness, then comprehensively exploring a number of important realities connected with breathing in and out, we cultivate a highly refined mindfulness. A crucial fruit of mindfulness with breathing in and out practice is mindfulness sufficient for stopping the flow of dependent co-arising. We will discuss the practice of *ānāpānasati* in a later chapter. Here, we will focus on how the fruits of mindfulness with breathing regulate or dam the flow of dependent co-arising and prevent suffering.

The point, place, or moment that is most important for using mindfulness to block dependent co-arising is the moment of sense contact. Mindfulness is required at each moment of contact. However, we generally lack such quick and consistent mindfulness. If we have not trained mindfulness, we will lack it when and where it is needed the most, that is, to regulate contact. This is a fundamental problem: the mindfulness we need is not adequately developed. Please cultivate mindfulness so there will not be foolish contact. Then, there will not be any further foolish *vedanā*, foolish craving, and the rest of the foolishness that ends up in dukkha.

Four Necessary Dhammas

As mentioned in chapter 9, the word *mindfulness* implies speed—fast as a lightning bolt or laser beam. The quickness and immediacy of mindfulness is needed to be immediately present at the arising of contact. Then, mindfulness is able to deliver wisdom to the point of contact, at the moment of contact, so that contact is governed by correct understanding and not by ignorance. Mindfulness prevents foolish contact and enables wise contact.

A central function of mindfulness is to deliver wisdom. This requires that there be wisdom and understanding to deliver at the point of contact. Without wisdom, mindfulness has nothing to deliver and works for nothing. Thus, it is necessary for there to be correct understanding, whether we call it wisdom (*paññā*), true knowing (*vijjā*), insight knowledge (*ñāṇa*), clear seeing (*vipassanā*), or whatever else. And from where does this intuitive wisdom come? Such insight and true, direct knowing are studied, trained, and cultivated through the practice of mindfulness with breathing in and out. Through it, mindfulness is developed and naturally matures in correct understanding.

Mindfulness with breathing also brings about *sampajañña*, or the specific application of wisdom to a particular situation or event, and *samādhi*, mind that is firm, clearly focused, stable, calm, clear, and active. These essential ingredients are discovered and thoroughly developed through mindfulness with breathing in and out. With a sufficiently developed practice, these four essential dhammas—mindfulness, wisdom, clear comprehension, and well-focused stability—will be ready to do their work at the moment of contact.

Let us look at these again. The primary function of mindfulness is to bring wisdom in to regulate contact. Then, contact will not be foolish and distorted. We can call it "wise contact"—sense contact that is watched and regulated by wisdom. Contact that is not foolish does not lead to foolish *vedanā*. When there is no foolish feeling, the *vedanā* that arises is intelligent. Any wanting that arises in response to intelligent feeling will be intelligent, too, rather than being more foolish craving. If mind holds onto or focuses on anything, it will not be foolish, either; it will be correct, the intelligent sort of holding or focusing that does not cause trouble. In this way, mindfulness brings correct understanding to contact, and the flow of dependent co-arising is controlled or regulated right there.

Higher Training Is Needed

There is a level of wisdom, although rather basic, that occurs naturally and should not be overlooked. It is instinctual and occurs even among animals. We naturally learn our lessons when we make mistakes and suffer pain or discomfort as a result. We do not like the pain of it, are chastened by the experience, and remember it. We do not dare to repeat that mistake again. Even animals learn in this way and avoid things that cause pain, harm, and death. This level of wisdom comes from the lessons nature continuously teaches us. Nevertheless, it is not all that much and not nearly enough to resolve this enormous problem of human suffering. Thus, we need to train wisdom to a higher level than the naturally occurring kind.

A crucial problem regarding mindfulness is that usually it is not fast enough to be fully present at the moment of contact. It lacks immediacy and arrives too late. Ordinarily, mindfulness is sluggish, or non-existent, or shows up a couple days after the damage has been done. What's the benefit in that? Consequently, mindfulness needs to be trained and developed until fast enough to be fully present whenever needed. Then it can deliver wisdom to the moment of contact and contact can be mastered.

Once there is quick enough mindfulness and it brings wisdom, the wisdom specific to the needs of the situation is called *sampajañña*. Accumulated wisdom can be great; the wisdom needed at any given moment is more specific and focused on resolving the problem at hand. In the Pāli texts, *sampajañña* usually appears in partnership with mindfulness—*sati-sampajañña*. When mindfulness is sufficiently present, it applies the special, particular wisdom needed in each moment of contact. This mindful, clear, specific, and appropriate understanding is what regulates contact and keeps it from becoming a foolish problem. Mindfulness brings that particular wisdom to contact, which acts to regulate the contact so that nothing foolish occurs.

Wisdom is vast. No matter how much knowledge and understanding one has, for it to be relevant and useful, mindfulness must select the right wisdom for the contact of the moment. Clear comprehension is this specific, applied wisdom. Wisdom in general is called wisdom. The relationship and difference between these two aspects of wisdom can be illustrated by a medicine cabinet. The medicine cabinet may be filled with all kinds of different medicines. When we have an illness, we need to choose the right medicine to treat that specific illness. Only a fool would take all the medicine in the cabinet or grab a bottle randomly. The intelligent person only uses the medicine specifically needed for his illness, and he takes it properly and in the right amount. We might have many weapons in our arsenal to fend off and destroy our enemies, but we do not use them all at once. The skilled warrior chooses the weapon specific to the enemy. The activity of selection is the duty of mindfulness. Therefore, mindfulness must be well trained in a wide variety of situations so that it is able to function quickly enough, that is, immediately, and deliver the appropriate wisdom to the specific situation, the particular case, of the contact happening right now. As wisdom is vast, and there are many possible situations and contacts, mindfulness chooses the specific element of wisdom appropriate for a particular case of contact so that ignorance does not turn it into a problem.

The Antithesis of Ignorance

This requires true knowing (*vijjā*), the kind of knowledge that is intuitive, subjective, and internal. In Pāli, we describe it as *sandiṭṭhiko*, to be seen clearly and known truly within oneself in a way that is subjective and intuitive. Only this kind of knowledge can be called true knowing, the true, genuine knowledge that can solve our problem. May we all have this kind of true, direct knowledge.

The word for true knowing, *vijjā*, has a most excellent meaning. The particle *vi-* means clear, bright, distinct, and directly intuitive, and *jā* means "to know." Consequently, *vijjā* means simply to know clearly, directly, intuitively. For the most part, our knowledge is the ordinary kind made up of information, memories, and common sense, which never reach the level of true knowing—mind knowing clearly, directly, intuitively within itself.

Buddhism cultivates such true knowing in order to regulate and master the flow of dependent co-arising. For the most part, however, we people have ignorance—not true knowing—that is, unclear knowing or ignorance. When direct inner understanding is immediately present at contact, nothing foolish can arise. With ignorance—non-knowing or unclear knowing—we cannot manage that flow of concocting. If our knowledge is incorrect, unclear, and incomplete, we are helpless to stop the flow of dependent co-arising. Consequently, please see the importance and necessity of improving our ordinary knowledge to the level that is true knowledge and wisdom.

True knowing is like daytime; ignorance is like nighttime. With true knowing we see clearly, as in the clear light of day. With ignorance everything is dark and we cannot see what we need to see. True knowing and ignorance oppose each other in this way. Sunlight (*āloko*) is a synonym for true knowing. Wisdom, sunlight, and true knowing are synonyms that can be used interchangeably. They all refer to the understanding that is clear, direct, correct, and sufficient.

In short, true knowing is the means for regulating and controlling the flow of dependent co-arising through the power of mindfulness. Mindfulness brings correct understanding to bear upon the flow of dependent co-arising and governs it so that no dukkha can arise.

Setting the Record Straight with Not-Self

The highest, most developed understanding of Dhamma in India before the Buddha's time is found in the Upanishads. The word *upanishad* means "sitting close to the truth" or "approaching the truth intimately." However, an important truth taught in the Upanishads is that there is a Self (*atmān*, in Sanskrit) that is reincarnated endlessly through a long series of existences through which it progresses and improves until becoming an eternal, unchanging atmān. The Upanishads affirm the self in very clear terms. Obviously, this concept was developed in India before the Buddha appeared.

What benefit or purpose would there be in the Buddha teaching the same thing already being taught? The Buddha did not appear in the world to teach the same old thing; we could not call him the Buddha if he had. The Buddha appeared to teach something subtler and liberating, that no true self can be found in anything anywhere. He taught that everything is not-self (*anattā*) and there is only the flow of dependent co-arising.

The usual flow of dependent co-arising is suffering. Although it is all not-self, ignorance leads to clinging to self. Still, no self that suffers can be found. The flow of dependent quenching (*paṭiccanirodha*) has no dukkha. Ignorance, craving, and clinging to self are quenched and this quenching, too, is not-self. The Buddha disposed with self and the self system. This is the new understanding introduced by the Buddha: not-self is wisdom and self is ignorance.

The Buddha appeared after the Upanashadic teachings to counter their emphasis on self or atmān, and thus taught not-self. This is the understanding of dependent co-arising that is original. It is essential that we interpret it correctly in line with his purpose. Use it to eliminate the illusion of self so that suffering will not occur. And be careful of dependent co-arising explanations that smuggle self back into dependent co-arising. After all, dukkha depends on the birth of self. Understanding dependent co-arising properly, we will make the most of the Buddha's appearance in this universe.

Real World Peace Requires Mindful, Wise Education

I do not know if it is amusing or pitiable that we modern people are so broadly and sophisticatedly educated that our intelligence and wisdom ends up so entangled and confused. Not only is it mixed up, it is excessive. We have a huge surplus of knowledge. We know so much more than we need, yet we obsessively seek even more information and knowledge. How is mindfulness to find and apply the right knowledge fit for the contacts we experience throughout daily life? How can mindfulness make the right choice amidst the cerebral mess we have created? Let us improve our education, learning, and search for knowledge so that our wisdom is appropriate, sufficient, and correct—the kind of understanding that is practically useful at each contact we face. The cultivation of mindfulness with breathing in and out can help us do so. It develops sufficiently quick mindfulness and correct, practical wisdom.

You can see for yourselves that although we have our marvelous educational systems and thousands of universities all over the world, we are as yet unable to create peace in our world. While we know so many things, the world lacks peace. This is because we lack the proper sort of wisdom that is able to deal with real problems of human suffering. Nor are we mindful enough. We do not have the kind of intelligence that gets to the bottom of dukkha. All our wonderful creativity leads to increasing excess and excessive problems.

If we cannot cope with the personal suffering of individuals in this world, there is no way we can bring about peace in the world. This is one clear example of how all our great learning and knowledge is neither correct nor sufficient for solving the problems of humanity. Often, this vast knowledge is used to create newer, bigger, fancier, more enticing things—that is, newer, bigger, fancier, more enticing problems. Consequently, instead of solving our problems modern education creates new ones. Let us take a good look at our situation and get interested in making the required improvements.

If each one of us has the mindfulness and wisdom to be able to regulate our contacts, there will not be any dukkha. There will not be any problems. Then, you will not have to worry what will happen to peace in the world. Peace will be part and parcel of our lives together. If each person can regulate contact and defeat suffering there will be peace. Peace will be complete, comprehensive, and simple—right here and now (*sandiṭṭhiko*). This is all it takes to have genuine world peace. So please give adequate attention to this central human problem: in our world we lack the necessary mindfulness and wisdom to control contact.

To make this important point completely clear, we must say that when we can control sense contact, we can control the world. We can have power over the entire world just by controlling contact through the power of mindfulness, wisdom, calm mental focus, and the specifically applied wisdom of *sampajañña*. This may sound strange but it is most assuredly true: if we can control sense contact, we can control the world. When we keep contact under control, everything in the world that appears and makes contact will be powerless to cause distress. Nothing in the world torments those who can control sense contact, and so we may say that the world is within our control. Should not you be interested in this?

13 ✻ Dependent Quenching

Venerable Friends, comparable to how space surrounded and enclosed by trees, vines, clay, and grasses is considered a dwelling, similarly, space surrounded and enclosed by bones, ligaments, muscle, and skin is considered "form (body)."

Friends, even though the eyes, the internal medium, are not destroyed, if visual form, the external medium, has not entered the channel of the eyes and foolishly adverting mind[72] that depends on those two media does not occur, then the consciousness arising due to those two media does not occur.

Friends, even though the eyes, the internal medium, are not destroyed and visual form, the external medium, has entered the channel of the eyes, if foolishly adverting mind that depends on those two media does not occur, then the consciousness arising due to those two media still does not occur.

Friends, when the eyes, the internal medium, are not destroyed and visual form, the external medium, has entered the channel of the eyes, and furthermore there is foolishly adverting mind depending on those two media, then the consciousness arising due to those two media naturally occurs.

Any form that has arisen together with foolishly adverting mind is categorized within the form aggregate of clinging. Any feeling that has arisen together with foolishly adverting mind is categorized within the feeling aggregate of clinging. Any recognition-perception that has arisen together with foolishly adverting mind is categorized within the perception aggregate of clinging. Any thinking that has arisen together with foolishly adverting mind is categorized within the concoction aggregate of clinging. Any sense consciousness that has arisen together with foolishly adverting mind is categorized within the consciousness aggregate of clinging.

A practitioner clearly knows and hears how the gathering, the meeting, and collecting together of these aggregates of clinging occurs in this way.

The Tathāgata himself has said, "Whoever sees dependent co-arising sees Dhamma; whoever sees Dhamma, sees dependent co-arising." All these phenomena—namely, these five clinging together aggregates—are known as "dependently co-arisen phenomena."[73]

Anything that is delight, longing, obsession, or infatuation regarding these five clinging together aggregates is known as "the origin of dukkha."[74]

Anything that is the removing of passionate desire[75] or abandoning of passionate desire regarding these five clinging together aggregates is known as "the quenching of dukkha."[76]

Venerable Friends, through this extent of practice the Bhagavā's teaching is developed and well cultivated.

[The exact same exploration is done with the other sense media: ears, nose, tongue, body, and mind.][77]

In the last chapter, we considered how to regulate or manage dependent co-arising. Now, we will consider a more profound level of practice. When dependent co-arising can be controlled, something new becomes possible, which can be called *paṭiccanirodha*, the quenching of dependent co-arising. While the term *paṭiccanirodha* does not literally appear in the Pāli scriptures, we find its meaning in numerous important passages where the Buddha speaks of *nirodhā* and *nirodho* repeatedly, as in the passage below. Thus, we feel quite justified in calling this *paṭiccanirodha*. Specifically, dependent co-arising refers to the dependent, conditioned arising (*samuppāda*) of suffering, while *paṭiccanirodha* refers to the dependent, conditioned quenching (*nirodha*) of suffering. Please give these terms significant interest in that they are opposite aspects of dependent conditioning.

The Sequence of Dependent quenching

The sequence with which students of the suttas are familiar is as follows:

Through the remainderless quenching of ignorance, concoctings quench;	Avijjāya tveva asesavirāganirodhā saṅkhāranirodho;
with the quenching of concoctings, consciousness quenches;	saṅkhāranirodhā viññāṇanirodho;

with the quenching of consciousness, mind-body quenches;	viññāṅanirodhā nāmarūpanirodho;
with the quenching of mind-body, sense media quench;	nāmarūpanirodhā saḷāyatana-; nirodho;
with the quenching of sense media, contact quenches;	saḷāyatananirodhā phassanirodho;
with the quenching of contact, feeling quenches;	phassanirodhā vedanānirodho;
with the quenching of feeling, craving quenches;	vedanānirodhā taṅhānirodho;
with the quenching of craving, clinging quenches;	taṅhānirodhā upādānanirodho;
with the quenching of clinging, becoming quenches;	upādānanirodhā bhavanirodho;
with the quenching of becoming, birth quenches;	bhavanirodhā jātinirodho;
with the quenching of birth, aging and death, sorrow, grief, pain, lamentation, and despair quench thoroughly.	jātinirodhā jarāmaraṅaṃ sokaparidevadukkhadomanass-upāyāsā nirujjhanti.
The entire mass of suffering quenches in just this way.	Evametassa kevalassa dukkha-kkhandhassa nirodho hoti ti.

One quenching after another is why we speak of *paṭiccanirodha*, the dependent quenching of suffering. In many of the suttas that explore dependent co-arising, *paṭiccanirodha* is implied though not expressly labeled so. Often, after explaining how things arise according to the law of dependent co-arising, the Buddha explained how things quench according to the same law. For clarity's sake, we call the latter *paṭiccanirodha*, the opposite or reverse of dependent co-arising.

The Ceasing of Function, Not Death or Destruction

Let us interject a crucial point here, which if not understood risks confusing the whole issue. This word *nirodha* is sometimes translated as cessation or extinction. *Nirodha*, quenching, or cessation does not mean that something is completely obliterated. Instead, *nirodha* means that something does not perform its usual function, is unable to perform that function, or has no function. This is what we mean by quench, in this context, which is speaking in the highest Dhamma terms rather than material terms. When something performs its function, we say it is born or arises, as in the elements of dependent co-arising. When it cannot perform that function, there is no point in speaking of it existing, at least not in Dhamma language. When eyes or ears do not perform their functions, they are said to quench, even though the nervous system and other physical apparatus remain intact. They do not disappear, they are not destroyed, but they do not function in their usual ways. In Dhamma language, we say they have quenched. When they actively function we say they are born, in particular, when they function ignorantly such that positivity and negativity, liking and disliking, and their ilk follow. Consequently, eyes, ears, and other senses arise and quench, arise and quench, over and over again, each time they function and then cease functioning. The words arising and quenching have this meaning in Dhamma language.

This way of speaking can be used even with the thing called "life." When life is not performing a function, we can say that life quenches. When life performs a function again, we can say that life arises or is born. This is how we speak in Dhamma language, which is not primarily about material functioning. To say that life ceases or quenches does not mean that somebody has died. In Dhamma language, we can speak of life being born and life ceasing many times each day. When it performs a function it is born; when it stops functioning it ceases. Ordinary people easily misunderstand this manner of speaking, as it deals with a subtler level of observation and focuses on the mental or spiritual aspect of things. From the Dhamma perspective, functioning life is a basis for clinging as "my life," while quenched life has no sense of ego-me.

When Ignorance Ceases . . .

The Buddha's standard description of the quenching process begins with this:

Through the remainderless fading away and quenching of ignorance, concocting quenches.
Avijjāya tveva asesavirāganirodhā saṅkhāranirodho.[78]

When ignorance quenches, the power that concocts this and that into being "something" quenches. In other words, the illusory appearance of something being a separate object quenches. When concoctings quench, the sense consciousness concocted by ignorance also quenches (*saṅkhāranirodhā viññāṇanirodho*). This is difficult to understand if you are not familiar with Dhamma language. Consciousness, here, is something that *saṅkhāra* has concocted for the sake of action via body, speech, or mind (*kāyasaṅkhāra*, *vacisaṅkhāra*, or *manosaṅkhāra*). If this sort of consciousness occurs, it has the function of concocting physical, verbal, and mental actions. When concoctings quench, this kind of consciousness is not concocted and does not perform the function of stirring up physical, verbal, and mental actions.

When the consciousness that comes from ignorance quenches, mind-body must quench (*viññāṇanirodhā nāmarūpanirodho*). Obviously, as the Buddha was teaching this after having experienced it, *nāmarūpanirodho*, or quenching of name and form, does not mean anything like physical death. When mind-body that has arisen successively from ignorance quenches, the sense media—eyes, ears, nose, tongue, body, and mind-sense—that are conditioned by such mind-body must quench—this is quenching of mind-body, quenching of the sense organs (*nāmarūpanirodhā saḷāyatananirodho*). But do not think this means the person is blind, deaf, cannot smell or taste, has no sense of touch, and has destroyed the nervous system. That is not at all what the Buddha is describing. The quenching of the senses simply means that they do not function in the old ignorant way, not that they are destroyed.

The especially profound aspect of dependent co-arising is right here: How is ignorance to quench? How are concoctings to quench? How is consciousness to quench without us becoming unconscious? How is mind-body to quench without having to die? These aspects of dependent co-arising are why the Buddha insisted it is so profound. Venerable Ānanda just thought it was "pretty deep," but we should agree with the Buddha saying it is "most profound." There is nothing more profound.

When these sense media—eyes, ears, nose, tongue, body, and mind—

that have been created by ignorance quench, the sense contact created by ignorance also quenches (*saḷāyatananirodhā phassanirodho*). In the same way, when this ignorant contact quenches, the *vedanā* conditioned by ignorance—"ignorant *vedanā*"—quench (*phassanirodhā vedanānirodho*). Consequently, all the other products and symptoms of ignorance—ignorant craving, clinging, becoming, birth, aging, and death—that condition each other in dependent co-arising quench one after the other, until dukkha itself quenches. Quenching continues down the line until distress and suffering quench, too. Everything concocted under the power of ignorance quenches one after the other.

Quenching from Ignorance: Theoretical

Ignorance (*avijjā*) itself quenches through true knowing (*vijjā*). Dependent co-arising is governed by ignorance or false knowing. Dependent quenching (*paṭiccanirodha*) is governed by true knowing. When ignorance is the commander-in-chief of life, there is dependent co-arising. When the commander-in-chief is true, correct knowing, there is dependent quenching and life carries on without craving, clinging, and suffering. Please study and compare the two—dependent co-arising and dependent quenching—until you can immediately tell them apart. When is life dependent co-arising and when is it dependent quenching?

It is necessary that we experience personally and observe carefully whether or not true knowing or ignorance commands life. Ordinarily and naturally life is dominated, controlled, and mastered by ignorance. This is because ordinarily there is a lack of true knowledge; we normally lack the true knowing that knows correctly according to reality. When true knowing is missing, ignorance takes over. This is why the Buddha said that ignorance exists generally throughout the universe, always ready to drop in and take over as soon as it has an opportunity. Ignorance exists widely, ever ready to run life, to run the universe, when it is empty of true knowing, just as darkness takes over as soon as daylight disappears. Remove light and you have darkness immediately.

In the previous chapter we spoke of regulating dependent co-arising through true knowing. There, the solution was temporary, contingent. When wisdom is fulfilled, however, the resolution is lasting. When true knowing governs contact, it is not foolish. There is wise contact rather than foolish contact from the very start. With wise contact, *vedanā* is not foolish and there is not any foolish craving, clinging, becoming, and birth—thus, no suffering. Through the power of true understanding, none of these foolish conditions exist. This is what true knowing governing dependent co-arising means.

Now, we can see how necessary it is to have true knowing or intuitive wisdom. We practice mindfulness with breathing in order to develop this necessary knowledge and wisdom, and to be always ready to use it with mindfulness delivering it to the moment of contact. If mindfulness is sufficiently developed that it is fast and sensitive enough and wisdom is complete and strong enough, they can be applied exactly at the moment of contact. Then every contact is wise contact, governed as it is by true knowing. Instead of ignorant contact we have wise contact; the result is the complete opposite and suffering cannot arise. True quenching is when the problems no longer need to be regulated because they do not even arise.

Quenching from Contact: Actual and Practical

When speaking theoretically, we say that true knowing enters and ignorance quenches. With ignorance quenched, concoctings quench, consciousness quenches, mind-body quenches, and so on through the rest of the sequence. It is easy to speak in this theoretical way. When it comes to practical application, however, it is sufficient to speak of contact. To put this into practice in actual life circumstances, we focus on contact. At the moment of contact, of sense experience, have mindfulness bring true knowing or wisdom into play so that contact belongs to true knowing rather than ignorance. With wise contact no problems arise.

There are two words that express the heart of the matter; please remember them: ignorant sense contact, meaning to experience contact through ignorance, and truly knowing sense contact, meaning to experience contact through correct knowledge. With sense contact there are these two options, one under the power of ignorance and the other under the power of true knowing. Manage contact carefully so that there is only wise contact and you will be able to quench suffering. Instead of the usual stuff, there will be quenching of dependent co-arising; the quenching of suffering can arise.

At this point, we must ask ourselves whether our lives are governed by ignorance or by true knowing, by not knowing or by true knowing? When understanding is lacking, there is ignorance. When there is no light, there is darkness. It is the same for all human beings. This life muddles along in the darkness of ignorance. So we study dependent co-arising, then we study how to regulate dependent co-arising, and finally we quench dependent co-arising, which can be called the stream of successively dependent quenching. This is the benefit and value of studying, exploring, and understanding dependent co-arising.

To See the Dhamma of Dependent Co-arising Is to See the Buddha

Perhaps you have heard the Buddha's words to Venerable Vakkali saying, "Seeing the Dhamma is to see me. Seeing my physical body, even holding onto it for days, does not mean you have seen me."[79] These words mean that seeing the Dhamma is what lets us see the Buddha. Elsewhere he said, "Seeing the Dhamma means seeing dependent co-arising."[80]

One must realize dependent co-arising to see the Dhamma, and only by realizing the Dhamma can we meet the real Buddha. Children, fools, and others lacking in wisdom see the Buddha in the Buddha's physical body. However, the Buddha's physical body is not actually the Buddha; it is merely the skin or outer covering. To take his body, his skin, to be the real Buddha is mistaken. The Buddha himself disagreed. Even more foolish is to take Buddha images to be the actual Buddha. Now that there are Buddha images all over the world, does anyone really see the Buddha? People see the Buddha in terms of his body or in the inanimate images fashioned by people, but those are not the real Buddha. One sees the real Buddha by seeing the Dhamma, and one sees the Dhamma by seeing dependent co-arising. Seeing dependent co-arising means seeing how suffering is born and how it is quenched. Seeing both dependent co-arising and dependent quenching means seeing the Dhamma and seeing the genuine Buddha.

We do not have to go to India or to any other special place in order to find the Buddha. We simply need to go to the place where we find dependent co-arising, that is, in our own hearts. When we see dependent co-arising there in our own minds, we meet the Buddha. Right now, we do not see the Buddha. A curtain of ignorance blocks our vision. If we pull aside this veil of ignorance in our hearts just a bit, we will discover that the genuine Buddha is sitting right here, not anywhere else. Just brush the veil aside a little bit to see the Buddha; leave the veil in place and you will not see at all. The true Buddha is sitting behind this veil of ignorance.

The true knowing we discover behind the curtain is simply the clear profound vision of conditionality and dependent co-arising flowing from moment to moment. When everything—all dhammas—is seen in this light, ignorance can do no damage. Such true knowing is also describable in terms of impermanence and inconstancy; unsatisfactoriness, stressfulness, and undependability; not-self; the conditioned nature of all phenomena; and emptiness and thusness.[81] The descriptions of true knowing are varied but overlapping and interpenetrating. Penetrate any of them—especially dependent co-arising and dependent quenching—deeply and the rest will be revealed.

These true knowings apply to the inner and outer sense media, sense consciousness, and contact. They apply to feeling, craving, clinging, becoming, and birth. They apply to all thoughts, emotions, memories, dreams, and experiences. They apply to all of the aggregates of clinging, to everything on which we base our identities and conceits of self. Most of all, they apply to suffering. Contact is a most excellent place to focus the light of true knowing, yet anywhere it arises is worth contemplating deeply.

Where is your veil of ignorance? Have you found it yet? We require understanding of dependent co-arising that comes from our own study and investigation to be able to see this curtain of ignorance. Once you have found it, you can brush it aside or cut through it by this understanding of dependent co-arising. Clear seeing, thorough understanding, true knowing, will destroy the curtain of ignorance completely.

We can see immediately that the topic of dependent co-arising is profound. Merely to study it requires a profound study. Its actual practice is even more profound. To realize the fruits of practicing dependent co-arising is incredibly profound. If anyone should say that it is not profound or is only moderately profound, we would have to respond:

Do not talk crazy! Do not go saying such a foolish thing!

14 ❋ Training Mindfulness through Mindfulness with Breathing

Friends, mindfulness with breathing in and out that one has developed and made much of has great fruit and great benefit. Mindfulness with breathing in and out that one has developed and made much of fulfills the four applications of mindfulness.

The four applications of mindfulness that one has developed and made much of fulfill the seven factors of awakening. The seven factors of awakening that one has developed and made much of fulfill true knowing and liberation.

How does mindfulness with breathing in and out that one has developed and made much of have great fruit and great benefit?

Friends, a practitioner within this training, having gone into the forest, to the base of a tree or to an empty dwelling, having sat cross-legged with body upright, securely maintains mindfulness. Ever mindful that practitioner breathes in, ever mindful she breathes out.[82]

In the previous chapters, we consider how to slow, dam, and eventually quench the stream of dependent co-arising. Now, we will discuss in more detail the mindfulness that stops the stream of dependent co-arising. In particular, we will explore the mindfulness that goes by the name development of mindfulness with breathing in and out (*ānāpānasati-bhāvanā*)—the development of mindfulness every time one inhales and exhales. This is another branch of knowledge that deals with the mental or conscious side of life. Mindfulness (*sati*) concerns mind, especially awareness of our experience of life. When there is understanding of mind, it is possible to manage all kinds of problems, both material and mental. Nature makes such understanding of mind necessary, so that we humans have knowledge concerning both material and mental matters.

Understanding of Body and Mind Go Together

Do not think that understanding of mind is something new that just began with modern psychology and science. Please recognize that mind has accompanied body throughout the evolution that has led to human beings. From the beginning of human life, both physical and mental experiences developed together. However, though mind and body are always paired together and cannot be separated, the mental side of life is subtler. Consequently, it has often been overlooked, leading some people today to think that it is brand new or has just been discovered. Please recognize that mental knowledge has evolved together with physical matters all along.

If we really speak the truth, mental knowledge has always been paired together with physical knowledge, even on the level we speak of as instinct. We have an instinctual level of mindfulness that enables us to walk, to put food into our mouths, and do other survival activities. Also, we have sufficient intelligence (*paññā*) to deal with life's obstacles; if a thorn punctures a foot, we are able to remove it. We have sufficient instinctual *samādhi* to throw a stone on the mark. These are examples of natural *samādhi*, mindfulness, intelligence, and *sampajañña* that already exist in us on an instinctual level, as a bare minimum.

However, the instinctual level of these essential virtues is not sufficient to solve the most important problem of life, namely, the suffering that arises from the stream of dependent co-arising. Therefore, we must develop mindfulness, intelligence, and focused stability from the natural level to the degree that can solve the problem of life, in order to be a complete human being or Arahant. This involves body and mind together. Consequently, it is necessary to develop body and mind, and our understanding of them, in tandem, simultaneously.

Even if only by accident, knowledge accrued, such as when our ancestors discovered that cooking meat decreased gastrointestinal problems, or when they found that the tastes of different plant juices and leaves could improve the flavor of food. Such material knowledge—discovering various seasonings and sauces—occurred even while we were still running naked in the forests. The same is true with the mental side of life. For example, our ancestors found that breathing in certain ways was better, more beneficial, healthier, or more powerful. We developed understanding of ways to breathe that calmed, cleared, and settled mind. We learned to solve our inner problems as well. Successively over time, knowledge and understanding accumulated through accidental and stumbled upon lessons. Nonetheless, the knowledge inherited from our ancestors is not enough; we must develop that inheritance further until we both understand these matters and are clear about the methods and techniques for developing them. Development of mindfulness with breathing in and out has an important role within that body of knowledge.

Breathing Benefits Both Body and Mind

Humanity has learned to use breathing to beneficially influence both body and mind. We've learned to use the breathing, to regulate the breathing, and to train the breathing in all the ways necessary to realize the fruits to which we aspire. When we want to control mind's power, there are methods to do so. If we need to uplift mind, there are methods for that. However we might want to change mind, there are appropriate methods to do so.

On the physical level, if you want to suppress mind's energy, there are drugs for doing so, such as the opiates. If you want to increase mind's energy, you can take various stimulants, such as amphetamines. You can use tranquilizers to calm mind. When you want it to behave strangely you can take LSD. Drugs can trick mind in all sorts of ways. However, the old hermits in the forests did not need any such drugs, which are material methods. Besides, they did not have any of these modern drugs to begin with. Yet they knew how to train and control their minds. They could suppress or stimulate or tranquilize or whatever they needed using meditation.

This is ancient knowledge, much older than our modern use of pills. Our ancestors had the intelligence to use mind itself, and its power of *samādhi*, to suppress mind or elevate it or change it or enhance its ability to solve problems, including illnesses. Please do not think that psychology or understanding of mind is a recent occurrence; it has been around since ancient times. If we choose the aspects of mind and mind-training that are most essential, one part will make mind calmly blissful and another will lead to wisdom.

In short, mind and body have always gone together and must work together. Nowadays, people only know how to solve their problems using material methods. In the old days, people knew how to solve their problems using mental methods.

Finally, the knowledge and technique concerning mind has just two basic forms. Other miscellaneous matters are unimportant and can be left aside. The first necessary aspect is for calming mind, for developing *samādhi*. The second involves intelligence and realizing vital matters, which lead to insight and wisdom. The *samādhi* side brings inner peace and happiness; the intelligence side eliminates the various problems that trouble us.

Though there are these two aspects, they are intimately connected and can be combined. First make mind peaceful; then see clearly into the true nature of things. The method called development of mindfulness with breathing in and out that the Buddha improved and systematized includes both aspects together, developing a peaceful, stable mind and understanding things as they actually are. This is the most valuable thing left behind by our ancestors. It is a monument to the understanding of mind from the days of those who lived in the forest. We come here to study and practice this.

Contemplating Four Areas of Life

Those of you who intend to train in mindfulness with breathing in and out should be prepared to understand four things. The first is body (*kāya*); second are the feelings of pleasure and pain (*vedanā*) that arise with sensation; third, mind (*citta*) that is concocted by such feelings; and fourth, the things (*dhamma*) that deceive mind into ignorance and suffering. The last group is all the things that trick mind into foolishness and clinging to self with clinging, which always leads to suffering no matter what those things may be.

The four areas are known collectively as applications or establishments of mindfulness (*satipaṭṭhāna*), and individually as contemplating body so that all aspects of body are thoroughly understood (*kāyānupassanā*), contemplating *vedanā* so that all feelings of pleasure and pain based in sense experience are thoroughly understood (*vedanānupassanā*), contemplating mind so that all aspects of mind are thoroughly understood (*cittānupassanā*), and contemplating nature-truth so that all phenomena that can delude and trick minds into suffering are thoroughly understood, ignorance is abandoned, and suffering ends (*dhammānupassanā*). There are these four matters to understand clearly: body, feeling, mind, and Dhamma.

Naturally Normal Bodies

The first category is about body and concerns material things that are the basis for consciousness and mind. We start with understanding body as it is fundamental. Body includes the flesh and blood aspects made up of the four primary elements of earth, water, fire, and wind.[83] We can call those aspects the flesh-body or flesh-collection. There is another kind of body known as the breath-body or breath-collection, consisting of all aspects of breathing. Together, these two kinds of body make up *kāya*.[84] The flesh-body of muscles, sinews, skin, and organs is nurtured and sustained by the breath-body. We come to understand these two kinds of body and how one nurtures the other. We learn how to breathe correctly so that the relationship between the two is also correct. Then we'll have a body that is healthy, strong, and of most benefit to life.

When breath-body is natural and normal, flesh-body is normal and natural (*pakati*). The reverse is also true: when flesh-body is normal and natural, breath-body is natural and normal. This shows how connected these two physical collections are. If breath-body is abnormal, flesh-body is abnormal. Just as well, if flesh-body is abnormal, breath-body is abnormal. They will be disturbed, distressed, and disordered immediately. This relationship makes it possible to train the flesh-body through the breath-body. On this level of practice—that is, in meditation—it is not possible to train the flesh-body directly, but we can do so indirectly through the breath-body. So we train the breathing to be calm, normal, and healthy, and the flesh-body will also be calm and normal.

An essential part of this training is experiencing and understanding how the two collectives are interrelated. Through this understanding, we'll be able to cultivate a body that is healthy, strong, peaceful, and most appropriate for life, especially for deeper aspects of meditation practice. That is what the first section is about.

Feelings of a Sensible Body

The second area concerns the *vedanā* sensible through body. Body does not just exist materially; it is sensate, it feels. In life, feelings of pleasure and pain, comfort and discomfort cannot be escaped. While negative *vedanā* irritate us, positive *vedanā* satisfy us. Such contentment or satisfaction has two levels that are mentioned in connection with mindfulness with breathing. The first, known as rapture (*pīti*), is more intense; these can be strong and disturbing. Once that level of pleasure or satisfaction calms down, happiness or joy (*sukha*) remains. After calming body in the first section, these two kinds of vedanā become available for further study and training. One is busier, more energetic and tumultuous. The other is subtler, calmer, and cooler. Both rapture and joy are pleasurable but in different ways. It is important to mindfully taste the flavor of each until we are thoroughly familiar with them, because they lead to difficulties in life. As we've already explored, *vedanā* leads to craving, clinging, egoism, and suffering. If we are unable to regulate feelings of pleasure and pain, we will not be able to regulate the flow of dependent co-arising. In other words, we will not be able to regulate suffering. That we must regulate pleasure, satisfaction, and happiness to be free of dukkha may seem strange to you. So it is important to explore this matter carefully.

We will investigate and study *vedanā* until seeing clearly—and this is important—that the feelings of body and its senses concoct the inner experiences we call mind. The ability to regulate the sensible feelings makes it possible to regulate the power they have over the experiences of mind. We call this understanding "knowing that *vedanā* are fabricators of mind," and we are able to regulate that power so it does not lead to craving, clinging, and suffering. Being able to regulate the *vedanā* is the path to regulating mind. Thus, we first get to know feelings, then we train in mastering their power to concoct mind. That is the core lesson of the second area of practice.

Mind that Feels and Knows

The third section concerns mind (*citta*). Mind is the most important thing because it is the place where everything comes together. It is both cause and fruit. Mind both acts and experiences. In fact, it is conditioned by *vedanā*. Feelings of pleasure and pain make it think in this way or that. All this thinking is called mind. And what people in the West call emotion is included here, too. If we cannot keep it under control, it can get off track, go down wrong paths, and suffer. When wisely regulated, it stays on track, is true to the path, and does not suffer. Consequently, it is necessary to understand what we call mind, which is an important aspect of life. Please pay special attention to it.

We begin the lessons of this area of practice by knowing all the diverse kinds of mind that can occur. At times, it might look like mind is beyond our ability to know directly, but actually there are ways we can know different kinds of mind.

Mind that is suffering, what is it like?

Mind that is not suffering, what is it like? Know it.

Mind polluted by egoism, what is it like? Know this.

Sometimes there is no pollution by egoism. Know what that is like.

Deduce or imagine what it would be like to never be subject to egoistic pollution (defilements, or *kilesa*) again. We are capable of knowing what mind free of defilements is like. Mind that has realized the end of suffering cannot yet be directly known, but it can be estimated or imagined indirectly. The better we understand the polluted mind, the closer we are to understanding mind completely beyond such pollution and egoism. Certain kinds of mind can be experienced and known directly. Others can be known by deducing from what we know to estimating the opposite. Thus, we can know every kind of mind, which is the first lesson of this group.

The second lesson in this section is making mind joyful. We already gained experience with the feelings of rapture and joy. Now we train in being able to use those lessons to make mind joyful, glad, and delighted, however we may wish. (Before, the emphasis was on the actual feeling; here, the emphasis is on the kinds of mind that are delighted in various ways.) We train to have this within our power so that a joyful mind is accessible whenever we want. We needn't use any pills or drugs to make us happy; we can delight mind through its own power.

The third lesson is making mind *samādhi* (calm, stable, collected, concentrated). Here, *samādhi* has a deeper meaning than is understood by most people, so please pay careful attention to what *samādhi* is like. The first factor of *samādhi* is that mind is clean and free with nothing disturbing it, which is called "pure mind" or "clean mind." The second factor is that it is firmly established, its energy is gathered and focused on a single thing, there is great stability and singularity. In other words, it has the highest equilibrium. The third factor is activeness; it is thoroughly fluid, flexible, ready, and lively in its present duty. Real *samādhi* is more than concentration, it must have all these factors and qualities: cleanliness or purity (*parisuddho*), stability or firm-establishment (*samāhito*), and activeness or liveliness (*kammaniyo*). In mindfulness with breathing in and out these factors are cultivated and integrated.

This brings us to the fourth lesson of this group: liberating mind, making mind release, freeing mind. It lets go of any objects or it just releases itself. Practicing the various lessons till reaching this point, mind lets go of anything clung to or grasped.

The group concerning mind is made up of these four lessons: experiencing all kinds of mind, delighting mind, concentrating mind, and liberating mind. When these four are completed, contemplating mind (*cittānupassanā*) is fulfilled according to the principles of mindfulness with breathing in and out.

No Longer Tricked by Phenomena

The final group is contemplating dhammas. Dhamma means all things and phenomena that are bases for tricking ourselves into clinging to them as me or mine. All those delusory things, whether positive or negative, fool mind into clinging. Even God, forgive me for saying so, is a basis for clinging. Nibbāna of Buddhism can be a basis for clinging, also. Without exception, everything is a basis for clinging, both conditioned, changeable phenomena (*saṅkhata*) and that which is unconditioned and unchanging (*asaṅkhata*). This section is for understanding everything until there is no clinging to anything.

To put it simply, from the lowest, crudest phenomena to the highest, most exalted, supreme thing, whatever meanings may be given to it, all are bases for clinging. Here, we will not cling to any of them. The highest Dhamma, the highest truth, that we must realize for the sake of complete non-clinging is thusness (*tathatā*). Phenomena are naturally "simply thus," "just like that," "merely such." When all these things are seen as simply thus—just like that—there will not be any clinging, either to the positive or to the negative.

We do not realize thusness by waiting around for it to appear. There is a sequence of insights and realizations that culminate in realizing thusness. That is, we begin with experiencing and seeing impermanence or inconstancy (*aniccaṃ*), which is the initial lesson of the fourth and final section, contemplating impermanence and the impermanent, non-lasting nature of conditioned things (*aniccatā*). *Aniccatā*, the state or fact of not lasting, refers to the perpetual change and flux of things because they are conditioned by causes and conditions (*hetu-paccaya*), carry on according to these causes and conditions, and must change as these causes and conditions change. Seeing impermanence is the start of seeing thusness.

Looking further into the matter, we see that we must live with all these impermanent things. Having to endure impermanent, uncertain things is called *dukkhatā* (suffering-ness, unsatisfactoriness), which literally means "difficult to bear," inconstant things are hard to endure. This is seeing thusness on a deeper level. Next, we see that impermanent, conditioned things that are always changing and difficult to endure cannot be found to have a real, substantial self (*attā*). This insight is "not-self" that such things cannot establish themselves independently as lasting selves. Seeing the fact of being not-self (*anattatā*) is to see thusness even more deeply.

All three of these characteristics together are seen as "just like this," thus, and naturally such. The term for this is a little strange, *dhammaṭṭhitatā*, (lit. standing in Dhamma or nature), the natural standing, ordinariness, or naturalness of these facts. Further, one contemplates why things are this way. One realizes that this is simply the natural, ordinary way of things (that we overlook because of ignorance and craving). At the same time, all dhammas are subject to natural law, such as the law of dependent co-arising that controls everything. This is called insight into the lawfulness of all nature (*dhammaniyāmatā*). When insight deepens in this sequence, we realize conditionality (*idappaccayatā*), the fundamental principle of dependent co-arising. Seeing conditionality is to see dependent co-arising.

When we clearly see that there is only the stream of dependent co-arising, we see that there cannot be a self in any of this, which is to realize emptiness (*suññatā*). This is the highest Dhamma and it must be realized if true liberation is to happen. Emptiness is a most difficult to understand word; please investigate, reflect, explore, observe, and strive until you are able to realize emptiness. Do not fool around with it. Thoroughly realizing this most important Dhamma brings the supreme fruits of Buddhism. Whether Mahāyāna or Theravāda Buddhism, realizing emptiness is the shared essential core of all Buddhism. Its realization is the end, the fulfillment, of Buddhism.

Emptiness is not nothingness or nihilism. Everything is what it is but nothing has anything that can truly be called self. All things are void of self. The universe is full of all kinds of things and all of them are void of self. In this body, in this life, and in this flow of mental experience, all kinds of things happen and every one of them is void of self. This is the meaning of seeing emptiness.

When the sequence of insight and realization deepens to the degree of seeing the emptiness of all things, then suchness (*tathatā*) is fully realized. That is all there is. Conditioned or unconditioned, positive or negative, all are characterized by emptiness, everything is empty of selfhood.

Not Concocted by Anything

Seeing thusness, or suchness, is the culmination. Mind will be disinterested, no longer under the influence of positive and negative. Phenomena and noumena have no meaning for this mind.[85] This kind of mind is described as "having unconcoctability." This *atammayatā* (unconcoctability) is a wonderful word. Realizing thusness leads to penetrating unconcoctability.

Literally, *atammayatā* means "the state of not being affected by anything." Nothing can produce, affect, or concoct this mind. Mind that has fully penetrated this is the highest mind because it dwells in unconcoctability. Some of you may see this as bland or tasteless, to which I will not respond. I hope some of you will understand what it is to be unconcoctable. The deepening of realization starts with the insights of impermance, unsatisfactoriness, and not-self; continues with seeing the naturalness of these facts, the lawfulness of all nature, and conditionality; and fulfills itself in emptiness, thusness, and unconcoctability. Altogether there are three groups of three insights amounting to nine insights or Dhamma Eyes. What a fine way to see life!

Please remember these nine eyes and discuss them among your Dhamma friends regularly. These nine eyes are the most direct shortcut to penetrate to the heart of Buddhism, which is the end of Buddhism. They make up the first, all-important lesson of this final section of practicing mindfulness with breathing in and out.

From this profound basis of sequentially seeing impermanence, unsatisfactoriness, selflessness, and so on, the clinging that we've had toward all things begins to dissolve. This gradual fading away is *virāga*. Contemplating the dissolution of clinging is the second lesson of this fourth group. Fading away leads to quenching (*nirodha*). The habits of clinging that once were well-entrenched have weakened, dissolved, and faded into quenching. Contemplate this as the third lesson here.

Finally, the fourth lesson of this group is liberation (*vimutti*). Interestingly, the mindfulness with breathing in and out teaching calls this throwing back (*paṭinissagga*). All the things we've ever clung to are thrown back, that is, they are returned to nature, their rightful owner. Previously we were thieves, appropriating life, our bodies, experiences, virtues, vices, and everything else as me and mine. Now we relinquish them all, return them all to nature, to emptiness. Previously we were rather stupid, but not any more. Everything positive and negative is tossed away. Now we are free and mindfulness with breathing in and out is completed.

For ease of understanding this overview of mindfulness with breathing, let me summarize one more time. Please take this to heart. In the first section we understand body well enough to have mastery over body. In the second section we understand feelings of body well enough to have mastery over body's feelings. In the third section, we understand mind well enough to have mastery over mind. In the fourth section, we understand everything that tricks us into clinging well enough that none of them can deceive us again, and consequently, we have mastery over everything. Once again, even more concisely:

One, mastery over body;
Two, mastery over sensible feelings;
Three, mastery over mind;
Four, mastery over everything that can trick us into foolish clinging.

These four sections are each comprised of four exercises or lessons, making a total of sixteen.[86] These are the sixteen phases of mindfulness with breathing in and out as originally taught by the Buddha.

15 ❋ Dependent Co-arising Controversies

Friends, that young child, relying upon the growth and development of the sense faculties plays with childish playthings, namely, with toy plows, with pots and pans, with spinning tops, with pinwheels, at scooping sand with leaves, with toy carts, and with toy bows and arrows.

Friends, that child, relying upon the growth and development of the sense faculties is delighted with and immersed in the five sensual values.[87] These cause him to pander to himself through the eyes with forms, through the ears with sounds, through the nose with odors, through the tongue with flavors, and through the body with touches, all of which are desirable, delightful, pleasing, loveable, provocative of sensuality, and the bases of lust.

That child, on seeing a form with the eyes . . . , on hearing a sound with the ears . . . , on smelling an odor with the nose . . . , on tasting a flavor with the tongue . . . , on experiencing a touch with the body . . . , on cognizing an "idea" with mind, is lustily pleased with the form, sound, or whatever that is agreeable and is offended by the form, sound, or whatever that is disagreeable. Consequently, that child's mind is deficient in virtue, lives without mindfulness regarding body, does not clearly realize according to reality the liberation of mind and liberation through wisdom that are the remainderless quenching of the multitude of evil, unwholesome dhammas.

That child, once conditioned by liking and disliking in this way, when partaking of any feeling whether pleasant, unpleasant, or neither-pleasant-nor-unpleasant, becomes infatuated with, indulges in, and is intoxicated by that feeling. When infatuated with, indulging in, and intoxicated by that feeling, lustful delight in one's desire[88] arises. Any such delight toward any of these feelings is clinging. Dependent on the child's clinging, there is becoming. Dependent on becoming, there is birth. Dependent on birth, aging and death, sorrow, grief, pain, lamentation, and despair arise completely. The dependent co-arising of the entire mass of dukkha naturally happens in just this way.[89]

In the Pāli suttas there are two descriptions of what occurred under the Bodhi tree at the time of the Buddha's great awakening (*sambodhi*). In one version, appearing in various texts, the Buddha realized the three supreme knowledges (*tevijjā*). In the first true knowing, as it is generally understood, he recollected his former lives (*pubbenivāsānussatiñāṇa*, lit. "knowledge through recollection of previous dwellings"). In this account, as traditionally understood, he is able to recall his own previous births far into the distant past. These are invariably described as happening to the same person. In the second true knowing, he reviewed how beings carry on according to their actions (*cutūpapātañāṇa*), how beings pass away and reappear according to the karma they have done. Through the third true knowing, he realized the destruction of the impulses (*āsavakkhyañāṇa*). The out-flowing fermentations (*āsavas*) are the deepest level of defilement; when they are completely ended, no further defilement, egoism, or suffering is possible. This is the more commonly recounted description of the night of the Buddha's awakening.

The Buddha Awakened to Dependent Co-arising

Elsewhere the Pāli texts state that the Buddha awakened to dependent co-arising.[90] There also are accounts of the Buddha contemplating dependent co-arising immediately after his awakening, while he was still sitting under the Bodhi tree.[91] Together, these give a second description of the Buddha's great awakening. In the immediate aftermath, during the first four-hour watch one night, the Buddha examined dependent co-arising in the forward order (*anuloma*), starting with ignorance, then concoctings, and so on, one after the other. During the second watch of the night, he reviewed dependent co-arising in the reverse order (*paṭiloma*), starting from suffering, then birth, becoming, clinging, and so on all the way back to ignorance. Then for the third watch, he examined dependent co-arising in both forward and reverse orders until dawn.[92]

Between these two versions, the second is more reasonable and acceptable in light of the overall themes and threads of the Pāli suttas. In the other account, the first knowledge concerning the recollection of past lives (*pubbenivāsānussatiñāṇa*) is in the language of eternalism (*sassataditṭhi*), just as in the pre-Buddhist Upanishads, which speaks of a self or individual being born again and again over many lives. The belief that the same person is repeatedly reborn is eternalism, which Buddhism aims to eliminate. This idea has more in common with popular beliefs and the philosophy of the Upanishads than with the core of the Buddha's message.

The second knowledge is about beings passing away and reappearing according to karma (*cutūpapātañāṇa*). This is generally understood in people language to mean that the same being disappears from one existence (*bhava*) and reappears in another according to karmic influences somehow carried over from one existence to the next. However, this is not directly or specifically a Buddhist teaching. At heart, Buddhism teaches the end of karma, living beyond karma, rather than carrying on according to karma. The noble path is for freedom from karma; living under the sway of karma is limiting, distressful, and burdensome. It is not good enough to merely surrender to karma, to die and be reborn according to the fruits of our actions. In Buddhism, liberating insight must go further than that.

Neither of these first two knowledges can be considered truly Buddhist principles. Why then are they included in the Pāli scriptures? My own view is that perhaps the compilers of the discourses may have included these passages for the benefit of ordinary people. They are expressed and commonly understood in people language. For those people unable to understand dependent co-arising and the end of karma, these passages were included for the sake of morality. Consequently, this is an account of the Buddha's awakening for the moral benefit of ordinary people.

The second account puts dependent co-arising at the center of the Buddha's awakening. Not only did he express his awakening in these terms, he described how he pondered and contemplated dependent co-arising both before the awakening and immediately after. After experiencing the bliss of liberation for a week, he examined and investigated dependent co-arising throughout at least one night, the first watch of which focused on how dependent co-arising occurs. He repeatedly investigated this in the forward order from ignorance to concoctings on through suffering. He spent four full hours thoroughly penetrating this truth. In the next four hours, he investigated the causality of dukkha in careful detail all the way back to ignorance. In the final four hours, he examined dependent co-arising in both directions, forward and backward. This shows the central importance of dependent co-arising. The formula recorded is brief and succinct; the Buddha looked into it forward and backward for twelve hours without a break. He had the most profound spiritual experience of this through each of the watches: forward order, reverse order, and both forward and backward, each for four full hours. Please consider how profound, how difficult, how subtle, and how important this is. This ought to be of great interest to all serious meditators.

The words we have translated as "forward order" and "reverse order," or "forward" and "backward"—*anuloma* and *paṭiloma*—can be understood rather broadly. Thus, for clarity's sake, we can explain *anuloma*, with the hairs, as the examining of the arising sequence, that is, dependent co-arising. The reverse, *paṭiloma*, against the hairs, is the quenching of dependent co-arising, that is, dependent quenching (*paṭiccanirodha*). In the first watch, the Buddha investigated and reviewed how dependent co-arising arises. In the second watch, he investigated and reviewed how it quenches. In the final watch, he investigated and reviewed both. This understanding is eminently reasonable and fully supported by the core themes of the discourses.

Please consider this important question: Have you ever practiced like this? Have you ever investigated dependent co-arising in the way that the Buddha did before, during, and after his awakening? We suggest that you examine and scrutinize dependent co-arising in the same great detail, with the same sincerity and intensity. Then, you might understand it like he did. You will find it worth your while to follow the Buddha's example.

Two Understandings of Karma

This is a good place to consider karma. After all, it parallels the dependent co-arising teaching, though with less precision and depth. Above, we discussed the second knowledge (in the first account of the Buddha's awakening) that beings carry on after death according to their karma. The difficulty with this understanding is that we cannot take this as the understanding of karma in line with core Buddhist principles. Rather, this understanding is simply the standard version of karma that existed in India before the Buddha's time. Before the Buddha's awakening, the Upanishads already taught that beings are reborn after death according to the workings of karma. Even Christianity, at least mainstream forms, teaches pretty much the same. If that is not the true Buddhist teaching, then what is?

In Buddhism, the central teaching on karma is about that practice that makes karma meaningless, "the karma that ends karma." This karma transforms us beyond all the influences of karma, which is the unique, more profound aspect of the Buddha's karma teaching. The idea that doing good deeds leads to good results and doing bad deeds leads to bad results was a general teaching that existed before the Buddha's time. The Buddha did not deny or object to such karma doctrines (*kammavādi*) that were already common before he appeared and are found in some form in all religions. However, such teachings were not sufficient for his purpose—the end of suffering. Therefore, the Buddha went further: his real teaching is about not being trapped by karma, thus transcending karma and its consequences.

Allow me to reiterate that most of the books on Buddhism with chapters on "Karma and Rebirth" are not correct, if they really intend to represent Buddhism. Their understanding of "rebirth" is not correct, as we explained earlier, and their accounts of karma are at best incomplete. If we are to explain "Karma in Buddhism," it is not enough to teach that good actions bring good fruits, bad actions bring bad fruits, and we inevitably receive the fruits of our good and bad karma. Properly, a Buddhist explanation must focus on "the karma that ends all karma." The practice of the noble eightfold path is that karma that ends all karma. The Buddha's teaching on karma is to be free of karma, not trapped by it, so that karma has no more power over our lives. If you come across those books and interpret what they say about karma in line with the understanding presented here, you will have a much better chance of getting it right and thus eliminating karma and dukkha.

The Buddha Perfected the Teaching of Karma

The teachings that existed in India before the Buddha's awakening are known as *sanantanadhamma*, traditions that had been around long enough that no one could say for how long. When the Buddha appeared, he did not deny or reject all of those teachings, only those that conflicted with the middle way of teaching and practice. He accepted any that were sufficiently correct and useful; there were a fair number that went along with his awakening. He then continued, completed, and perfected such teachings, such as he did in the case of karma, by extending it to encompass "the end of karma."

The teaching that human beings experience life according to our karma was not entirely correct. This lower teaching is correct on a certain level, appropriate for the understanding of ordinary people and supportive of morality. It was correct in terms of morality and relative truth. For a full and complete understanding of karma, however, it must directly liberate from suffering.

To be trapped forever in the prison of karma is not Buddhism. If everything constantly happens to us according to karma, there could never be any liberation (*vimutti*). For a teaching and practice to be Buddhism, we must be liberated from the power and oppression of karma. A teaching that merely reiterates the old approach cannot be the true Buddhist teaching. It must be completed to the extent of liberation to be Buddhism. Thus, the Buddha needed to teach the karma that ends karma. He took the kind of karma that does not explain liberation and perfected it so that liberation from karma became the central point.

"Beyond karma" is a teaching above and beyond the world, or a *lokuttara* teaching. The ordinary karma teachings are part and parcel with the world (*lokiya*). *Lokiyadhamma* is for mind still trapped in worldly conditions. *Lokuttaradhamma* is for mind free of and beyond worldly conditions. The Buddha accepted a number of the old teachings, perfecting them within his *lokuttaradhamma* system as he did so. The Buddhist teaching on karma—the noble eightfold path that ends karma—is a perfect example of how the Buddha completed the old teachings and traditions.

Other *sanantanadhamma* accepted by him include non-vengeance (*avera*), non-harming or nonviolence (*avihiṁsa*), the five *sīla*, various *samādhi* practices, and the form and formless *jhānas*. All of these are older teachings and practices that he did not reject. Instead, he further developed, completed, and perfected them. Please be aware that Buddhism contains a certain amount of older teachings and practices that the Buddha included, deepened, and completed for the sake of quenching dukkha. Understanding this fact is important so that we will not confuse the old versions of such teachings with the new, perfected versions.

Jesus Christ said more or less the same thing: "I did not come to abolish the old teachings but to fulfill them."[93] Jesus did not try to get rid of Judaism, with its law and its prophets, but he found it incomplete. Instead of opposing all Jewish traditions, he did what he could to complete them. Jesus's attitude and practice was similar to how the Buddha completed the Upanishadic teaching on karma and the like. To do so, he taught the end of karma.

Two Levels of Teaching

These examples clearly show that there are two levels of teaching, both of which are necessary. One is for the sake of morality, for those who still believe in and hold to self. The moral level of teaching is necessary for those who can only understand things in terms of me and mine, who require moral and therapeutic teachings that operate on a worldly level. It teaches people how to live in the world morally and peacefully, to be less selfish about the selves to which they cling, and thereby suffer less.

For those aiming higher, the Buddha's teaching focuses on letting go of self, that everything is not-self and nothing is worth clinging to as me or mine. This level does not ignore or reject the moral teachings; it simply goes beyond them. This is the more comprehensive transcendent level (*lokuttara*) of ultimate truth (*paramatthadhamma*) that truly liberates from all suffering. Dhamma teachings come in *lokiya* and *lokuttara* forms or levels. If both are understood, there is no conflict between them. They can coexist for the sake of both those who want to live in and of the world (*lokiya*) and those aiming to live above and free of the world (*lokuttara*), in it but not of it.

Each person decides their own preference and way. If you want to travel the paths of the world and have no wish to transcend the world, you can follow the worldly teachings and receive the moralistic explanation of dependent co-arising given by various commentators. You can continue rebirthing yourself in a worldly way, but with healthy morality, not harming others and living relatively peacefully. If you want to be free, to transcend the world and no longer be caught by all its trappings, you must study the transcendent teachings such as "the end of karma" that do not involve self. For this, we have the dependent co-arising of ultimate truth that enables us to see through all the concoctings of self. Dependent co-arising also has these two levels or two models. The choice of which to follow is yours.

The *Visuddhimagga* Orthodoxy

Have you ever before heard dependent co-arising explained in terms of this life here and now? Most of the literature explaining dependent co-arising—whether Singhalese, Indian, Tibetan, European, or American—follow the interpretation of Venerable Buddhaghosa, the chief commentator of Theravāda Buddhism, in the hugely influential *Path of Purity* (*Visuddhimagga*).

This interpretation of dependent co-arising is in terms of past lives, present lives, and future lives. We call it "the three life times interpretation." In it, birth is understood literally, materially, as physical birth from a mother's womb. Further, as we are already alive now, birth is assumed to mean a "rebirth" into another lifetime. Becoming and other terms are taken in the same literal way. Thus, dependent co-arising is dragged out over at least three lifetimes—past, present, and future.

The commentators that followed Venerable Buddhaghosa and most subsequent writers have clung to this interpretation and passed it along without critical thinking. Even the Westerners who have studied dependent co-arising mostly follow that interpretation, whether they consider themselves Theravāda, Mahāyāna, or Vajrayāna. May I challenge you, them, and all the Westerners who write about dependent co-arising in the old conservative vein? Go look for yourselves. Almost all the books written about dependent co-arising follow the *Visuddhimagga* line.[94] Maybe you've read some of them already. Or you might purchase some or all of them to read and see what they have to say. When you consider these descendants of the *Visuddhimagga*, ask yourself if their explanations can be applied to the complete quenching of suffering. Can you apply their explanations in actual practice today? I think you will find that it is not possible.

This multiple lifetimes interpretation is not, however, without value. While it is not applicable to ultimate truth, we can credit it with certain ethical benefits. As it speaks in terms of a self[95]—the same person being born and reborn, which is relative truth—it is not the dependent co-arising of the Awakened One. In the Buddha's time, there was only one explanation of dependent co-arising—the Buddha's. Later, the alternative explanation appeared in the relative language that ordinary people could understand more easily. It supports a moral worldview considered necessary for people to see future benefits in doing good and refraining from evil—happy, heavenly rebirths and woeful, hellish rebirths. Such conventional truths, explained in terms of selves, are valuable but do not qualify as the ultimate truth that can quench dukkha. For that, we need an interpretation and understanding of dependent co-arising that we can study and practice right now, here in this life and at this moment, without reference to beings that carry over from one life to the next. We ought to hold onto the later version for its moral value, but do not confuse it with the Buddha's original understanding, which is of ultimate value.

The Buddha Is about the Ultimate Truth of Not-Self

In the Pāli suttas—the primary source of Buddhist teachings—we find the Buddha's original system of describing dependent co-arising. The later explanation is from Venerable Buddhaghosa's commentarial system, which we must admit is a dependent co-arising outside the suttas. Now, we have both the sutta version for the sake of ultimate truth and the commentarial version for the sake of relative, moral truth. Relative truth speaks in terms of selves, persons, and beings, while the Buddha's ultimate truth is in terms of not-self—all things are not-self.

The Buddha's original teaching is for the sake of eliminating self, for removing the sense of being a separate self. On the other hand, the later commentarial teaching affirms that there is self in order to promote people being good, that is, good selves. This is a simple means to distinguish between the two main explanations of dependent co-arising. If the genuine dependent co-arising, it must lead to realizing not-self and letting go of self. If it seeks moral benefits and fruits, it affirms self, a person or being who acts and receives the fruits of those actions in this life or the next.

We are not suggesting that you should choose one version over the other or argue about which one is right. Rather, we are concerned to understand the proper application of each version. Personally, I am most interested in the original version, as it is most directly relevant to the quenching of suffering. The version that is most appropriate for you, and in what ways, and when, is for you to determine yourself.

Please review dependent co-arising all the way through from the very beginning: starting with ignorance, then concocting, consciousness, name and form, sense organs, sense contact, feeling, clinging, becoming, birth, and aging and death. In the true dependent co-arising there is nothing that can be taken as self. Each is conditioned by and dependent upon other things. Further, it clearly shows how craving gives birth to clinging, to grasping at me and mine, that there is merely an illusion of self concocted by craving. A truly existing and lasting self cannot be found anywhere. There is only the delusional self of clinging that has been concocted by ignorance. The entire sequence of dependent co-arising demonstrates that there is no self to be found anywhere.

For our practical purposes, we uphold the principle that the true dependent co-arising must eliminate views about and clinging to the existence of self. This is the heart of Buddhism, which emphasizes not-self and emptiness. All the Buddha's teachings are centered on not self and emptiness, so the genuine teachings must clearly illuminate the truth of not-self and emptiness. By now, you will have seen that the teaching of dependent co-arising will destroy the concept that there is self. Eliminating the belief in self eliminates suffering, because dukkha comes from clinging to notions and concepts about self.

Whenever there is clinging to any aspect or combination of the components of life as me or mine there is distress. Traditionally, we describe the components of life as the five aggregates (*pañcakkhandha*), namely, body, feeling, perception, thought-emotion, and consciousness. These are the five basic components or functions that make up a human being. A human being is just these five subsystems functioning interdependently. When we realize dependent co-arising we see that none of these aggregates or functions can be self, they all are not-self, they are all void of selfhood. Clear, correct understanding of dependent co-arising removes clinging to the concept of self in regard to any of the aggregates, so we stop taking them personally, stop seeing them as me or mine, and thus dissolve dukkha. Penetrating dependent co-arising gets rid of suffering directly. This is the essential import of the dependent co-arising that the Buddha intended us to understand.[96]

16 ❋ The Beginning and End of Spiritual Life

Friends, if one practices for disenchantment with, the fading away of, and the remainderless quenching of aging and death, it is appropriate to speak of that practitioner as "one practicing Dhamma according to Dhamma."

Friends, if one practices for disenchantment with, the fading away of, and the remainderless quenching of birth, it is appropriate to speak of that practitioner as "one practicing Dhamma according to Dhamma."

Friends, if one practices for disenchantment with, the fading away of, and the remainderless quenching of becoming, it is appropriate to speak of that practitioner as "one practicing Dhamma according to Dhamma."

Friends, if one practices for disenchantment with, the fading away of, and the remainderless quenching of clinging, it is appropriate to speak of that practitioner as "one practicing Dhamma according to Dhamma."

Friends, if one practices for disenchantment with, the fading away of, and the remainderless quenching of craving, it is appropriate to speak of that practitioner as "one practicing Dhamma according to Dhamma."

Friends, if one practices for disenchantment with, the fading away of, and the remainderless quenching of feeling, it is appropriate to speak of that practitioner as "one practicing Dhamma according to Dhamma."

Friends, if one practices for disenchantment with, the fading away of, and the remainderless quenching of contact, it is appropriate to speak of that practitioner as "one practicing Dhamma according to Dhamma."

Friends, if one practices for disenchantment with, the fading away of, and the remainderless quenching of sense media, it is appropriate to speak of that practitioner as "one practicing Dhamma according to Dhamma."

Friends, if one practices for disenchantment with, the fading away of, and the remainderless quenching of mind-body, it is appropriate to speak of that practitioner as "one practicing Dhamma according to Dhamma."

> Friends, if one practices for disenchantment with, the fading away of, and the remainderless quenching of consciousness, it is appropriate to speak of that practitioner as "one practicing Dhamma according to Dhamma."
>
> Friends, if one practices for disenchantment with, the fading away of, and the remainderless quenching of concoctings, it is appropriate to speak of that practitioner as "one practicing Dhamma according to Dhamma."
>
> Friends, if one practices for disenchantment with, the fading away of, and the remainderless quenching of ignorance, it is appropriate to speak of that practitioner as "one practicing Dhamma according to Dhamma."[97]

At the close, we should say something about the formulas of dependent co-arising, of which there are many variations.[98] There are two basic formulas to consider here. The first model is the full, complete formula beginning with ignorance; following through concocting, consciousness, mind-body, sense media, contact, feeling, craving, clinging, and becoming; and then culminating in birth and suffering. This long formula includes twelve terms or modes (*ākāra*) of dependent co-arising and is theoretically complete. In the second model, the Buddha begins with sense contact, and then follows the process of dependent co-arising through to dukkha. Here there are nine terms. We have both models from which to work. The first is theoretically most complete but a bit too much for most people. The second—starting with sense contact—is eminently practical. Please be aware that there are these two basic formulas or models of dependent co-arising, in order to select the one most appropriate for daily practice.

The Humming Version of Dependent Co-arising

There is something quite amusing and interesting about the second model. Although already perfectly awakened, the Buddha still recited dependent co-arising to himself. He chanted and reviewed it out loud, similar to how ordinary people, when in a good mood, will sing or hum to themselves, sometimes not quite consciously. When the Buddha was in a good mood, or whatever his motivation may have been, he recited dependent co-arising like this:

> Through the interaction of eye and form, eye consciousness arises. These three conditions together are contact. Contact conditions feel-

ing, feeling conditions craving, craving conditions clinging, clinging conditions becoming, becoming conditions birth, and birth conditions aging and death. Thus arises the entire mass of suffering. (This is repeated for each of the six sense media pairs.)[99]

I like to call this version of dependent co-arising the Buddha's "humming dependent co-arising."

One day the Buddha thought he was alone in a quiet place and hummed this version of dependent co-arising to himself. It is not recorded where he was, but there happened to be a monk standing nearby listening in on the Buddha. When the Buddha noticed this monk, he did not startle or reprimand the monk. Instead, the Buddha asked the monk if he had heard. When the latter answered affirmatively, the Buddha instructed the monk to learn, master, and remember this humming dependent co-arising. Today, we might imagine the Buddha giving the same advice to us. We can take this story to heart ourselves in order to learn, master, and remember this humming dependent co-arising.

We might consider how a school child must memorize her multiplication tables. If she cannot yet remember them, she will be afraid of forgetting. For the Buddha, however, there is no such fear. He's already a Buddha and he cannot forget something so central to his awakening experience. Why then did he recite it to himself? There must have been something important about it that it would come out in this way.

Please consider how important this must have been for him, and for us today. We have this concise formulation to learn and memorize like multiplication tables or phone numbers. It is not too long to remember. Once memorized, we can examine it repeatedly in all sorts of circumstances. We can study it in our daily lives. Please remember that there are two dependent co-arising formulations. The long version is more theoretical. For practice, you will do better with the humming version, which is sufficient for our needs.

The Starting Point of the Brahmacariya

Next, we may consider the term *ādibrahmacariya*, the starting point of true Dhamma practice, the beginning of life lived in the highest possible way (*brahmacariya*). *Ādi-* is a prefix meaning "starting point" or "beginning."

Brahmacariya means "supreme practice" or "supreme way of living." It is often synonymous with the noble eightfold path.[100] At the end of the same sutta, the Buddha declared "humming dependent co-arising" to be the *ādibrahmacariya*, the beginning of the supremely lived life and Dhamma practice. This means that dependent co-arising is the starting point of our study, investigation, and practice.

Unfortunately, this is hardly ever taught. Buddhist teachers are afraid it is too difficult, so it is often overlooked, especially with beginners. Otherwise, it is taught following the old, cumbersome, explanation of Ven. Buddhaghosa—spanning various lifetimes—which is overly theoretical, speculative, complicated, and virtually impossible to understand. What a pity that we ignore the *ādibrahmacariya* of "humming dependent co-arising," and consequently waste the starting point of the supreme spiritual practice. So please make it your starting point for Dhamma study and practice.

Study and practice both begin with dependent co-arising. Let me stress this again, that we start by studying and practicing dependent co-arising, especially the practical formula beginning with sense contact. Is it not strange, then, that the Buddha also declared dependent co-arising to be the most profound teaching? Yet, he called this the starting point. Marvelously, dependent co-arising is both the starting point and the most profound thing we can study and investigate. Still, there is no conflict or contradiction between the two.

The Buddha advises us to start with knowing the eyes and visual forms, then knowing the visual consciousness that arises dependent on them. This is not beyond our abilities to mindfully observe and understand. When eyes, forms, and visual consciousness work together, we call it contact. Sense contact is happening every day, all the time. We start here, knowing contact, then observing and knowing the arising of feelings of pleasure and pain and whatever follows. We investigate this continuously and increasingly deeply. It is difficult to understand, especially the modes of clinging and existence, which are extremely profound, but is within our capacities. Please, in this way practice with the starting point of the supreme way of living.

As it is with eyes, so it is with the ears, nose, tongue, body, and mind. With the ears there are sounds. Ear consciousness arises dependent on the two, and the three together are ear-contact. Feeling occurs regarding contact and then craving arises toward the contact and feeling. From there, clinging and the rest follow. It is the same process with nose and odors, tongue and flavors, body and sensations, and even mind and mental experiences. They are all conditions for the arising of sense consciousness, contact, feeling, craving, clinging, becoming-existence, birth, and suffering.

We are sentient beings with nervous systems. We rely on this nervous system as the base for studying dependent co-arising. The dependent co-arising of the sense media and the things dependent on them is *ādi*, fundamental or the starting point, in this sense, too. We do not study and practice from books or rituals. We begin with the nervous system that gives rise to spiritual experience step by step. We have all the tools needed for investigating dependent co-arising right here. We are alive and they are functioning normally. What a shame that we do not make the highest use of them? Please focus your study here—eye-contact, ear-contact, nose-contact, tongue-contact, body-contact, and mind-contact—with the experiences provided by the nervous system in our daily lives.

Allow me to declare to you that all the spiritual experiences of the past have great value. Do not ignore or abandon them. Use them as aids and supports for studying all the ins and outs, steps and stages of dependent co-arising. All the spiritual experiences that you can remember since birth until today can be taken up as aids for your study-practice. With such help, it will not be too difficult for you. Use them in this study rather than let them go wasted.

Essential Points to Remember

At this point, we have provided enough of the necessary details of dependent co-arising. You have all the details that you need for good practice. Henceforth, we will summarize essential points and meanings of dependent co-arising. Please give this your full attention.

1. Conditionality (*idappaccayatā*) applies to all things, especially to all material things. Dependent co-arising applies to mental matters and the concerns of mind, especially problems regarding mind, that is, suffering.

2. We use the Buddha's original dependent co-arising of the early Pāli suttas as *paramatthadhamma*, for the sake of ultimate truth and full liberation. The later version of the commentaries may be used as relative, conventional truth, for the sake of morality.

3. The Buddha's original version of dependent co-arising occurs many times, many thousands of rounds, in one life; while one cycle of the later

version covers three lifetimes. The truest, most liberating version has many rounds in one lifetime while the conventional, ethical version has many lifetimes in one round or birth.

4. If one round of dependent co-arising spans a number of lifetimes, how can we manage it? How can we practice with it, if one round takes many lifetimes? On the other hand, even though the right understanding and practice involves many rounds in a single lifetime, regulating it is still within the realm of possibility. One approach is beyond practice, the other is something we can practice with daily. One version of dependent co-arising is impractical, while the other is practical.

5. Dependent co-arising has the aim of destroying clinging to self (*attā*) and clinging to words and concepts about self (*attāvādūpādāna*). Clinging to ideas and terms of "I" and "mine" is the basic root attachment. Dependent co-arising is an exquisitely refined teaching of how everything is not-self (*anattā*).

6. Dependent co-arising introduces us to the genuine Buddha. We discover the true Buddha, as he himself said, "Whoever sees dependent co-arising, sees the Dhamma; whoever sees the Dhamma, sees dependent co-arising" and "whoever sees the Dhamma, sees me; whoever sees me, sees the Dhamma." Dependent co-arising tears down the curtain of ignorance so that we discover the genuine Buddha that has been sitting here all along.[101]

7. Dependent co-arising is not a philosophy, it is science. If one wants, one can speak of it in philosophical terms, turn it into philosophy and metaphysics, enjoy speaking philosophically, and become addicted to the drug of overly rational, speculative philosophy. However, we do not rely on logic, deductive or inductive reasoning, or philosophical speculation. Understanding dependent co-arising relies on scientific methodology alone. It is empirically and personally verifiable through investigation, experiment, and direct experience. It is not philosophy.

8. Dependent co-arising is a matter of spiritual science, rather than material science. It demonstrates that real birth and death occur spiritually, while physical birth and death are not the real problem. Dependent co-arising is a teaching of the most profound Dhamma language rather than the literal, material meanings of people language.

9. Finally, dependent co-arising is the great noble truth (*mahāriyasacca*). Dependent co-arising explains dukkha and the conditionality of dukkha. Dependent quenching explains the quenching of dukkha, and

the way of quenching dukkha. Together, these two cover the four noble truths in exquisite detail, depth, and subtlety, so we call them the "great noble truths." The "little" or ordinary noble truths are a shorter, more compact explanation of suffering, the origin of suffering, the quenching of suffering, and the way leading to the quenching of suffering. We are fortunate to have both the extensive investigation of the great noble truths and the concise form of the little noble truths.

To study and investigate the great ennobling truths, you must expend a great deal of effort and energy. To thoroughly understand it requires more time, patience, and energy. Please be aware that there are the ordinary noble truths that require a moderate amount of time and effort, while the great noble truths require much more. We sincerely hope that you have the requisite time, energy, diligence, and patience to investigate and come to fully understand this great noble truth.

A Guide to Source Texts for *Under the Bodhi Tree*

In preparing this edition, many passages from the Pāli record of the Buddha's early discourses (*suttas*) were collected and translated from Ajahn Buddhadāsa's own translations from the Pāli into Thai. Only a quarter of them could be included above. The rest are being published separately by Liberation Park Press as *Companion to Under the Bodhi Tree* (available through www.liberationpark.org). Given the on-going debates concerning the interpretation of *paṭiccasamuppāda* both in overall meaning and in details, we highly recommend that dedicated student-practitioners investigate the source texts for themselves. To encourage this we here offer suggested readings by way of brief introductions to the passages included in *Companion to Under the Bodhi Tree*. We aim to link Ajahn Buddhadāsa's explanations to his Pāli sources and to provide translations free of the interpretive biases of the commentarial tradition. While the headings are in the main his, the translator-editor is responsible for these summaries. We also give standard references so that you can read these passages within the suttas from which they are taken, such as those found in Wisdom's published translations and in online sources such as www.accesstoinsight.org and www.suttacentral.org.

Abbreviations Used

AN	Aṅguttara Nikāya
DN	Dīgha Nikāya
MN	Majjhima Nikāya
SN	Saṃyutta Nikāya
It	Itivutakka (from the Khuddaka Nikāya)
Ud	Udāna (from the Khuddaka Nikāya)
CDB	*The Connected Discourses of the Buddha*

LDB	*The Long Discourses of the Buddha*
MDB	*The Middle Length Discourses of the Buddha*
NDB	*The Numerical Discourses of the Buddha*
Ireland	*The Udāna & The Itivuttaka*

Chapter 1: Buddhism Is Natural Truth

Only Abandon or Practice When You Know for Yourself What's What

Reading *Kesaputti (Kālāma) Sutta* (AN 3:65)
NDB, pp. 279–83

The Kālāma (or Kesaputti) Sutta stresses the pragmatic and experiential focus of the Buddha's Dhamma. When wise examination arrives at sufficiently clear understanding of what is harmful and what is healthy, then one knows what to do. Knowledge for its own sake does not liberate. Knowledge that leads to appropriate action frees us from reactive emotions and suffering.

This teaching is one of the many from the suttas that aims at cultivating right view, which Ajahn Buddhadāsa took to be the focus of his life's teaching work. Chapter 1 and all the chapters that follow it are for the sake of stimulating and encouraging reflection, intelligent thought, and discernment. He neither wanted to be believed nor rejected, just to serve the Buddha.

Frequently cited as the Buddha's permission for "free thinking," important parts of this sutta are often glossed over. Rather than encouragement for thinking whatever one likes, having whatever opinions one likes, or the idea that one doesn't have to believe anything, this sutta is about finding out in one's own experience, along with that of companions in the way, what is wholesome and what is not, what is conducive to suffering and what leads to liberation. Kneejerk rejection of teachings, beliefs, and practices is no better than uncritical or blind belief. Neither is encouraged by this sutta or any of the Early Buddhist teachings.

The Buddha Taught Only Dukkha *and the Final Quenching of* Dukkha

Reading *Alagaddūpama Sutta* (MN 22)
MDB, pp. 224–36

This simple statement maps out the territory of the Buddha's message, the beginning and end of his teaching. A teaching cannot be considered the

Buddha's unless related to *dukkha* and its quenching. Staying within this domain of concern eliminates the time-wasting speculations and excessive philosophizing that the Buddha discouraged. We must share this primary concern for these teaching to be meaningful. The *paṭiccasamuppāda* teachings are based in it and elaborate further.

Conditionality: The Most Basic Law of All

Reading *Cūḷasakuludāyi Sutta* (MN 79)
MDB, pp. 654–62

The law of *idappaccayatā*, found at the beginning of the preface, is one of the fundamental perspectives to which the Buddha awakened. When explored within the parameters of *dukkha* and its quenching, this law generates the four noble truths. When *idappaccayatā* is applied to the origin and quenching of *dukkha* in detail, we have *paṭiccasamuppāda* in its arising sequence and its quenching sequence. While it is sometimes treated as synonymous with *paṭiccasamuppāda*, Ajahn Buddhadāsa prefers to distinguish *idappaccayatā* as the universal principle of conditionality from *paṭiccasamuppāda* as the detailed application of conditionality to *dukkha* and its quenching.

Newly Awakened, the Buddha Reviewed Paṭiccasamuppāda

Reading *Bodhi Suttas* (Ud 1:1–3)
Ireland, pp. 13–15

The Buddha's experience of full awakening is described in various ways. This sutta passage links that experience with a thorough realization of *paṭiccasamuppāda*. Although he elaborated the usual formulations of *paṭiccasamuppāda* later, it's clear that from the beginning this way of seeing was unique to the Buddha and central to his realization. Furthermore, he stated in other suttas (such as Nagara Sutta, SN 12:65, CDB 601) that he had explored *paṭiccasamuppāda* prior to the great awakening.

Chapter 2: Independently Investigating Causes and Conditions

The Buddha Challenged Beliefs about Old Karma and a Creator

Reading *Titthāyatanādi Sutta* (AN 3:61)
NDB, pp. 266–70

Perspectives and beliefs that attribute our current well-being and distress to actions in the past or a creator god have no support in Early Buddhism.

Instead, the suggested reading describes how well-being and *dukkha* occur based upon six fundamental elements of experience, six avenues for sense contact, and eighteen ways mind interacts with sense experience. Due to these and *paṭiccasamuppāda*, there is feeling. Therefore, the Buddha laid out the four ennobling truths, here in a form that incorporates *paṭiccasamuppāda* and gives his perspective on how well-being and distress come about. In short, happiness and suffering are a matter of natural phenomena and conditionality.

With Dhamma, Be Lights and Refuges for Yourselves

Reading *Mahāparinibbāna* Sutta (DN 16)
LDB, pp. 231–78

Rather than depending on him over much, the Buddha advised that we become lights and refuges for ourselves, which is to have Dhamma as our lights and refuges. This advice is as applicable for us in later times as it was for those who were alive in the Buddha's time. To consistently contemplate the applications of mindfulness is the means to follow his advice. Such practice is a more excellent foundation than depending on someone else for our understanding.

This Natural Element of Truth Is "Just So"

Reading *Paccaya Sutta* (SN 12:20)
CDB, pp. 55–52

These teachings are not concocted out of speculative views, logic, or ideologies. Rather, they point to basic facts of human experience. These natural facts are "just so," whether or not buddhas appear to point them out. Further, even a single dependent relation is called *paṭiccasamuppāda*. We need not get stuck on a particular formulation of this teaching; each is a skillful pointing to the way things are.

Sahampati Brahmā Begs the Buddha to Have Compassion

Reading *Bodhirājakumāra Sutta* (MN 85), MDB, pp. 704–9
Ariyapariyesanā Sutta (MN 26), MDB, pp. 253–68

At first, the profundity of his realization and awakening, and of *paṭiccasamuppāda*, made the newly awakened Buddha reluctant to teach. His decision to point out these realities and the way to others is portrayed in this encounter with Sahampati Brahmā, who came down from his Brahmā-world to implore the Buddha to teach. The compassionate decision to tirelessly do so blossomed into humanity's most profound legacy.

Chapter 3: Training in Direct Experience of Freedom

Reactive Tendencies Accumulate in Those Who Do Not Understand

Reading *Chachakka Sutta* (MN 148)

MDB, pp. 1129–36

Teachings on the dependent co-origination of *dukkha* take many forms. Teachings on the senses, sense contact, and accompanying feelings are always central and provide an important practice clue. In this passage, indulgence in such feelings due to lack of mindfulness leads to accumulating patterns of lust, aversion, and ignorance, which obstruct the arising of true knowledge and liberation. Thus, suffering continues through habituation to these three basic toxic energies. Observing these patterns in ourselves is an essential practice.

Avoid Metaphysical Assumptions

Reading *Jāṇussoṇi Sutta* (SN 12:47)

CDB, p. 584

Human societies are awash in metaphysical opinions about human beings and the universe, the past and the future, and what happens after death. Holding to such views entraps us in positions that distract us from Dhamma and lead us off the Middle Way. In this passage, a young Brahmin wonders whether things exist or don't exist. The Buddha considers such views to be extremes. Rather than answering the brahmin's statements, the Buddha reviews his middle way of teaching concerning the conditionality of *dukkha* and its quenching.

All Buddhas Teach Action, Activity, and Effort

Reading *Kesakambala Sutta* (AN 3:137)

NDB, pp. 364–65

The Buddha once declared that he merely points out the way and that the path requires our own effort. At other times he described his teaching as a "doctrine of effort." In this passage, the Buddha condemns a wanderer's claim that actions don't exist and there are no meaningful spiritual endeavors. This is compared to a trap that merely inflicts pain and torments its victims. Unfortunately, such pseudo-Dhamma is still heard today by certain sophisticates.

Chapter 4: Beyond Positive and Negative

Don't Get Excited or Annoyed with Worldly Stuff

Reading *Lokadhamma Suttas* (AN 8:5 and AN 8:6)
NDB, p. 1116–18

Worldly experience is a constantly shifting terrain of conditions that seemingly oppose and compete against each other. Ajahn Buddhadāsa often referred to sadness and gladness as positiveness and negativeness. Reacting and clinging to these worldly conditions stirs up our minds. The wise see more deeply than the world's transitory appearances.

Rely on Unconcoctability to Abandon Even Equanimity

Reading *Saḷāyatanavibhaṅga Sutta* (MN 137)
MDB, pp. 1066–73

To give up the things that cause us suffering, we may rely upon more refined phenomena. The sadness, gladness, and equanimity of spiritual practice are more refined than those of sensual experience. The equanimity of spiritual practice is more refined than the sadness and gladness of spiritual practice. The equanimity of deeper absorptions is more refined than that of the lesser absorptions. Finally, *atammayatā*—unconcoctability—is more refined than any form of equanimity.

Avoid Being Confused about Self and Other

Reading *Timbarukha Sutta* (SN 12:18)
CDB, pp. 548–89

Do we create our own pleasure and pain? Or do others cause us to suffer and be happy? Or might some combination of self and other be responsible? As we all seek to avoid suffering and be happy, knowing who is able to bring this about is crucial. The Buddha's response to this issue might surprise you. His middle way teaching concerning the conditionality of *dukkha* and its quenching is once again central.

Chapter 5: The Natural Law of Conditionality

The Tathāgata Understands the World

Reading *Loka Sutta* (AN 4:23)
NDB, pp. 410–11

One who appears in this world neither to reject it nor be trapped in it is called the Tathāgata. Such a one thoroughly understands the world in terms of the four ennobling truths and *paṭiccasamuppāda*. If we aspire to freedom in this world, to live "just so," the guidance of the Tathāgata is of the greatest value.

The World's End Is Right Here

Reading *Rohitassa Sutta* (AN 4:45)
NDB, pp. 434–36

In the material world we expect that a path leads from one physical location to another and requires physical travel to reach the destination. The Buddha pointed out a path followed within this living body without physically going anywhere. Here, the world's end and quenching is found.

Have No Doubts Concerning the Origin and Quenching of the World

Reading *Dutiya-ariyasāvaka Sutta* (SN 12:50)
CDB, pp. 585–86

The noble follower of the Buddha's way has no doubts about how experience arises and occurs, is quenched and ceases. The world of experience, especially experiences of distress, arises and is quenched through *paṭiccasamuppāda*.

Dhamma that Cannot Be Rebuked or Disputed

Reading *Titthāyatanādi Sutta* (AN 3:62)
NDB, pp. 270–72

Here the Buddha lays out basic experiential facts about which he sees no grounds for dispute: the basic elements of experience, the sense doors through which contact takes place, the sense objects that the mind resorts to, and the feelings that depend on sense contact. He gives four ennobling truths as a framework for investigation and practice regarding these realities that recycle within "feeling beings" countless times each day.

Chapter 6: Conquering Ignorance, Selfishness, and Superstition

Disentangling Inner and Outer Tangles

Reading *Jaṭā Sutta* (SN 1:23)
CDB, p. 101

The Buddha's image of tangles and entanglement is an apt metaphor for the human condition. Here, he outlines how anyone can untangle the knots and *dukkha* created by lust, hatred, and ignorance. This passage is quoted at the beginning of the *Visuddhimagga*, the classic fifth century Singhalese manual that is honored as a bible by Theravāda orthodoxy.

How to Stop Feeding Ignorance

Reading *Avijjā Sutta* (AN 10:61)
NDB, pp. 1415–18

Ignorance is both active false knowing and the absence of true knowing. Especially in the more basic form, the beginning of ignorance cannot be discovered. Yet, as a conditioned phenomenon like just about everything else, it can be investigated in terms of *idappaccayatā*. Feed ignorance its food and it becomes well fed; stop feeding ignorance and it will starve.

The Bases of Dukkha *Are Dependently Co-Arisen Stuff*

Reading *Mahāhatthipadoma Sutta* (MN 28)
MDB, pp. 278–85

To see Dhamma is to see everything as arising, changing, and passing through *idappaccayatā* and that all things implicated in *dukkha* are dependently co-arisen phenomena. All the stuff of our distresses, which have to do with one or another of the five clinging-together aggregates, is a matter of *paṭicca-samuppāda*. This applies to both the causal and the quenching aspects.

The Five Heaps Are Heavy Burdens for "Me"

Reading *Bhārā Sutta* (SN 22:22)
CDB, pp. 871–72

The heaps of human existence, the aggregates or bundles of our lives, become burdens when we take them personally and experience them in terms of self. We create stress for ourselves by weighing ourselves down with such burdens. The wise lighten their loads and know how to leave new burdens alone.

Chapter 7: Dependent Co-arising: Birth into Suffering

Consider the Dhamma Meaning of Each Mode of Paṭiccasamuppāda

Reading *Vibhaṅga Sutta* (SN 12:2)
CDB, pp. 534–36

As this chapter presents Ajahn Buddhadāsa's lucid exposition of the twelve modes of *paṭiccasamuppāda* that make up the classic formula, this sutta's analysis of the modes is in order. Take time to go beyond common or literal meanings and ponder the Dhamma meaning of each mode.

Understand the Activities of Concoctings (Saṅkhāra)

Reading *Khajjanīya Sutta* (SN 22:79)
CDB, pp. 914–18

Of the varied interpreted and disputed terms of *paṭiccasamuppāda*, *saṅkhāra* has the most influence on how *paṭiccasamuppāda* is understood. One perspective places ignorance and *saṅkhāra* in a past life. For Ajahn Buddhadāsa, they are repeatedly operating in this life and, in observable fact, every day.

This Body Is Neither Yours nor Another's

Reading *Lokāyatika Sutta* (SN 12:37)
CDB, pp. 575–76

This body with which we so easily identify, scheme for its pleasures, and fight to defend, is also known as "old karma." What is it made of? Who does it really belong to? *Paṭiccasamuppāda* provides a deeper perspective than people language can.

Chapter 8: Dimensions and Streams of Dependent Co-arising

Try Humming this Basic Paṭiccasamuppāda *to Yourself*

Reading *Ñātika Sutta* (SN 12:45)
CDB, pp. 582–83

In the passage preceding this chapter the Buddha gives us a straightforward and practical version of *paṭiccasamuppāda*. He explains that based in the senses, sense experience occurs along with feeling. In the absence of sufficient mindfulness and wisdom, craving, clinging, and the other conditions for *dukkha* follow. Ajahn Buddhadāsa called this "humming *paṭiccasamuppāda*," as the Buddha was heard reciting it to himself. The Buddha advised an interloping young monk to rely on this as "the beginning of the spiritual life." Ajahn Buddhadāsa considered it to contain all that is necessary for understanding the fundamentals of practice, which makes it the basis of spiritual life.

See Buddha through Dhamma

Reading *Saṅghāṭikaṇṇa Sutta* (It 92)

Ireland, pp. 217–18

In our materially minded moments, we consider the Buddha an embodied person or present in images. Sometimes we try to know the Buddha through words from ancient texts. Yet these are not the places to look. The Buddha is seen only through and in Dhamma.

See Dhamma through Paṭiccasamuppāda

Reading *Mahāhatthipadopama Sutta* (MN 28)

MDB, pp. 278–85

The heart of Dhamma is *paṭiccasamuppāda*. To see *paṭiccasamuppāda* is to see Dhamma and therein Buddha, no matter how many centuries have passed since a certain prophetic individual died.

See beyond Conceptions of "Existence" and "Nonexistence"

Reading *Kaccānagotta Sutta* (SN 12:15)

CDB, p. 544

"Being" and "nothing," "existence" and nonexistence," "I am" and "I am not" are dualisms that we conceive and grasp. The Buddha's middle way teaching of *paṭiccasamuppāda* enables us to avoid the extremes of such dualisms by rightly seeing that the nature of all phenomena is to arise and pass away. With this wisdom one does not take a stand on "my self."

Chapter 9: Dependent Co-arising for Children

Craving, Indulging, and Clinging to Pleasing Experiences Obstruct Liberation

Reading *Sakkapañha Sutta* (SN 35:118)

CDB, pp. 1192–93

Even the gods are interested in Dhamma practice. Sakka asks the Buddha the difference between those who become thoroughly cooled (liberated from *dukkha*) here in this life and those who don't. Those who do not indulge in or cling to sense experiences are liberated soon enough to directly experience it without physically dying.

Experience Fully and Simply without Fabricating Anything Extra

Reading *Māluṇkyaputta Sutta* (SN 35:95)

CDB, pp. 1175–78

An aged monk seeks a succinct Dhamma teaching. Rather than dwelling in past experiences or conjecturing about future ones, the Buddha advises him to be present fully and simply to experience here and now. In this way we do not fabricate ourselves anywhere or in anything; hence, there is nobody to suffer.

Distinguish the Subtle Difference between Two Levels of Contact

Reading *Mahānidāna Sutta* (DN 15)

LDB, pp. 223–30

Having two aspects, or levels of contact, is one of *paṭiccasamuppāda*'s many subtleties. This insight illuminates the distinctions made in the two preceding sutta passages. Sense experience in itself is not necessarily *dukkha*. Craving manifests through designations or meanings based on qualities and signs.

Paṭiccasamuppāda *Is Apparently and Actually Profound*

Reading *Nidāna Sutta* (SN 12:60)

CDB, pp. 593–94

The Buddha scolds his cousin and personal attendant Ānanda for proudly declaring that *paṭiccasamuppāda* is not as profound as many believe. The Buddha declares that *paṭiccasamuppāda* is in fact truly profound. We remain entangled with *dukkha* as long as we fail to penetrate its truth.

Chapter 10: Three Existences Are the Basis of Self

The Quenching of Craving and Clinging Disestablishes Dukkha

Reading *Dukkha Sutta* (SN 12:43)

CDB, pp. 580–81

This variation of *paṭiccasamuppāda* refers to the four ennobling truths. Ajahn Buddhadāsa observes that this sutta and others like it show how *paṭiccasamuppāda* is quenched in the middle by quenching craving without needing to cross over into another life. This and similar sutta passages indicate that there is no reason to assume that *paṭiccasamuppāda* is about past and future lives.

Cultivate Samādhi *to Clearly Understand Reality*

Reading *Samādhi Sutta* (SN 22:5)
CDB, pp. 863–64

When mind is focused, stable, and clear, it sees the five clinging-together aggregates according to reality. That is, such a mind understands how taking pleasure in, exalting, and indulging in the five aggregates leads to delight, and such clinging supports becoming, and so on. The Buddha also describes the reverse process.

Without Training We Get Stuck in Feelings and Accumulate Harmful Tendencies

Reading *Sallatha Sutta* (SN 36.6)
CDB, pp. 1263–65

How we respond to feeling distinguishes ordinary people from well-trained disciples of the Buddha. We all experience the gamut of pleasant, painful, and neither painful-nor-pleasant feelings. We can become stuck in the feelings we experience and strengthen unhealthy tendencies that perpetuate suffering. The wise don't get stuck, don't harbor tendencies, and don't perpetuate suffering.

Four Ennobling Truths of Paṭiccasamuppāda *Cannot be Rebuked or Censured*

Reading *Titthāyatanādi Sutta* (AN 3:62)
NDB, pp. 270–72

This passage explicitly links the Buddha's core teaching framework of the four noble truths with *paṭiccasamuppāda* in both the arising and quenching modes. Here he also points out that these teachings are for embodied sensate beings. These teachings are not abstract metaphysical propositions; they are practical guidance for those recognizing and facing the consequences of being alive and sensate.

Chapter 11: Heavens and Hells

Karma Bears Fruit or Ends in this Individuality

Reading *Nidāna Sutta* (AN 3:34)
NDB, pp. 230–32

Actions based in selfishness—greed, hatred, and delusion—bear fruit within the collection of aggregates (human life) where the sense of individuality arises. Egoistic action occurs with a sense of separate existence and agency that acts, and the fruits of the action fall to that individuality, too. Unselfish action—action without greed, hatred, and delusion—doesn't bear such fruit. When we consider this teaching in light of "birth" within *paṭiccasamuppāda*, while recognizing that the fruits of some actions may have a time lag, we need not assume they are spread out over various "lives," understood conventionally.

New Existences Depend upon Underlying Tendencies

Reading *Cetanā Sutta* (SN 12:38)
CDB, p. 576

Thinking about, pondering, and inclining toward something creates an object or basis for consciousness to rest upon and take hold. Growth here is the means for entering a new existence and the changes and suffering that follow. Even without active thinking and pondering, remaining tendencies toward something or patterns of habituation are a sufficient basis for becoming and entering a new existence (*bhava*). Becoming, birth, and *dukkha* have no basis when such tendencies are absent.

The Five Clinging-Together Aggregates Manifest with Passion and Infatuation

Reading *Mahāsaḷāyatanika Sutta* (MN 149)
MDB, pp. 1137–39

In the absence of true understanding, we react passionately to the factors of experience, such as contact and feeling. With such passion and fixation, the five clinging-together aggregates—life with distress and suffering—fully manifest. This is described in terms of agitation, roasting, and burning. This *paṭiccasamuppāda* perspective highlights the rebirth of suffering within daily experience.

Chapter 12: Damming the Streams of Suffering

Regarding the Clinging-Together Aggregates as Self

Reading *Samanupassanā Sutta* (SN 22:47)
CDB, pp. 885–86

Our habitual ways of regarding things are usually bound up with the five clinging-together aggregates and taking them personally, that is, in terms of self. The untrained mind is still infected with ignorance and identifies with these basic life functions, assuming "I am" in regard to them. With the natural functioning of the sense faculties, ignorant contact arises and the feelings conditioned by it give rise to such appropriations and attachments. Noble disciples see all of this in light of *paṭiccasamuppāda*, without appropriations and attachments to "I am."

Happiness and Suffering Are Neither a Matter of Our Own Actions Nor of Others'

Reading *Bhūmija Sutta* (SN 12:25)
CDB, pp. 559–61

This passage illuminates the early links of *paṭiccasamuppāda*, specifically ignorance and concoctings. Whatever claims disparate teachers may make about happiness and distress being caused by oneself or by others, we can observe that all happiness and distress arises dependent upon sense contact. Ignorance is the significant factor that insinuates itself into volitions related to body, speech, and mind, and the concocting of happiness and distress that follow. With the remainderless quenching of ignorance, body, speech, and mind no longer function in ways subject to troublesome volitions.

Set Aside Questions about Past and Future Aggregates; Dhamma Is in Conditionality Right Here

Reading *Cūḷasakuludāyi Sutta* (MN 79)
MDB, pp. 654–62

The Wanderer Sakuludāyi asks a question about the past. The Buddha responds that discussing matters of the past and future requires having the psychic powers of recollecting past births and the divine eye that sees beings disappearing and moving on according to karma. The Buddha recommends setting aside questions about the past and future in order to contemplate *idappaccayatā* here and now.

Chapter 13: Dependent quenching

How to Quench the Clinging-Together Aggregates in this Life

Reading *Mahātthipadopama Sutta* (MN 28)
MDB, pp. 278–85

The Buddha points out with subtlety and sophistication how the aggregates of life come to be taken personally (clinging together; together with clinging) and how this process constitutes suffering. Conversely, he shows how the quenching of *dukkha* is found in the removal or abandoning of passionate desire regarding the five clinging-together aggregates. Ajahn Buddhadāsa takes this as further evidence that the Buddha's intention was liberation within this life: to die (halting the process of self-centered rebirth) before dying (physical death).

The Buddha Describes the Quenching Sequence of Paṭiccasamuppāda

Reading *Paṭiccasamuppāda Sutta* (SN 12.1)
CDB, pp. 533–34

Buddhist practice is about the quenching of *dukkha* and *paṭiccasamuppāda* describes the quenching process. Here is the standard "quenching sequence" of the twelve links or modes. Elsewhere in the suttas are found many variations on this theme. With the quenching of ignorance, all the links are quenched, culminating in the quenching of *dukkha*, distress, and suffering.

The Noble Eightfold Path Is Karma That Ends Karma

Reading *Kukkuravāditka Sutta* (MN 57), MDB, pp. 493–97
Ariyamagga Sutta (AN 4:237), NDB, pp. 604–5
Bojjhaṅga Sutta (AN 4:238), NDB, p. 605

We hear a lot about karma in Buddhist circles but seldom about the Buddha's unique teaching on karma. The conventional karma teachings are more moralistic than Buddhist. The distinctive feature of Buddhist teachings about karma is the karma (action) that ends karma. The noble eightfold path is the culmination and end of karma as it frees life of the "actor" that is responsible for karma. The "actor" is quenched within *paṭiccanirodha*.

Chapter 14: Training Mindfulness with Breathing

Mindfulness with Breathing Is a Complete Path of Practice

Reading *Ānāpānasati Sutta* (MN 118)
MDB, pp. 941–48, paragraphs 15–17

In guiding the international retreats at Suan Mokkh, Ajahn Buddhadāsa instructed us to emphasize two teachings: *paṭiccasamuppāda* for the sake of right understanding and *ānāpānasati* to cultivate the conditions and skills for living freely. He investigated these topics himself and regularly explained how they go together. Accordingly, it is important to understand the full liberating scope of *ānāpānasati*.

Mindfulness with Breathing Is the Full Application of Mindfulness

Reading *Ānāpānasati Sutta* (MN 118), MDB, pp. 941–48, paragraphs 23–28

Pathamānanda Sutta (SN 54:13), CDB, pp. 1780–85, section i

While acknowledging other ways of being mindful while breathing, the Buddha consistently presented his approach as encompassing all four applications (establishments, foundations) of mindfulness. Unfortunately, this is often overlooked when modern teachers present a truncated version of "*ānāpāna*." Ajahn Buddhadāsa felt we should have the whole picture encompassing all four applications of mindfulness as the Buddha taught.

Mindfulness with Breathing Nurtures the Seven Factors of Awakening

Reading *Ānāpānasati Sutta* (MN 118), MDB, pp. 941–48, paragraphs 29–40

Pathamānanda Sutta (SN 54:13), CDB, pp. 1780–85, section ii

The factors of awakening describe a high level of practice that brings one to the cusp of awakening. Ordinary mindfulness matures to a level ready for awakening and is accompanied by six other highly developed factors of awakening. When these are sufficiently developed, true knowing brings about liberation from *paṭiccasamuppāda*, that is, *paṭiccanirodha*. All this is possible while breathing in and out.

Chapter 15: Dependent Co-arising Controversies

Ignorance and Infatuation Begin in Young Children

Reading *Mahātaṇhāsankhaya Sutta* (MN 38) MDB, pp. 349–61

Unlike the traditional commentaries on the suttas that place the beginnings of *paṭiccasamuppāda* in past lives, in this sutta the Buddha describes its beginning in the young child. At some point in our lives, *paṭiccasamuppāda* is concocted out of ignorance for the first time. Once the child's senses are developed to the extent they can be indulged, they become the basis for liking and disliking, which gives rise to clinging and egoism. This perspective may confuse those from cultures that idealize children's innocence. Nevertheless, the Buddha pointed out that the ignorance that underlies suffering is present in both children and adults. In other words, underlying innocence there is also ignorance. Note again the crucial role of the senses and feeling.

The Buddha-to-Be Investigated Paṭiccasamuppāda *before the Great Awakening*

Reading *Nagara Sutta* (SN 12:65)
CBD, pp. 601–4

The Bodhisatta (Buddha-to-Be) thought about, reflected upon, and investigated the details of *paṭiccasamuppāda* even before the ultimate awakening under the Bodhi tree. In this sutta, he asks what makes aging and death possible, and has the certain insight that birth is the condition for aging and death. He continues to investigate the conditions one after another until culminating in mind-body and consciousness circling back upon each other. Concurrently, he realizes that all this is process and *anattā*, rather than discreet phenomena that happen to somebody. This discovery is compared to a man finding the remains of a long-lost ancient city deep in the forest.

The Paṭiccasamuppāda *that Transcends* Paṭiccasamuppāda

Reading *Upanisa Sutta* (SN12:23)
CDB, pp. 553–56

One of the most profound suttas in the entire Pāli Canon traces the *paṭiccasamuppāda* sequence from ignorance to *dukkha* and then describes how profound knowledge and liberation arise out of *dukkha*. The realization of *dukkha*'s end is also a matter of causes and conditions, just like everything else (almost) we experience. Many other suttas examine these conditions for liberation, but only this one links them with the sequence of *dukkha*'s origin. Faith emerging from *dukkha* is a crucial turning point. This teaching is the epitome of the Buddha's four ennobling truths.

Chapter 16: The Beginning and End of Spiritual Life

Practicing for Remainderless Quenching Is Dhamma Practice According to Dhamma

Reading *Dhammakhatika Sutta* (SN 12:16)
CDB, p. 545

The phrase "Dhamma practice" has become a well-worn synonym for meditation. It might appear that meditation, then, is Dhamma or the way. However, the Buddha's teachings stress that practice is to be guided by right understanding of Dhamma. As seeing Dhamma is a matter of seeing *paṭiccasamuppāda*, practicing according to right understanding of *paṭiccasamuppāda* is crucial. Consequently, right understanding of *paṭiccasamuppāda* is the purpose of both the Buddha's teaching and this book.

Explore Inner Conditions in this Life Here and Now

Reading *Sammasa Sutta* (SN 12:66)
CDB, pp. 604–7

In this passage, "inner conditions" refer to *dukkha* (aging and death), acquisitions, craving, and lovely and gratifying sense experiences; as such, "inner conditions" are an abridged version of *paṭiccasamuppāda*. If these are to be actively explored, the overall thrust of Buddha-Dhamma would explore them in this life, while they are happening. This is yet another passage that supports Ajahn Buddhadāsa's understanding that the traditional interpretation in terms of past, present, and future lives misses the main import of *paṭiccasamuppāda*. Spreading "inner conditions" over three lifetimes puts them beyond direct experience, turning them into an intellectual pursuit or a matter of faith. The primary reason for interpreting *paṭiccasamuppāda* in "this life" is the ability to explore it in our lives here and now.

The Buddha Fulfilled his Duty and Encouraged Us in Ours

Reading *Asaṅkhatasaṃyutta* (SN 43)
CDB, pp. 1372–80

The Buddha offered himself as a guide not a savior. He compassionately shared the Dhamma and path he had discovered and formulated a multitude of expressions and presentations fitting the needs and abilities of his listeners. In fulfilling the duty (Dhamma) of a Perfectly Self-Awakened One, he did not presume to save anyone. Instead, the Buddha taught that practicing wisely according to Dhamma is the duty of each one of us. *Dukkha* is to be quenched wherever its conditions arise.

Notes

The majority of these notes refer to Pāli suttas and give the name of the sutta; the sutta number in what has become the standard reference form; the Pāli Text Society collection, volume, and page numbers; and the most widely available English language translation. These citations use the above abbreviations.

1. Alagaddūpama Sutta, MN 22, M.i.140, MDB 234 (also SN 22:86, S.iii.119, CDB 938 and SN 44:2, S.iv.384).
2. Cūḷasakuludāyi Sutta, MN 79, M.ii.32, MDB 655 (also SN 12:21, S.ii.28, CDB 552; SN 22:57, S.iii.63, CDB 898; AN 10:92 A.v.184, NDB 1463; and others).
3. Mahhatthipadopama Sutta, MN 28, M.i.191, MDB 294.
4. Vakkali Sutta, SN 22:87, s.iii.120, CDB 939.
5. Nidāna Sutta, SN 12:60, S.ii.92, CDB 594. See *Companion to Under the Bodhi Tree.*
6. See Buddhadāsa Bhikkhu's *Heartwood of the Bodhi Tree: The Buddha's Teaching on Voidness* (Boston: Wisdom, 1994), 14–17.
7. He had previously compiled similar works on the Buddha's Life and the Four Noble Truths at a time when extensive translation of these texts were not available in Thai.
8. In early texts of the Pāli Canon, the term used for this is *punabbhavo*, "again becoming" or "repeated existence." It occurs only a few times.
9. Six talks given by Venerable Ajahn Buddhadāsa during a ten-day retreat at Suan Mokkh in December 1988 have been supplemented with talks given during two subsequent retreats, November 1990 (chapters 10 and 11) and July 1991 (chapter 14).
10. This list is often misused to reject aspects of traditional Buddhism, which is to wander off the middle way.
11. Kesaputti (Kālāma) Sutta, AN 3:65, A.i.189, NDB 279.
12. *Idappaccayatā*, conditionality, the state (*tā*) of having this (*ida*) as condition

(*paccaya*). See the glossary for further explanation of this and other Pāli terms.

13. The term "Buddhism" was coined by European scholars who viewed Buddha-Dhamma teaching and practice externally and in terms foreign to it. Here, Ajahn Buddhadāsa de-emphasizes such externals and social science perspectives for the core that liberates.
14. Ajahn Buddhadāsa's frequent use of the term *correct* and its derivatives should be understood in the context of the noble eightfold path, where each factor is qualified as *sammā* (right, appropriate). Here, it means sufficient to get the job done, appropriate to the situation, in harmony with Dhamma, and leading out from suffering. This usage of *correct* does not include externally imposed righteousness or rule-following legalism.
15. Titthāyatanādi Sutta, AN 3:61, A.i.173, NDB 266.
16. *Hetu* (cause) refers to the primary influence and *paccaya* (condition) to other influences. Both terms are frequently combined as *hetupaccaya*, as in this paragraph. Used alone, *paccaya* often has a broad, general meaning that includes *hetu* and other forms of relationship. Hence, we use the term "conditionality" for *idappaccayatā,* which is more inclusive than "causality" or "cause and effect," especially the limited linear causality often assumed in the West.
17. Titthāyatanādi Sutta, AN 3:61, A.i.173, NDB 266. This passage is abridged above.
18. This must not, of course, be confused with a merely material, genetic, or biological law (nor should this understanding of natural law be confused with how this term has been understood in Western religious thought). Ajahn Buddhadāsa's understanding of this natural law is fundamentally spiritual or Dhammic, which in his understanding encompasses material and mental.
19. AN 3:65, A.i.188, NDB 64. See passage preceding chapter 1. Also known as the Kesaputti Sutta. See *Messages of Truth from Suan Mokkh* for further discussion of this sutta: http://www.suanmokkh.org/books.
20. The criteria given here also apply to rejecting teachings. Today, we should consider how rejecting teachings on the basis of anything but direct personal experience is also a form of blind belief expressed negatively.
21. Chachakka Sutta, MN 148, M.iii.285, MDB 1134.
22. Similarly, we need not worry about the diversity and apparent differences among the various schools and traditions of Buddhism.
23. *Citta* encompasses mind, heart, consciousness, awareness, and psyche. The distinctions between heart and mind, and emotion and thought, are foreign to early Buddhism. Nonetheless, in modern English the connotations of "heart" and "mind" tend to confuse us. Please see the glossary for further explanation.

24. This is not meant as an insult to those who study such matters. Tan Ajahn himself was an expert in the local archeology and history of Ban Dorn Bay, the part of southern Thailand where he lived almost all of his life. If one has the time for such studies and can use them constructively, they need not be a distraction. His concern is with such factors becoming such a focus that they obscure or dominate the heart of Buddhism.
25. This is a simile used by the Buddha himself and preexists modern imaging technology.
26. Some readers may find this criticism harsh. For those who might object that humanistic and transpersonal psychologies are different, or that psychotherapy helps people with their problems, Ajahn Buddhadāsa might respond that all of these are limited by the individualism that gave rise to them and the privilege of those who can avail themselves of such services. Anyway, psychotherapies receive smaller budgets than marketing psychology. Psychology is famously employed by militaries and large corporate bureaucracies. Again, he points out that something seen by the educated middle-class as good is by no means an unmitigated good and may be harmful in ways we prefer to ignore.
27. Ajahn Buddhadāsa consistently uses the abstract form of these terms. They could be rendered as "the positive" and "the negative," but the definite article would imply a reality that these terms do not have, so I have used "positivity" and "negativity" instead, though they are regrettably clumsy.
28. Do not confuse this meaning of "doubt," which refers to doubting what is true and being skeptical about reality, with "uncertainty" when information is insufficient.
29. Lokadhamma Sutta, AN 8:5, A.iv.156, NDB 1116.
30. Genesis 3:3.
31. Love, *rak*, is a rather ambiguous word in Thai. Unlike the Pāli terms *karunā* (compassion) and *mettā* (loving kindness), which are much purer in meaning, *rak* ranges widely, encompassing passionate attachment, selfish demanding affection, the love of a mother for children, and sublime *agape*. Tan Ajahn uses it here to provoke and challenge, rather than unmindfully assume that love is always good. Central to the discussion here is that love is conditioned and limited, especially the personal love of one egoistic being for another.
32. One who has arrived in thusness, one who is just so: the Buddha's preferred term of self-reference.
33. Celestial beings, tempter beings, and gods.
34. Loka Sutta, AN 4:23, A. ii.23, NDB 410.
35. Some translators render the Pāli, "because this exists, that arises; through

the arising of this, that happens." Nevertheless, "this . . . this" is more true to the original.

36. The vowel is a long "o" as in goat, while the final consonant isn't fully aspirated and is thus cut off short.
37. *Vedanā* is a central term in the *paṭiccasamuppāda* teaching and Buddha-Dhamma generally. Translating it as 'feeling' is both appropriate and misleading. Please the glossary entry for *vedanā* to avoid confusion.
38. The same applies to the overly broad use of the terms "law of karma" and "karma." Properly, karma means "action" not the ethical law governing actions. The law of karma is limited to the ethics of volitional actions and their consequences (*vipāka*), which is not as broad as conditionality or as profound as dependent co-arising.
39. Jaṭā Sutta, SN 7:6, S.i.165, CDB 259.
40. *Sayasāstra*, the science of sleeping (in ignorance): misunderstanding how natural law and duty operate, attributing causal efficacy where it doesn't actually exist, and behaving accordingly (though some understanding may be lurking within it).
41. The key Thai term here is *saksit* (from Sanskrit *sakti* and *siddhi*), which can be translated as "sacred" or "holy," though neither is entirely satisfactory. The Thai term carries connotations of miraculous or mysterious power. Please see the glossary.
42. Which is not to say that such beliefs are bad. Interestingly, some of them did a better job of protecting Thai forests than the scientific knowledge taught in modern schools and used by industry to cut down trees far faster than less technologically advanced people could have done.
43. Found in many Sutta passages—MN 79, M.ii.32, MLD 655; SN 12:21, S.ii.28, CDB 552; AN 10:92, A.v.184, NDB 1463; and others. In some of these, the conditionality formula is followed by an exposition of dependent origination. Following Ajahn Buddhadāsa, I've translated the pronouns as "this" and "this," while some translators render them "this" and "that."
44. Vibhaṅga Sutta, SN 12:2, S.ii.2, CDB 534.
45. Khajjanīya Sutta, SN 22:79, S.iii.87, CDB 915. The quotation marks are meant to convey a mental conception abstracted from reality as it is.
46. This includes ignorance regarding the ennobling truths, impermanence, dukkhaness, selflessness, voidness, and thusness, all of which are connected with conditionality in the original teachings.
47. Some suttas refer to the sense media in the plural, collective sense, which describes the overall structure. In moment-to-moment experience, the specific sense bases are given, each giving rise to a specific sense contact, giving rise to a specific *vedanā* , and so on.
48. *Vedanā* is frequently misunderstood as emotion and can be confused with

physical sensations. Due to these muddles, we prefer the Pāli term. Please see the glossary for a fuller explanation.

49. Clinging to "mine" is more easily and commonly recognized, as well as more frequently acknowledged in Dhamma talks, whereas clinging to "me" is more basic, central, and important, yet less frequently acknowledged. We hope that serious practitioners will give more attention to clinging to our own subjectivity, not just to possessions, acquisitions, and externals.
50. Kaccānagotta Sutta, SN 12:15, S.ii.17, CDB 544.
51. *Ñātika Sutta,* SN 12:45, S.ii.74, CDB 582 (identical with Upassuti Sutta, SN 35:113 S.iv.90). Except for the ending, this passage appears a number of times in the Pāli Suttas. Because the Buddha recited these words to himself while alone in the forest, Ajahn Buddhadāsa called this "humming dependent co-arising."
52. The practical purpose of distinguishing these two levels is to allow the first level to remain "merely seeing" and to not cling to the meaning or value of the second level, as in the Buddha's famous advice to Bāhiya (Udāna 1:10, Ireland 20) and the teaching to Māluṇkyaputta (Māluṇkyaputta Sutta, SN 35:95, S.iv.72, CDB 1175).
53. This ought not to be taken as "natural contact," which would assume that foolishness, no matter how common, is the natural state or nature of human beings.
54. Vakkali Sutta, SN 22:87, S.iii.120, CDB 939.
55. Post-Vedic Hindu scriptures, the earliest perhaps as old as the seventh century BCE, that is, pre-dating the Buddha, with others much later. (See the glossary.)
56. *Diṭṭhadhamma*, directly and immediately seeable, without needing to wait for the future. "Thoroughly cool" is a verb form of *parinibbāna*, traditionally associated with death, although in many sutta passages it is experienced while very much alive. Ajahn Buddhadāsa often rendered *nibbāna* as "coolness" and emphasized that it can be realized here in this life and without physically dying first.
57. Ajahn Buddhadāsa comments: Consciousness *(viññāṇa)*, here, refers to the consciousness of mental phenomena *(manoviññāṇa)* that experiences pleasure and infatuation regarding that form. This does not refer to the eye-consciousness *(cakkhuviññāṇa)* that sees the form in the ordinary functioning of the visual sense.
58. Sakkapañha Sutta, SN 35:118, S.iv.101, CDB 1192.
59. Right aspiration *(sammāsankappa)* or wise want corresponds to the second factor of the noble eightfold path.
60. Now that "mindfulness" has gone mainstream, its meaning often diverges

from its Buddhist sources and contexts. Please see the glossary for further explanation.

61. Suan Mokkh International is across the Asian Highway from the main monastery where these talks were given.
62. Dukkha Sutta, SN 12:43, S.ii.72, CDB 580 (also Dukkhasamudaya Sutta, SN 35:106, S. iv.86). The following sutta of this section speaks in exactly the same way about the origin and disestablishment (passing away) of the world: Loka Sutta, SN 12:44, S.ii.73, CDB 581 (also Dukkhasamudaya Sutta, S. iv.87).
63. Ajahn Buddhadāsa's discussion here and later about housewives, husbands, and marriage reflect Thai Buddhist ideals. While he considered them to be a good model to follow, he was open-minded about other relationship models, his bottom line always being whether something is skillful (lessens dukkha) or unskillful (increases dukkha).
64. This is Ajahn Buddhadāsa's own neologism "although we know that 'form-ish' cannot be found in any English dictionary."
65. Rohitassa Sutta, AN 4:45, A.ii.48, NDB 434.
66. We have used more literal translations here for the Pāli terms *diṭṭhadhamma*, *uppajja*, and *aparapariyāya*, which are often interpreted to mean "this life," "the next life," and "subsequent lives." Ajahn Buddhadāsa comments that "this sutta demonstrates how all three causes of actions occur in this life, before physical death within this individuality, which corresponds to birth *(jāti)* in the language of *paṭiccasamuppāda*. That is, any time there is clinging, there is a birth, which can happen many times each day. Thus, *diṭṭhadhamma* means immediately, *uppajja* means a moment later, and *aparapariyāya* means some time later. Note that the last term does not preclude "future lives."
67. Nidāna Sutta, AN 3:34, A.i.134, NDB 230.
68. This term is difficult to render in English, as the ancient Indian cosmology is from a different cultural background than the one that produced the English language. Such gods have no form and it is difficult to imagine what sort of existence they have, though they are said to last for very long periods of time.
69. Here, Ajahn Buddhadāsa refers to one of the simplest forms of dependent co-arising: *kilesa, karma,* and *vipāka*. Each gives rise to the next, with defilement being a reaction to fruit such that it tends to spin over and over. The *Visuddhimagga* explanation of this is too complicated to practice. However, all three basic aspects of dependent co-arising can be seen clearly in the many spins of dependent co-arising that take place each day.
70. *Samanuppassati*, to seize, grasp, examine, explore, and know thoroughly.
71. Samanupassanā Sutta, SN 22:47, S.iii.46, CDB 885.

72. *Samannāhāracitta* is the aspect of mind that becomes conscious in order to cognize the object striking a sense door and is accompanied by ignorance, lacks mindfulness, and lacks true knowledge regarding liberation.
73. *paṭicca-samuppanna-dhamma*
74. *dukkhasamudhaya*
75. *chandharāga*
76. *dukkhanirodha*
77. Mahātthipadopama Sutta, MN 28, M.i.190, MDB 283.
78. Ibid.
79. See note 52.
80. Mahāhatthipadopama Sutta, MN 28, M.i.191, MDB 284.
81. Further teachings on the voidness of dependent co-arising can be found in Ajahn Buddhadāsa's *Heartwood of the Bodhi Tree.*
82. Ānāpānasati Sutta, MN 118, M.iii.82, MDB 943.
83. The four elements signify solidity, cohesion, temperature or combustion, and movement.
84. *Kāya* is usually translated "body," but also means a group or collection of things, an aggregate of individuals or collective mass, as in body of water or troop of soldiers. To avoid confusion about the sense being used here, think in terms of a collection or group of related phenomena that make up a functional system.
85. "Meaning" here refers to mind-made meaning leading to clinging and suffering.
86. For a detailed discussion of all sixteen lessons or domains, please see Buddhadāsa Bhikkhu, *Mindfulness with Breathing: A Manual for Serious Beginners* (Boston: Wisdom, 1997).
87. *kāmaguṇa*
88. *nandi*
89. Mahātaṇhāsankhaya Sutta, MN 38, M.i.266, MDB 358. Ajahn Buddhadāsa comments: This passage shows, first, how the child must mature enough to experience clinging in regards to *vedanā* in order for the stream of dependent co-arising to arise in the child's mind through the power of ignorance. Second, the passage clearly shows that becoming and birth arise only after there is clinging to *vedanā*, and not immediately at birth from the mother's womb, as is generally understood in ordinary people language. This passage uses the language of dependent co-arising, that is, Dhamma language. *Bhava* and *jāti* arise every time there is clinging to *vedanā*. In Dhamma language, aging and death occur even for a child, that is, the heavy-hearted problems connected with the meaning of "aging and death," which genuinely cause dukkha when clung to such that they have power over the child's mind.

90. See, for example, the *Ariyapariyesāna Sutta* (MN 26, M.i.167, MDB 253) and the Nagara Sutta (SN 12:65, S.ii.104, CDB 601).
91. Udāna, Bodhi Suttas 1–3, Ud 1–3, Ireland 11–13, and Vinaya-piṭaka, Mahāvagga, V.iv.1. The latter has both arising and quenching sequences for all three watches. See *Companion to Under the Bodhi Tree.*
92. Literally, "with the hairs" *(anuloma)* and "against the hairs" *(paṭiloma)* respectively.
93. Matthew 5:17.
94. This was true for most of Ajahn Buddhadāsa's life. However, decades after his own pioneering re-examination of these teachings, various Asian and Western writers have offered their own re-examinations. Prominent among them are Macy, Ñāṇānanda, Ñāṇavira, Wettimurti, Bucknell, and Swaris (please see Further Reading). Still, one finds the old orthodoxy repeated far more often than not.
95. Apologists for this interpretation try to explain how it does not conflict with *anattā* and *suññatā*. Nevertheless, the language they use is replete with persons, beings, and somethings that carry over from one life to the next. If not fully explicit, self (*attā*) is implicit in their explanations.
96. With these perspectives of Dhamma language, dependent co-arising, and not-self, we might return to the *tevijjā* teaching and understand the first two knowledges (*vijjā*) in less conventional or literal terms. The third *vijjā* does not present any problems of interpretation, because it is not expressed in people language. It is about the end of the *āsava*, not about persons carrying on here and there. Just remember that ultimately nobody has *āsava* and nobody ends them. What might a Dhamma language reading of the first two *vijjā* look like? How might "previous dwellings" be understood without reference to past lives? How might "passing away and reappearing according to karma" apply to experience today? We leave that for the reader to ponder and explore. We still prefer the Buddha's dependent co-arising description of the awakening. It is both more straightforward and more profound, not to mention more practical.
97. Dhammakhatika Sutta, SN 12:16, S.ii.18, CDB 545. In this sutta, each mode of dependent co-arising is also used to describe "one who is a speaker of Dhamma" and "one who has realized Nibbāna in this very life." Here, Ajahn Buddhadāsa has selected the middle section of each paragraph, which deals with the practice of Dhamma.
98. Ajahn Buddhadāsa's *Dependent Co-arising From His Own Lips* runs over 800 pages, containing hundreds of passages that express conditionality and dependent co-arising in more and less detail, and from many different angles. You have seen some of them between the chapters of this book. More are collected in *Companion to Under the Bodhi Tree* (www.liberationpark.org).

99. *Cakkhuñca paṭicca rūpe ca uppajjati cakkhuviññāṇaṃ. Tiṇṇaṃ saṅgati phasso. Phassapaccayā vedanā; vedanāpaccayā taṇhā; taṇhāpaccayā upādānaṃ; upādānapaccayā bhavo; bhavapaccayā jāti; jātipaccayā jarāmaraṇaṃ sokaparidevadukkhadomanassupāyāsā sambhavanti. Evametassa kevalassa dukkhakkhandhassa samudayo hoti.* (Ñātika Sutta, SN 12:45, S.ii.74, CDB 582)

100. Ibid. S.ii.75. See sutta passage preceding chapter 8.

101. A reference to one of the paintings in Suan Mokkh's Theater of Spiritual Entertainments.

102. *Dhammānukrom Dhammaghosana*, ed. Pinit Raktonglor (Dhammadāna Foundation, Chaiya: revised 1997).

Glossary

In passages from the Pāli, as well as in Ajahn Buddhadāsa's commentary throughout this book, I have adhered to his understanding of key Pāli terms, which at times differs from that of other teachers and translators. Readers are cautioned to remember that Pāli is a language created in the process of recording orally transmitted texts and never existed separate from those texts.

While terms have been explained in the later commentaries, these are not always as trustworthy as we might wish, and their explanations can be misleading. Many sutta passages leave much room for interpretation, which depends on the understanding, beliefs, and biases of the interpreter (including this translator as well as you the reader). Ajahn Buddhadāsa worked to derive his understanding primarily from the original Pāli sources. Unlike more "orthodox" scholars and traditionalists, he chose the original Pāli sense over the later commentarial gloss whenever there was discrepancy or confusion. In conveying Ajahn Buddhadāsa's understanding of these terms I draw on his own explanations scattered throughout his lectures and which have been collected in a Dhamma Glossary to his major Thai works.[102] Certain English terms are also included in order to clarify and remind how Ajahn Buddhadāsa understood them or to help clear up common confusions. A few terms are discussed in detail because of their importance and frequent misuse.

Alphabetization follows the order of the English alphabet, as many readers may be unfamiliar with the Pāli alphabet. A few well-known terms are not included when their meanings are noncontroversial. Chapters are noted when a term has been discussed there in some detail or depth.

Key to the Pronunciation of Pāli

The Pāli Alphabet

Vowels:	a, ā, i, ī, u, ū, e, o
Consonants:	
Gutterals	k, kh, g, gh, ṅ
Palatals	c, ch, j, jh, ñ
Cerebrals	ṭ, ṭh, ḍ, ḍh, ṇ
Dentals	t, th, d, dh, n
Labials	p, ph, b, bh, m
Other	y, r, ḷ, l, v, s, h, ṃ

Pronunciation

a as in "cut"
ā as in "father"
i as in "king"
ī as in "keen"
u as in "put"
ū as in "rule"
e as in "way"
o as in "home"

Of the vowels, *e* and *o* are long before a single consonant and short before a double consonant. Among the consonants, *g* is always pronounced as in "good," *c* as in "church," ñ as in "onion." The cerebrals (or retroflexes) are spoken with the tongue on the roof of the mouth; the dentals with the tongue on the upper teeth. The aspirates—*kh*, *gh*, *ch*, *jh*, *ṭh*, *ḍh*, *th*, *dh*, *ph*, *bh*—are single consonants pronounced with slightly more force than the nonaspirates, e.g., *th* as in "Thomas" (not as in "thin"); *ph* as in "putter" (not as in "phone"). Double consonants are always enunciated separately, e.g., *dd* as in "mad dog," *gg* as in "big gun." The pure nasal (*niggahīta*) *ṃ* is pronounced like the *ng* in "song." An *o* and an *e* always carry a stress; otherwise the stress falls on a long vowel—ā, ī, ū, or on a double consonant, or on *ṃ*.

A

adibrahmacariya. The beginning or basis of the supreme way of living (see *brahmacariya* below). Some translators render *ādi-* as "fundamentals," hence, "fundamentals of the holy life" (chapter 16).

ānāpānasati-bhāvanā. Cultivation of and with mindfulness every time one inhales and exhales. In the Pāli suttas, *ānāpānasati* is much more than mere mindfulness "of" breathing. It is a comprehensive system of practice that fully develops the four *satipaṭṭhāna*, insight, and liberation. Ajahn Buddhadāsa's *Mindfulness with Breathing* examines the full scope of this practice in detail (chapter 14).

anattā. Not-self, not having self, not being self; all aspects of experience fail to reveal a self or *attā*. (See *attā* below.)

anattātā. The fact of being not-self; selflessness. Not to be confused with nothingness or nihilism.

anicca. Impermanent, inconstant, not lasting. Uncertainty (*aniyata*) is a close synonym.

aniccatā. Impermanence, inconstancy, the fact that nothing lasts; applies most of all to the constituents of experience and everything we might claim to be "me" or "mine."

anusaya. Underlying tendencies, familiarity with *kilesa*. Every instance of reactive emotion leaves a deposit. These accumulate as *anusaya*. When enough pressures build they flow out as *āsava*.

āsava. Ferments, pickles, outflows, infections; the condition of collecting and fermenting, the pickling spice of danger stored away in the unconscious. The *āsava* are the last, subtlest level of *kilesa*, the most difficult to see and abandon. The pressure of accumulated *anusaya* flows out as *āsava* and expand in consciousness as *kilesa* again. Their end is synonymous with liberation, and knowing this is the flowering of awakening. The Suttas generally list three: sensuality, becoming-being, and ignorance. Later texts add a fourth: views.

atammayatā. Unconcoctability (lit. "the condition of not being made up by that"). Ajahn Buddhadāsa colloquially explained as "I ain't gonna mess with you no more." The condition of not being affected or influenced by anything. Nothing can produce, affect, or concoct this mind, because it does not depend upon or react to positive and negative (chapters 4 and 14).

attā. Self; Atmān; more loosely, ego, soul. A thing, being, or entity that lasts, is separate and independent, and has agency and control. Though we speak of such a thing, the Buddha's teaching insists that it never can be found.

avacara. Wandering; awareness wandering in one of the forms of existence (*bhava*). Ajahn Buddhadāsa has explained *arūpavacara* as "mind that wanders among formless things," *rūpavacara* as "mind that wanders among and obsesses about formish things unconnected with sensuality; living with the flavors of purely material things, such as the formish absorptions," and *kāmāvacara* as "mind that spins around among the sensual and sexual stuff that is the basis for sensual desires" (chapter 10).

avijjā. Ignorance, non-*vijjā*. Ignorance can be passive (not knowing what ought to be known) or active (knowing incorrectly). *Avijjā* is often delineated in terms of the four ennobling realities; lacking insight into inconstancy, unsatisfactoriness, and selflessness is also *avijjā*. Views and opinions are more active *avijjā* (chapters 12 and 13).

awakened. Preferred to "enlightened," which has unfortunate philosophic connotations due to its use for a Western rationalist movement. Further, "awakened" is closer to the meaning of *bodhi* and *buddha*.

āyatana. Sense media, sense domains, "connectors." The six inner *āyatana* are the eyes, ears, nose, tongue, body, and mind (functioning as a sense door), and the six outer are the forms, sounds, smells, flavors, physical sensations, and mental experiences that correspond with the six sense doors. These are collectively known as *saḷāyatana*. The four *arūpa*s (cf. *jhāna*) are also termed *āyatana*. Nibbāna is described as *āyatana*, in that it can be experienced and realized (chapter 8).

B

Bhagavā. One of the primary epithets of the Buddha, often translated as Blessed One, or even Lord, though these smack of more theistic religions. From *bhāga*, to distribute, hence, one who distributes and disseminates Dhamma. We prefer to leave it untranslated.

bhava. Being, existence, becoming; in Dhamma language, to conceptually be or have in a certain way, to identify with, to take personally. In *paṭiccasamuppāda*, *bhava* parallels the gestation stage between conception (*upādāna*) and birth (*jāti*). Three kinds of *bhava* are sensual existence (*kāmabhava*), formish existence (*rūpabhava*), and formless existence (*arūpabhava*) (chapters 10 and 11).

bhāvanā. Cultivation, development of body, moral action, mind, and wisdom. Often in a compound with *samādhi*.

brahmacariya. Supreme way of life, highest faring; the way of life that is sublime, excellent, and able to solve all human problems. Some translators render *brahmacariya* as "holy life." Ajahn Buddhadāsa's rendering is more literal. In later Thai usage it has come to mean "celibacy." Ajahn Buddhadāsa uses it in the original sense of the path leading to the utter quenching of *dukkha*, such as, the noble eightfold path.

Buddha. Awakened One; life that has seen deeply into our human reality, engendered profound compassion, given up all clinging to self, awakened from the sleep of the *kilesa* (reactive emotions), and selflessly shown the way to beings in search of liberation from *dukkha*.

Buddha-sāsanā. Buddhism; originally, the Buddha's teaching, message, and dispensation.

C

citta. Mind, heart, psyche, character. The umbrella name we give to the capacity to experience, which thinks, has moods and emotions, reacts, understands, realizes, and is either caught within craving and clinging or is liberated and awakened. *Viññāṇa* (sense consciousness) and *mano* (the function of mind that experiences sense experiences and is counted as the sixth of the sense doors) are not equivalent to *citta*, though usage is seldom strictly separated. In the text, the definite article has been avoided as "the mind" implies something singular and independent that is too easily taken as "the self." Actually, *citta* is not a "something" in the ordinary ways we think of "things." Even more, it is not a "self."

clinging (*upādanā*). Tan Ajahn used "attachment" at the time of these talks and "clinging" at other times. Here, the latter is preferred as more active and also avoids confusion with psychological "attachment theory."

Commentaries (*aṭṭhakathā*). "Exposition or explanation of meaning." After the Pāli Canon was settled at the Third Council, later texts were developed, purportedly to explain the earlier texts. Traditional orthodoxy has assumed that these texts, standardized a millennium after the Buddha's passing, are fully harmonious with the suttas. Ajahn Buddhadāsa did not agree, nor do the majority of modern scholars.

D

dhamma. Phenomenon, natural thing, stuff.

Dhamma language. Non-personal language, speaking in terms of phenomena, processes, and conditionality. A more detailed explanation of these two levels of language is found in Ajahn Buddhadāsa's *Keys to Natural Truth*. He often used words somewhat metaphorically, teaching that the literal (usually material) meaning of words cannot adequately convey Dhamma, which requires Dhamma language.

dhammaniyāmatā. Natural lawfulness, the lawfulness of all nature; the impermanence, inconstancy, undependability, conditionality, and emptiness of phenomena is a matter of natural law rather than mere human conception (chapter 14).

dhammaṭhiṭatā. Lit. "standing in Dhamma or nature." The natural standing or naturalness of facts such as impermanence and conditionality.

dukkha. Suffering, distress, "bummers." The unnecessary pain and stress we undergo because of craving and clinging due to ignorance of dependent co-arising. One of the Pāli terms that serious students of Buddha-Dhamma will learn in all its facets.

dukkhatā. Dukkha-ness; this term is always used in terms of the universal characteristics of conditioned things (*sankhāra*). Thus, it is not about psycho-emotional pain or suffering (as in the first ennobling truth). Rather, *dukkhatā* refers to the inescapable burdensomeness, unsatisfactoriness, and stressfulness of impermanent, put together things that cannot endure and are subject to uncontrollable change.

dukkha-vedanā. Pain, discomfort, unpleasant feeling.

E

ego-me (Thai: *tua-goo*). Ajahn Buddhadāsa coined this Thai term to convey a sense of self-centeredness or narcissism that arises with a fully developed sense of self that we regularly identify with strongly. He variously associates *tua-goo* with *upādāna* and *jāti* in *paṭiccasamuppāda*. Very often selfish, *tua-goo* can be restrained though ethical practice and mindfulness. Unrestrained, it can develop in all sorts of unhealthy ways, primarily forms of *kilesa*. *Tua-goo* roughly corresponds to colloquial "ego," as in "so-and-so has a big ego."

emotion. The Pāli term that comes closest to the English word "emotion" is *saṅkhāra*, though there is no Pāli equivalent. *Kilesa* covers only the destructive or reactive emotions. As emotion plays a big role in modern psychology and for those influenced by European Romanticism, Western students of Buddha-Dhamma naturally wish to find the place of emotion in the Buddha's teaching. Further, emotions regularly show up in practice, often stealing the show, and we would like the Buddha to help explain them and guide our practice in response. Nevertheless, we must not mangle his terms to fit our wishes, as regularly happens to *vedanā*. The so-called "destructive emotions" or "reactive emotions" of greed, lust, aversion, anger, hatred, envy, boredom, anxiety, fear, confusion, and the like are captured by the Pāli *kilesa* (tarnishings of *citta*). These are unwholesome psychological states. The suttas do not consider these to fall under *vedanā*. The "virtuous emotions," "constructive emotions," or "healthy emotions" as some consider them, of kindness, gratitude, generosity, equanimity, patience, honesty, and the like are wholesome psychological states or phenomena. I refer to these as "virtues." In Pāli, they are referred to simply as *dhamma*.

H

hetu-paccaya. Causes and conditions. The two terms are roughly synonymous but *hetu* can be understood as the primary cause while *paccaya* are secondary or supporting conditions. Other synonyms relevant to *paṭicca-samuppāda* are *nidāna* (source), *ṭhāna* (basis), *samudhaya* (origin), and *upanissa* (support).

I

idappaccayatā. Conditionality (lit. the "fact of having this as condition"); the basic reality of conditioned, impermanent things, that they are dependent upon and conditioned by other things. Everything is conditioned by other things, which are also conditioned by other things.

Paccaya (condition) is broader than cause (*hetu*) and encompasses all forms of influencing relationship. Hence, we use the term "conditionality" for *idappaccayatā*, which is more inclusive than "causality" or "cause and effect," especially the limited linear causality commonly assumed by those unfamiliar with Buddhist teaching. *Idappaccayatā* is central to the Buddha's way of understanding experience and is the flip side of emptiness. Ajahn Buddhadāsa considers it the most fundamental natural law, the Buddhist counterpart of God (chapters 2 and 5).

J

jāti. Birth. In the *paṭiccasamuppāda* teaching, Ajahn Buddhadāsa usually takes *jāti* to mean the mental or spiritual birth of a fully formed ego (*tua-goo*), which is more often selfish than not. The context does not describe a material or biological birth and *jāti* cannot be assumed to mean "rebirth," which doesn't literally appear in the Pāli suttas, though terms such as renewed existence (*ponobbhava*, again becoming) are found (chapter 7).

jhāna. Absorptions: deep levels of *samādhi* in which mind is singularly focused on a particular aspect of inner experience. The Bodhisatta (pre-Buddha) was familiar with the four form *jhāna*s and the four formless states (*arūpa*) that can develop out of the first four. After awakening, he used them for rest and recreation, and taught them as a foundation for deeper insight and contemplation.

K

kāma. Sensuality; the basis of *kāma-sukha* (sensual pleasure) and the object of *kāma-chanda* (sensual desire) and *kāma-taṅhā* (sensual craving). Ajahn Buddhadāsa considered sexuality to be the core or essence of sensuality. In these talks, Tan Ajahn chose to stress the sexual aspect of *kāma-bhava* although it's generally translated as "sensual existence." Pleasures of eyes, ears, nose, tongue, and body not directly related to sex are nonetheless *kāma-bhava* when they have a sexual flavor. (Not to be confused with *kamma-bhava*, action ripening in a state of being.)

kamma (Sanskrit *karma*). Action; the Buddha emphasized *cetana* (volition, intention) as the active force of *kamma*. The fruits and consequences of actions are *kamma-vipāka*. *Kamma* does not mean "fortune" or "fate." Nor does *kamma* mean the "law of cause and effect," though *kamma-niyāma*, the "law of *kamma*," could be described as the "law of ethical cause and effect." Later usage often conflates the various meanings and nowadays there is much confusion due to shorthand uses of Anglicized "karma."

kāya. Body (lit. "group"); the complete bodily system as well as any collections or subsystems within it.

kilesa. Defilements, reactive emotions, selfish ego states. Most often categorized as three: lust (*rāga*) and greed (*lobha*), hatred (*dosa*) and anger (*kodha*), and delusion (*moha*). As ignorance underlies all kinds of defilement, *moha* should not be translated as "ignorance" (see *avijjā*) (chapter 3). The hindrances (*nivaraṇa*) are a subset of the *kilesa*. The *kilesa* are the full-blown reactive emotions that devour us like tigers. The *nivaraṇa* are half-formed moods that pester us like gnats.

L

loka. World; the universe of subjective experience, which naturally disintegrates. When the Buddha speaks of "the end of the world," he does not mean the physical planet Earth or the material universe. *Paraloka*, "other world," is often taken to mean other realms in which we might be reborn after death. In Dhamma language *paraloka* refers to the possibility of alternative realms of experience available here-now through a shift in causes and conditions.

lokiya. Worldly, of the world; mentally-emotionally bound up with worldly experience.

lokuttara. Above and beyond the world; to be free of the world even while living in its midst, fully sentient and active (chapter 15).

love (*rak*). A word of broad meaning in Thai. A standard dictionary has "to love, to care for, to be fond of." Unlike the Pāli terms *karunā* (compassion) and *mettā* (kindness, friendliness, benevolence), which are much purer in meaning, *rak* ranges widely, encompassing passionate attachment, selfish demanding affection, the love of a mother for children, and sublime agape. Tan Ajahn uses it here to provoke and challenge, rather than unmindfully assume that love is always good. Central to the discussion here is that love is conditioned and limited, especially the personal love of one egoistic being for another.

M

mano. Mind, mind-sense; mind as a sense door interacting with a mental phenomenon (*dhamma*). Cf. *citta* and *viññāṇa*.

N

nāmarūpa. Mind and body, name and form. In DN 15 a rather difficult passage discusses how *nāmarūpa* is discerned when the signs, marks, and qualities of *nāma* and *rūpa* are delineated and recognized so that it becomes the basis of sense contact (*phassa*). This parallels descriptions in the Vedic ritual literature.

Nibbāna (Sanskrit: *nirvāṇa*). Coolness. The end of all suffering and misery, of all things that burn and scorch, and of the egoistic reactions that cause them. This is the supreme reality according to Buddhism and the aim of spiritual practice. Often portrayed as a distant goal to be realized after many lifetimes of striving, Ajahn Buddhadāsa highlighted the possibility of "*nibbāna* at the tip of the nose" and its accessibility for everyone. *Nibbāna* is found in the midst of *dukkha* rather than in often imagined auspicious circumstances of ease and comfort (chapters 1 and 4).

nirodha. Quenching, cessation; that something does not perform its usual function, is unable to perform that function, or has no function. We prefer "quenching" to "cessation" as it better conveys Ajahn Buddhadāsa's understanding. Think of examples such as "thirst quenches" or to "quench a fire." *Nirodha* doesn't mean the utter ending, obliteration, or extinction of something. When something, or a life, quenches, it is no longer capable of flaring up into or as a basis for craving, egoism, and *dukkha* (chapter 13).

P

pakati. Normal, natural; how things, *dhamma*s, naturally and normally are in terms of *idappaccayatā* and the inter-relatedness of phenomena.

paññā. Wisdom, discernment, understanding, intelligence. The range of this term is wide, including book learning and profound spiritual insight. Ajahn Buddhadāsa uses *paññā* as an umbrella term encompassing more specialized terms such as *vipassanā*, *ñāṇa*, and *vijjā*. Ajahn Buddhadāsa often referred to three levels as listed in the Saṅgīti Sutta (DN 33, D.iii.219): *sutamaya-paññā*—understanding from listening to the words of others and reading books; *cintāmaya-paññā*—understanding from thought, reflection, and reasoning; and *bhāvanāmaya-paññā*—understanding from immediate spiritual experience (chapter 3).

paramadhamma. Supreme thing, supreme reality. See *Nibbāna*. Also the title of an influential series of lectures and book by Ajahn Buddhadāsa (1969).

paramatthadhamma. Supreme (*parama*) meaning, benefit, truth (*attha*); the highest, most profound Dhamma or truth. (The translation "absolute truth" doesn't fit with Buddhism's pragmatic, non-dogmatic approach.)

paṭiccasammuppāda. Dependent co-arising (depending upon + together + arising). Not "codependent." Explained throughout this work, especially in chapter 5 and afterward.

phassa. Sense contact, sense impression: the functioning together of inner and outer sense media (sense organ and sense object) and corresponding sense consciousness. There are six kinds of *phassa*, categorized according to the six senses. Ajahn Buddhadāsa also distinguished between foolish or ignorant contact and mindful, wise contact. See *āyatana* and *viññāṇa* (chapter 8).

S

saddhā. Faith, confidence; trust in Dhamma that is based in experience, never "blind," and is balanced and completed by wisdom. Most often expressed in terms of the Buddha's awakening, the Dhamma's veracity, and the Sangha's noble practice (chapter 1).

saksit (Thai, from Sanskrit *sakti* and *siddhi*). Sacred, holy, with an emphasis on power. In English, sacred means "set apart for or dedicated to some religious purpose, and hence entitled to veneration or religious respect; made holy by association with a god or other object of worship; consecrated, hallowed" (OED). In addition to that meaning, the Thai term carries connotations of miraculous or mysterious power (chapter 6).

saḷāyatana. Sense media, sense domains, "connectors." See *āyatana*.

samādhi. Collected, calm stability of mind. Primarily characterized by non-distraction, *samādhi* is clean, unhindered, clear, bright, unified, agile, and imperturbable (See standard descriptions of post-*jhāna samādhi*, e.g., MN 38). It provides the strength and stability for meditation practice. Classically exemplified by the *jhānas* (absorptions), *samādhi* is always present to some degree when we function with some coherence and can successively refine and deepen into "good enough *samādhi*" and the *jhānas*. It is not a synonym for *samatha* (serenity), nor is it opposed to *vipassanā* (insight). *Samādhi* supports both aspects of the path and is essential to each.

I am reluctant to translate this word, as the common "concentration" can be misleading. This is one of the Pāli terms that we encourage serious students to learn for themselves (chapters 10 and 14).

sampajañña. Clear comprehension, ready wisdom, intelligence; clear seeing and intelligence applied to specific circumstances. *Sampajañña* draws upon wisdom accumulated through inquiry, practice, insight, and contemplation. *Sampajañña* often forms a compound with *sati*.

sanantanadhamma. Ancient teachings and primeval traditions that had been around long enough that no one could say for how long (chapter 15).

saṅkhāra. Concocting, concoction; fabricating, fabrication; conditioning. The power to concoct various things into existence. *Saṅkhāra* has three primary uses in the suttas: most broadly, all concocted, created things; as a *khandha*, aggregate, thinking-emoting; and in *paṭiccasamuppāda* teachings the volitional influences upon sense consciousness.

sandiṭṭhiko. "To be seen personally by those who practice," to be seen clearly and known truly within oneself in a way that is subjective, intuitive, and here-now. Second of the virtues or qualities of Dhamma.

Sāsanā. Teaching, message, religion. Nowadays used as an equivalent of the Western term "religion," the original meaning was more straightforward. Combined with "Buddha" it can mean the Buddha's teaching or message, and also is equivalent to Buddhism, another Western creation.

sati. Mindfulness, recollection, recall, remembering, awareness, attentiveness. Keeping attention on what's happening at present, whether internally or "outside"; bringing something into awareness for reflection, investigation, or contemplation; keeping something in awareness in order to be fully present with it; delivering the required wisdom in time to do its work. Readers interested in Buddhist practice would do well to note when mainstream uses of "mindfulness" diverge from the original Buddhist understanding of *sati*. Liberating mindfulness is guided by right view and backed by skillful effort. *Sati* is hindered when lacking a solid ethical foundation (chapter 9).

satipaṭṭhāna. Applications or establishments of mindfulness; aspects of lived experience for training *sati*, categorized as four: body, *vedanā*, *citta*, and Dhamma. These are kept in mind for the sake of sustained and deepening contemplation. The Ānāpāsati Sutta (MN 118) is a better example of how to systematically cultivate *satipaṭṭhāna* than the often quoted but later Satipaṭṭhāna Sutta (chapter 14).

sayasāstra. Superstition, the science of sleeping (in ignorance); misunderstanding how natural law and duty operate, attributing causal efficacy where it doesn't actually exist, and behaving accordingly (though some understanding may be lurking within it).

stuff. A great Anglo Saxon word. Tan Ajahn often uses the word *reuang*, which can be translated "stories" or "matters." Here, I've chosen to translate it as "stuff." Although rather informal in current English usage, the term has a good pedigree and is less stuffy than "matters." Also, stuff (see its OED entry) is not a bad translation of dhamma, phenomena.

Sugata. One who Goes Well and Arrives Well. Another epithet of the Buddha that we prefer to leave untranslated.

summum bonum. Latin for "the greatest or supreme good" from which all others are derived; an expression used in philosophy, particularly in medieval philosophy, to describe the ultimate importance, the singular and most ultimate end that human beings ought to pursue. Ajahn Buddhadāsa was fond of applying it to the ultimate aim of Buddha-Dhamma.

suññatā. Voidness, to be empty of self and anything to do with self; more or less equivalent to *anattā*. See *attā* and *anattā* (chapter 4). The theme of Ajahn Buddhadāsa's *Heartwood of the Bodhi Tree* (Wisdom, 1994).

sutta. A discourse or dialogue attributed to the Buddha or his close disciples. Lit. "thread," the strands of Dhamma teaching collected within the second basket of the Tipiṭaka.

T

taṇhā. Craving (lit. "thirst," "hunger"); ignorant desire. Usually categorized as three: sensual, existential (to be or have), and nihilistic (to not be or not have). Sometimes as six, according to the six senses. Compare with "want" (*chanda*), which can be Dhammic or defiled depending on context, and wise aspiration (*sammāsankappa*).

tathatā. Thusness, suchness. Things, *dhammas*, are "simply thus," "just like that," "merely such." Phenomena don't really fall within any tidy category of positive, negative, or any other dualism. *Tathā* means "thus," "like that," "such"; the suffix *-tā* means "state of being" or "condition" as with the suffixes "-ness" and "-hood."

Tathāgata. An untranslatable epithet the Buddha used for himself and other indescribable beings. Variously explained "one who is thus come" and "one who is thus gone." Ajahn Buddhadāsa explains Tathāgata as one who has fully realized thusness (*tathatā*) and lives in thusness.

tevijjā. Three true knowledges. In some accounts, the Buddha awakened to these insight knowledges under the Bodhi tree: (1) *pubbenivāsānussati-ñāṇa*—knowledge through recollection of previous dwellings; (2) *cutūpapāta-ñāṇa*—knowledge of how beings pass away and reappear according to their actions; and (3) *āsavakkhya-ñāṇa*—knowledge of the end of the fermentations, the most basic impulses toward defilement. In the text, Ajahn Buddhadāsa critiques the first two *ñāṇa* or *vijjā* as unsuitable for the highest level of liberating insight. Metaphorically, the first knowledge can be taken as a people language representation of impermanence and the second as a people language representation of *dukkha*-ness (unsatisfactoriness, burdensomeness). See *vijjā* (chapter 15).

Tipiṭaka. Three Baskets: Vinaya (monastic code), Suttas, and Abhidhamma (an early level of commentary, accepted as canonical though clearly a later development, that attempts to analyze and express the Dhamma in impersonal terms). Also known as the Pāli Canon, the name comes from the baskets in which palm leaf manuscripts were kept. Ajahn Buddhadāsa considered the first basket unnecessary for ordinary non-monastic practitioners and the third basket as "Excess Dhamma," suitable for specialists and those who enjoy breaking things down into minutiae.

U

upādāna. Clinging, grasping. Four kinds are given: clinging to sensuality, to precepts and practices, to views, and to concepts of self. The last, the conception of self, clinging to "me" and "mine," is the core of the others and is of particular importance in Buddhism (chapter 7).

upādāna-kkhandha. Clinging-together-groups, bundles or aggregates of clinging. These five—body, *vedanā*, conceptualization-perception, thoughts and emotions, and consciousness—taken personally are the core of *dukkha*.

Upanishads. Regarded as part of the Vedas and as such form part of the Hindu scriptures. They primarily discuss philosophy, meditation, and the nature of God and form the core spiritual thought of Vedantic Hinduism. The oldest, such as the Bṛhadaranyaka and Chandogya Upanishads, may date to roughly before the 7th century BCE, while the youngest came after the Buddha. Ajahn Buddhadāsa refers to these non-Buddhist texts because of their importance within Indian religiosity in the centuries immediately preceding and following the Buddha's time. They are both part of the philosophical context toward which the Buddha applied his radical critique and a significant—largely unacknowledged and probably unintentional—influence on how early Buddha-Dhamma was reinterpreted by later Buddhists.

V

vedanā. The simple subjective feeling tone of an experience; any feeling of pleasure, pain, and neither-pleasure-nor-pain that occurs with sense contact (*phassa*). Some experiences are pleasant, agreeable, comfortable, attractive, or beautiful. Some experiences are painful, unpleasant, disagreeable, uncomfortable, repellant, or ugly. Some experiences don't feel either way, which may feel "neutral" or "ambiguous." *Vedanā* are generally distinguished in this threefold manner and also according to the six kinds of contact on which they are based. Within *paṭiccasamuppāda*, and as the second aggregate, *vedanā* has this limited meaning. *Vedanā* is not the same as physical sensation (*phoṭṭabba*, tangibles), which can be a basis for the various *vedanā*. In chapter 10, "sexual feelings" and "feelings of sensuality and form" are mentioned. These are not *vedanā* per se, although they will be felt as pleasurable or uncomfortable, which are *vedanā*. Such is the ambiguity of the Thai *ruseuk* and English "feeling." Unfortunately, emotion (see entry above) is often confused with *vedanā*, leading to superficial confusions of Buddha-Dhamma. Emotions, like other forms of experience, involve *vedanā*, that is, may feel pleasurable, painful, or ambiguous. And emotions are partly triggered by the *vedanā* of a sensible experience. Still, emotions are not *vedanā*. Causal relationship is not equivalence.

vijjā. True knowing, clear knowing. Ignorance (*avijjā*) is the absence or distortion of *vijjā*. Replacing ignorance with true knowing leads to liberation. *Vijjā* (true knowing) and *paññā* (intuitive wisdom) are effectively synonyms, as are *ñāṇa* (true knowledge), *āloka* (light), and, more or less, *vipassanā* (clear seeing, insight) (chapters 12 and 13).

vimutti. Liberation, emancipation, release, "salvation."

viññāṇa. Sense consciousness, discriminating consciousness; to cognize sense objects via the six sense media. There are six kinds of *viññāṇa*: eye-consciousness, ear-consciousness, and so on through mind-consciousness. *Viññāṇa* distinguishes a separate object within each sensory sphere. Readers should be careful to understand "consciousness" as used in the Pāli suttas and not confuse it with the various associations in English usage.

viriya. Effort, energy, perseverance. *Viriya* has numerous synonyms, all of which can be translated with overlapping meanings, such as *vāyāma* (effort), *padhāna* (striving), and *uṭṭhāna* (vigor, rousing, industry). *Viriya* is more common, although *vāyāma* is a factor of the noble eightfold path. Both may be translated as "effort." Ajahn Buddhadāsa explains: "In *viriya* there is effort, intelligence, and courage intermixed sufficiently and appropriately. Only then can we call it the *viriya* of the Buddha."

Visuddhimagga. *The Path of Purity*, "the Bible of orthodox Theravada Buddhism." *Visuddhimagga* serves as the lynchpin of the Theravāda commentarial system and subsequently has dominated Theravāda interpretation and orthodoxy to this day. Bhadantācariya Buddhaghosa, its author, lived in the 5th century, approximately 1,000 years after the Buddha's passing. Originally a brahmin from southern India, Ven. Buddhaghosa was converted to Buddhism and eventually moved to Sri Lanka. There, he was a central figure in the competition to control the interpretation of early Buddhist teachings. He joined the conservative Mahāvihāra and compiled his famous treatise. As a reward, he supervised the organization and translation into Pāli of existing Singhalese commentaries. Ajahn Buddhadāsa both acknowledged the tremendous contribution that Ven. Buddhaghosa made to Theravāda Buddhism and criticized some of the conservative interpretations that this dominant medieval Buddhist teacher represents: "Ninety-five percent of the *Visuddhimagga* is useful; five percent of it should be thrown out." More details can be found in Bhikkhu Ñāṇamoli's introduction to his translation of the *Visuddhimagga* (Kandy: Buddhist Publication Society, 1991).

W

wanderers and priests (*samaṇabrāhmaṇā*). Truth-seeking wanderers and brahmins, stay-at-home priests of the Vedic mantras and rituals. The Buddha and his *bhikkhu*s were home-leaving *samaṇa*, while the Buddha revalued brahmins within his new dispensation in terms of spiritual realization and freedom rather than ritualism and social caste.

Bibliography

Buddhadāsa Bhikkhu. 1988. *Keys to Natural Truth*. Translated by Ariyanando and Santikaro Bhikkhu. Bangkok: The Dhamma Study & Practice Group.

———. 1988. *Buddha-Dhamma for Students*. Translated by Ariyanando Bhikkhu, edited by Santikaro Bhikkhu. Bangkok: The Dhamma Study & Practice Group.

———. 1994. *Heartwood of the Bodhi Tree: The Buddha's Teaching on Voidness*. Translated by Dhammavicayo. Boston: Wisdom Publications.

———. 1997. *Mindfulness with Breathing: A Manual for Serious Beginners*. Translated by Santikaro Bhikkhu. Boston: Wisdom Publications.

Bodhi, Bhikkhu, trans. 1995. *The Middle Length Discourses of the Buddha: A New Translation of the Majjhima Nikāya*. Boston: Wisdom Publications.

———, trans. 1999. *The Connected Discourses of the Buddha: A New Translation of the Saṃyutta Nikāya*. Boston: Wisdom Publications.

———, trans. 2012. *The Numerical Discourses of the Buddha: A New Translation of the Aṅguttara Nikāya*. Boston: Wisdom Publications.

———, ed. 1999. *A Comprehensive Manual of Abhidhamma: the Abhidhammattha Sangaha of Ācariya Anuruddha*. Onalaska, WA: BPS Pariyatti Editions.

———, ed. 2005. *In the Buddha's Words: An Anthology of Discourses from the Pāḷi Canon*. Boston: Wisdom Publications.

Ireland, John D., trans. 1997. *The Udāna: Inspired Utterances of the Buddha; & The Itivutakka: The Buddha's Sayings*. Kandy: Buddhist Publication Society.

Walshe, Maurice, trans. 1995. *The Long Discourses of the Buddha: A New Translation of the Dīgha Nikāya*. Boston: Wisdom Publications.

Further Reading

Bodhi, Bhikkhu. 1983. *The Great Discourse on Causation: The Mahānidāna Sutta and its Commentaries*. Kandy, Sri Lanka: Buddhist Publication Society.

Buddhadāsa Bhikkhu. 1992. *Practical Dependent Co-Origination*. Chaiya, Thailand: Dhammadāna Foundation.

de S. Wettimuny, R. G. 1969. *The Buddha's Teaching: Its Essential Meaning*. Colombo, Sri Lanka: M. D. Gunasena.

Jurewicz, Joanna. 2005. "Playing with Fire: The Pratītyasamutpada from the perspective of Vedic Thought." In *Buddhism: Critical Concepts in Religious Studies, Vol. I*, edited by Paul Williams, 169–87. New York: Routledge.

Macy, Joanna. 1991. *Mutual Causality in Buddhism and General Systems Theory: The Dharma of Natural Systems*. Albany, NY: State University of New York.

Ñāṇamoli, Bhikkhu, trans. 1991. *The Path of Purification: Visuddhimagga*. Onalaska, WA: BPS Pariyatti Editions.

Ñānananda, Bhikkhu. 1971. *Concept and Reality in Early Buddhist Thought: An Essay on "Papañca" and "Papañca-Saññā-Saṅkhā"*. Kandy, Sri Lanka: Buddhist Publication Society.

Ñāṇavīra Thera. 2009. *Notes on Dhamma*. Rotterdam: Path Press Publications.

Payutto, P. A. 1994. *Dependent Origination: The Buddhist Law of Conditionality*. Translated by Bruce Evans. Bangkok: Buddhadhamma Foundation.

Swaris, Nalin. 1999. *The Buddha's Way of Human Liberation: A Socio-Historical Approach*. Nugegoda, Sri Lanka: Sarasavi Publishers.

Index

A

actions, 2, 9, 11, 40, 85–86, 90, 125, 127, 146, 152–53. *See also* karma

ādibrahmacariya, 135–36

Ajahn Buddhadāsa. *See* Buddhadāsa, Ajahn

anattā. *See* not-self

anger (*kodha*), 25, 28, 33, 90

animism, 48–49, 162*n*42

arising, 36. *See also* dependent co-arising

aspirations, 70–71, 163*n*59

atammayatā, 29–30, 120, 146

attā. *See* self.

attachment (*upādāna*), 53–54, 59–60. *See also* clinging

avacara, 82

awake, 4–5

awakening, the great awakening, 5, 111, 124–25, 143, 156–57

ā*yatana*, 58

B

birth (*jāti*), xiv–xv, 54–56, 62, 87, 159*n*8

- ego birth, 55–56, 71
- rebirth, 63–65, 127

bhava, 54, 75–76. *See also* existence

Bodhi tree, 124, 157

body, 52, 112, 114–16, 149, 165*n*84. *See also* mind-body; senses and sense organs

brahmacariya, 4, 135–36

breathing (*ānāpānasati*), 73, 94–95, 111–15, 155

the Buddha, xi, 4–5, 10, 61, 98–99, 108, 124–25, 131, 134–35, 138, 143–44, 150, 158

Buddhadāsa, Ajahn

- critics of, xix–xv
- lectures at Suan Mokkh, ix–x, 155–56, 159*n*7
- recovering core Buddhist perspectives, xiii
- teaching philosophy, xi–xii

Buddhaghosa, Venerable, 129–30, 136

Buddhism

- core concerns and teachings, x–xi, 74
- as discovered as opposed to created, 3
- distractions in the study of, 20–21
- freedom of, 15–17, 19
- meaning of the word, 3–5, 10, 160*n*13
- as a methodology, 14
- natural truth/natural law, 3–4
- original teachings, 131–32
- and other religions, 5–8
- practice of, 21
- scientific method of, 14–15, 20–21
- study of, 20–23
- teaching, two levels of, 129
- *See also* dependent co-arising

natural law/natural truth, 3–4, 11, 13–14, 160*n*18
negative, 24–33, 146, 161*n*27
Nibbāna, 5, 26, 31–34, 65, 80
nirodha, x, 102, 104. *See also* quenching
nirvana. See *Nibbāna*
noble truths, 22, 138–39, 143, 151–52, 157
not-self (*anattā*) xii, xv–xvi, 44, 47, 50, 74, 98–99, 119, 131–32, 138, 166*n*95. *See also* self

O

Old Testament, 28

P

paccaya, 160*n*16. *See also* conditionality
Pāli terminology and keys to pronunciation, xvii–xviii, 170
paññā, 7, 10, 22, 95, 112
paramadhamma, 5
paramatthadhamma, 61, 64, 129, 137
Path of Purity (*Visuddhimagga*), 129–30
paṭiccanirodha, 99, 102–3, 106, 156
paṭiccasamuppāda. *See* dependent co-arising
paṭipatti, 21
peace, 99–100
phassa. *See* contact.
pleasure, 9, 19, 38, 53, 67–68, 81, 114–16. *See also* senses and sense organs; sex and sexuality
positive, 24–33, 146, 161*n*27
psychology, 24, 161*n*26
puppy and lion metaphor, 12–13

Q

quenching, x–xi, 5, 35, 56, 75, 77, 99, 102–8, 126, 133–34, 138–39

R

rebirth, 63–65, 127. *See also* birth
religions, 5–8, 80
rūpa. *See* form

S

sacred, highest sacred, 48–49
saddhā, 7
Sahampati Brahmā, 144
saksit, 162*n*41
salvation, 31
samādhi, 73, 82, 88, 95, 112, 114, 117, 128
samannāhāracitta, 165*n*72
sammā, 160*n*14
sampajañña, 95–96, 112
sandiṭṭhiko, 23, 65, 97, 100
Sangha, 10
saṅkhāra, 51–52, 105, 149
sāsanā, 4
sati. *See* mindfulness
sayasāstra, 162*n*40
scientific method of Buddhism, 14–15
self (*attā*), xv, 43–47, 54, 60, 75, 99. *See also* existence; not-self
selfishness, 45–46
selflessness. *See* not-self
self-reliance, 10–11
senses and sense organs, 52, 57–58, 69–70, 105, 123, 136–37, 162*n*47. *See also* contact
sensual existence, 80–82, 88
sex and sexuality, 80–82, 88, 91
sikkhā, 21
the spirits are laughing at us (*phii buarau*), 47
Suan Mokkh, ix, xii, 164*n*61, 167*n*101
suchness. *See* thusness
suffering, ix–x, xii, 5, 55–56, 75, 142–43
  arising of, 11, 38–39
  causes, list of, 90–91
  and ego birth, 55–56

investigating like a surgeon, 21
prevention of, 94–100
and rebirth, 64–65
and the self, 44
suññatā, xii, 31, 119, 166*n*95
superstitions, 47–49
suttas
Ānāpānasati Sutta, 111, 155–56
Chachakka Sutta, 19, 145
Dhammakhatika Sutta, 133–34, 157–58, 166*n*97
Dukkha Sutta, 75, 151
Jāṇussoṇi Sutta, 145
Jaṭā Sutta, 41, 147–48
Kaccānagotta Sutta, 56
Kālāma Sutta, 1–2, 15–16, 142
Kesakambala Sutta, 145
Khajjanīya Sutta, 51, 149
Lokadhamma Sutta, 27
Loka Sutta, 35, 146–47, 164*n*62
Mahātaṇhāsankhaya Sutta, 123–24, 156–57
Mahātthipadopama Sutta, 101–2, 105, 108, 154–55
Ñātika Sutta, 57, 149, 163*n*51
Nidāna Sutta, 85–86, 152–53
Rohitassa Sutta, 77, 147
Sakkapañha Sutta, 67–68, 150
Samanupassanā Sutta, 93–94, 153–54
Titthāyatanādi Sutta, 9–10, 147
Upanisa Sutta, 157
Vakkali Sutta, 163*n*54
Vibhaṅga Sutta, 51

T
taṇhā. *See* craving
tathatā. *See* thusness
the Tathāgata, 35, 147
teaching, two levels of, 129
three lifetimes interpretation, xv, 130
thusness, xiii, 109, 118–20
Tipiṭaka, 19, 22, 29
transmigration, 62
true knowing (*vijjā*), 95, 97–98, 106, 166*n*96
true things, determination of, 1–2
truths, noble truths, 22, 138–39, 143, 151–52, 157

U
unconcoctability, 29–30, 120, 146. *See also* concocting
upādāna. *See* attachment.
Upanishads, 62, 98, 126, 163*n*55

V
vedanā, 52–53, 59, 114–16, 162*n*37, 163*n*48, 165*n*89. *See also* feeling
vijjā, 95, 97–98, 106, 166*n*96
vimutti, 31, 120
viññāṇa. *See* consciousness
vipāka, 162*n*38
viriya, 7
Visuddhimagga, 129–30, 148, 166*nn*94–95

W
wakefulness, 4–5
wandering (*avacara*), 82
wisdom (*paññā*), 7, 10, 22, 95–96, 112

About the Author

Buddhadāsa Bhikkhu ("Servant of the Buddha") is arguably the most influential Buddhist teacher Thailand has ever produced and one of the most controversial monks in twentieth-century Theravāda Buddhism. The range and depth of his teaching is unparalleled in modern Theravāda Buddhism, with dependent co-arising at the heart of all his work.

He was influential for his promethean output and reconciliation of the austere forest lifestyle with serious scholarship. After dedicating his life as "Buddha's Servant," he repeatedly called attention to the liberating core of Buddha-Dhamma, such as emptiness, dependent co-arising, and that "nothing is worth clinging to as 'me' or mine.'" He championed mindfulness with breathing as the Buddha's original and comprehensive system of meditation. He emphasized the aim of freedom from *dukkha* in this life.

The controversy had many aspects. He questioned the medieval orthodoxy based in the traditional commentaries, promoted lay practice and women teachers, and spoke out on a wide array of social issues. He also championed interreligious understanding and cooperation. At the height of the Cold War he proposed "Dhammic Socialism" as a middle way independent of the competing Western ideologies. His depth of Dhamma outlasted most of his critics, and he died in 1993 at the age of 87. Even then, the nationwide conversation concerning end-of-life care that occurred during his unnecessary hospitalization (he was unconscious) was a farewell teaching, as was the distinctly no-frills cremation ceremony stipulated in his will.

He had gone forth as a bhikkhu (a Buddhist monk-friar) in 1926, at the age of twenty. After a few years of study in Bangkok, he was inspired to live close to nature in order to investigate Buddha-Dhamma as the Buddha had done. Thus, he established Suan Mokkhabalārāma ("The Garden of the Power of Liberation") in 1932, near his home town in southern Thailand. At that time Suan Mokkh was the only forest Dhamma center in the region and one of a very few places dedicated to training in *vipassanā* (meditation that leads to "seeing clearly" into reality).

Along with his brother Dhammadāsa he founded *Buddha-Sāsanā Quarterly*, Thailand's longest running Buddhist journal. Word of Buddhadāsa Bhikkhu and Suan Mokkh spread over the years. He was invited to speak throughout southern Thailand and in Bangkok, he held special sessions for university students, and numerous books were published. Here, we can only mention a few of the more memorable services he has rendered to Buddhism.

Ajahn Buddhadāsa worked painstakingly to establish and explain the essential principles of pristine Buddhism. That work was based on extensive research of the Pāli texts (canonical and commentarial), especially of the Buddha's discourses (*suttanta piṭaka*), followed by personal experiment and practice with these teachings. From this, he uncovered the Dhamma that truly quenches *dukkha*, which he in turn shared with anyone interested. His goal was to produce a complete set of references for present and future research and practice. His approach was always "scientific"—straightforward, practical, and testable in daily life.

Although his formal education was limited to seven years, plus some beginning Pāli studies, Thai universities have given him eight honorary doctorates. Numerous doctoral theses have been written about his life and teaching. His books, both written and transcribed from talks, fill shelves at the National Library and influence all serious Thai Buddhists. Not only was he an intellectual pioneer and meditation master, he advocated "socially engaged Buddhism" even before the term was coined.

Progressive elements in Thai society have been inspired by his wide-ranging thought, teaching, and selfless example. Since the 1960s, activists and thinkers in such areas as education, social welfare, rural development, and ecology have drawn upon his teaching, advice, and friendship. His work helped inspire a new generation of socially concerned monks.

Since the founding of Suan Mokkh, he studied all schools of Buddhism and all the major religious traditions. This interest was practical rather than scholarly. He sought to unite all genuinely religious people, meaning those working to overcome selfishness, in order to work together for world peace. This broadmindedness won him friends and students from around the world, including Christians, Muslims, Hindus, and Sikhs.

Near the end of his life, he established an International Dhamma Hermitage for hosting courses to introduce foreigners to the correct understanding of Buddhist principles and practice. Monthly retreats are held in English at the beginning of every month. Retreats in Thai are also organized. Further, he hoped that meetings would be organized for Buddhists from around the world to identify and agree upon the "Heart of Buddhism." Third, he wanted to bring together all the religions to cooperate in helping humanity.

In his last years, he established projects for carrying on the work of serving the Lord Buddha and humanity. One was Suan Atammayatārāma, a small training center for foreign monks in a quiet grove near the retreat center. The guidelines he laid down aim to develop "Dhamma Missionaries" who are well versed in the Buddha's teaching, have solid experience of Buddhist meditation, and can adapt Buddha-Dhamma to the problems of the modern world. A sister project was named Dhamma Mātā (Dhamma Mothers). Society is suffering from the lack of women spiritual teachers; they exist but are not given adequate recognition. Dhamma Mātā is for raising the status of women by providing better opportunities and support in Buddhist monastic life and meditation practice. His wish was that we will have more women who can "give birth to others through Dhamma."

Ajahn Buddhadāsa died at Suan Mokkh on July 8, 1993. The work of Suan Mokkh in Thailand and abroad continues as before, according to the law of nature.

About the Translator

Santikaro trained for almost two decades as a Theravāda bhikkhu, mostly at Suan Mokkh in southern Thailand where he lived with Ajahn Buddhadāsa and became his primary translator, in print and especially orally (available on SoundCloud). Behind these translations are hundreds of hours of Dhamma conversation in which Ajahn Buddhadāsa explained his approach to Dhamma, the terms he used, and his practice understanding. Santikaro was accepted as a capable exponent of that approach. He remained at Suan Mokkh for a further five years after Ajahn Buddhadāsa's death, then returned to the USA in 2000. He remains in close contact with other students of Ajahn Buddhadāsa in Thailand and elsewhere.

Santikaro's training continues in the Midwest, as an *upasaka*, where he is cofounder of Liberation Park, a modern expression of Buddhist practice, study, and social responsibility, located in rural southwestern Wisconsin. He teaches actively around Wisconsin and the Chicago area, as well as other parts of the USA and world. He is committed to further deepening understanding of the practical brilliance of the original Pāli suttas, while living with the realities of "everything falls apart" modern America. Life's vicissitudes have given him some acquaintance with cancer, stroke, addictions, globalization, and other challenges that he explores regularly. Please visit www.liberationpark.org for more information, especially updates on the facilities being built to serve retreatants seeking deeper insight into Dhamma as Nature and dependently co-arising emptiness.

What to Read Next from Wisdom Publications

Mindfulness with Breathing
A Manual for Serious Beginners
Ajahn Buddhadasa Bhikkhu

"A precious yogic manual."
—Larry Rosenberg, author of *Breath by Breath*

Heartwood of the Bodhi Tree
The Buddha's Teachings on Voidness
Ajahn Buddhadasa Bhikkhu
Foreword by Donald Swearer and Jack Kornfield

"A remarkable and beautiful book that captures the spacious and profound teachings of the Thai Forest Tradition."
—*Inquiring Mind*

In the Buddha's Words
An Anthology of Discourses from the Pali Canon
Bhikkhu Bodhi
Foreword by His Holiness the Dalai Lama

"It will rapidly become the sourcebook of choice for both neophyte and serious student alike."
—*Buddhadharma*

Food for the Heart
The Collected Teachings of Ajahn Chah
Introduction by Ajahn Amaro
Foreword by Jack Kornfield

"In this book, you'll find Ajahn Chah's unique wisdom, which shone brilliantly from the stillness of his mind. These words will inspire, guide, and liberate you. It is Buddhism at its best."—Ajahn Brahm, author of *Don't Worry, Be Grumpy*

Sons of the Buddha
The Early Lives of Three Extraordinary Thai Masters
Kamala Tiyavanich

"Uplifting and, at times, magical."—*Buddhadharma*